PRAISE FOR

TINY HABITS

"Deeply researched and highly practical, this book will be a valuable resource to anyone interested in changing their behavior (that is, all of us)."

—Gretchen Rubin, *New York Times* best-selling author of *The Happiness Project*

"BJ Fogg's ideas on self-change are uniquely relevant, approachable, and powerful. I can't recommend this book highly enough."

—Ramit Sethi, *New York Times* best-selling author of *I Will Teach You to Be Rich*

"BJ Fogg's work is transformative . . . We use Tiny Habits at Amen Clinics with our patients, online students, and readers. It is simple, easy to implement, and it works."

—Daniel G. Amen, MD, *New York Times* best-selling author of *Change Your Brain, Change Your Life*

"[*Tiny Habits*] demystifies the little behaviors that add up to what is, in essence, our identity. Understanding these micro behaviors [is] critical if you want achieve big outcomes like losing weight or building a company."

—Tony Fadell, inventor of the iPod and coinventor of the iPhone

"Fogg's method has great potential to promote altered behavior in those who have sought help in other ventures with little success."

—*Library Journal*, starred review

"Myth-breaking and persuasive research . . . Balancing useful practices (including many charts, tables, and graphs) with his own story of personal transformation, Fogg's convincing method will help any reader reconfigure their habits."

—*Publishers Weekly*

TINY HABITS

TINY
HABITS

+

The Small Changes That
Change Everything

BJ Fogg, PhD

HARVEST

An Imprint of WILLIAM MORROW

Boston   New York

First Mariner Books edition 2020
Copyright © 2020 by BJ Fogg

Tiny Habits® is a registered trademark

www.harpercollins.com

Library of Congress Cataloging-in-Publication Data
Names: Fogg, B. J., author.
Title: Tiny habits : the small changes that change everything /
BJ Fogg, PhD.
Description: Boston : HarperCollins Publishers, 2019.
Identifiers: LCCN 2019023920 (print) | LCCN 2019023921 (ebook) |
ISBN 9780358003328 (hardcover) | ISBN 9780358003991 (ebook) |
ISBN 9780358362777 (pbk.)
Subjects: LCSH: Habit. | Change (Psychology)
Classification: LCC BF335 .F56 2019 (print) | LCC BF335 (ebook) |
DDC 158 — dc23
LC record available at https://lccn.loc.gov/2019023920
LC ebook record available at https://lccn.loc.gov/2019023921

Book design and graphics by Amy Sly

Printed in the United States of America
24 25 26 27 28 LBC 14 13 12 11 10

While all of the stories in this book are true, some names and identifying
details have been changed to protect confidentiality.

For references and resources related to this book,
go to TinyHabits.com/resources.

Contents

To the wonderful people
who inspired me to explore.

INTRODUCTION
Change *Can* Be Easy (and Fun)

Tiny is mighty.

At least when it comes to change.

Over the last twenty years, I've found that most everyone wants to make some kind of change: eat healthier, lose weight, exercise more, reduce stress, get better sleep. We want to be better parents and partners. We want to be more productive and creative. But the alarming levels of obesity, sleeplessness, and stress reported by the media—and seen in my Stanford lab's research—tell me there is a painful gap between what people want and what they actually do. The disconnect between *want* and *do* has been blamed on a lot of things—but people blame it on themselves for the most part. They internalize the cultural message of "It's your fault! You should exercise more, but you aren't doing it. Shame on you!"

I am here to say: It isn't your fault.

And creating positive change isn't as hard as you think.

For too many years, myths, misconceptions, and well-meaning but unscientific advice have set you up to fail. If you've attempted change in the past and haven't seen results, you may have concluded that change is hard or that you can't succeed because you lack motivation. Neither is accurate. The problem is with the approach itself, not with you. Think of it this way: If you tried putting together a chest of drawers with faulty instructions and parts missing, you would feel frustrated. But you probably wouldn't blame yourself for this, would you? You would blame the manufacturer instead. When it comes to failed attempts at change, we almost never blame the "manufacturer." We blame ourselves.

When our results fall short of our expectations, the inner critic finds an opening and steps on stage. Many of us believe that if we fail to be more productive, lose weight, or exercise regularly then something must be wrong with us. If only we were better people, we wouldn't have failed. If only we had followed that program to the letter or kept those promises to ourselves, we would have succeeded. We just need to get our act together and pull ourselves up by our bootstraps and *do better*. Right?

Nope. Sorry. Not right.

We are not the problem.

Our *approach* to change is. It's a *design* flaw—not a *personal* flaw.

Building habits and creating positive change *can* be easy—if you have the right approach. A system based on how human psychology really works. A process that makes change easier. Tools that don't rely on guesswork or faulty principles.

Popular thinking about habit formation and change feeds into our impulse to set unrealistic expectations. We know habits matter; we just need more good habits and fewer bad ones. But here we are, still struggling to change. Still thinking it's our fault. All my research and hands-on experience tell me that this is exactly the wrong mindset. In order to design successful habits and change your behaviors, you should do three things.

+ Stop judging yourself.

+ Take your aspirations and break them down into tiny behaviors.

+ Embrace mistakes as discoveries and use them to move forward.

This may not feel intuitive. I know it doesn't come naturally to everyone. Self-criticism is its own kind of habit. For some people, blaming yourself is just where your brain goes—it's like a sled in the snow, slipping into a well-worn path down the hill.

If you follow the Tiny Habits process, you'll start taking a different route. Snow will quickly start covering those self-doubting grooves. The new path will soon be the default path. This happens quickly, because with Tiny Habits you change best by *feeling good*—not by *feeling bad*. The process doesn't require you to rely on willpower, or set up accountability measures, or promise yourself rewards. There is no magic number of days you have to do something. Those approaches aren't based on the way habits really work, and as a result, they aren't reliable methods for change. And they often make us feel bad.

This book says good-bye to all that change angst and—even more important—shows you how to easily and joyfully bridge the gap (no matter the size) between who you are now and who you want to be. *Tiny Habits* will be your guide to disrupting the old approach and replacing it with an entirely new framework for change.

The system I'll share with you is not guesswork. I've road tested the process with more than 40,000 people during years of research and refinement. By coaching all these people personally and gathering data week by week, I know that the Tiny Habits method works. It replaces misunderstandings with proven principles, and it trades prescriptions for process. You'll take what the cofounder of Instagram, my former student, learned about human behavior to design a breakthrough app, and you'll use the same methods to create breakthrough changes in your own life—and the lives of others. And best of all, you get to have fun. Once you remove any hint of judgment, changing your habits becomes an uplifting journey of self-discovery. As you'll learn from the true stories in this book, a sense of exploration prepares the path to success.

Behavior Design

Welcome to Behavior Design! This is my comprehensive system for thinking clearly about human behavior and for designing simple ways to transform your life. My early work in Behavior Design helped innovators create products that millions of people use every day to get fit, save money, drive efficiently, and more. After seeing the power of these methods to successfully design business solutions, I shifted my focus to the personal: How do we change our *own* behavior? I got focused on changes that people want to make for themselves. And when I looked in the mirror, I saw plenty that could be improved on. I decided to do what every gung-ho scientist does at one time or another—I experimented on myself.

I tinkered with the behaviors I wanted to incorporate into my life. I did silly things that turned out to be wildly successful, like doing two push-ups after every time I pee. I did seemingly rational things that totally failed, like trying to eat an orange every day at lunch. Whenever something didn't work, I went back to my models and analyzed what happened. I started seeing patterns. I followed hunches. I pivoted. I iterated endlessly.

Even though I was a behavior scientist, I had to learn how to create habits in my own life. It wasn't obvious or natural for me; it was a deliberate process. But with practice I turned a weakness into a strength, and six months later, I had significantly changed my life. I lost twenty pounds and felt healthier and stronger. I was working more productively and more effectively than ever before. I started eating eggs and spinach for breakfast and cauliflower with mustard as an afternoon snack, and I weeded out foods that weren't helping me. I started each day with an uplifting series of habits, and I designed (and redesigned) my life and my environment to get better sleep. As I figured this out, with twists and turns along the way, I realized that my *ability* to change was increasing and my momentum was building. As I accumulated dozens of new habits—mostly tiny ones—they combined to create a transformation. Sustaining all this did not feel hard. Pursuing change in this way felt natural and oddly fun.

The results delighted me, and I started teaching my methods to others in 2011. My research showed this approach worked for other people, too, and it changed their lives. To my surprise and excitement, what started as a whimsical self-exploration in the Behavior Design universe became a proven method called Tiny Habits—the quickest, easiest vehicle for personal transformation.

Before I go on, let me set the record straight: information alone does not reliably change behavior. This is a common mistake people make, even well-meaning professionals. The assumption is this: If we give people the right information, it will change their attitudes, which in turn will change their behaviors. I call this the "Information-Action Fallacy." Many products and programs—and well-meaning professionals—set out to educate people as a way to change them. At professional conferences they say stuff like, "If people just knew the facts, they would change!"

As you look at your own experiences, you'll see that information alone did not transform your life. And that's certainly not your fault.

In my research on habit formation, dating back to 2009, I've found that there are only three things we can do that will create lasting change: Have an epiphany, change our environment, or change our habits in tiny ways. Creating a true epiphany for ourselves (or others) is difficult and probably impossible. We should rule out that option unless we have magical powers (I don't). But here's the good news: The other two options can lead to lasting change if we follow the right program, and Tiny Habits gives us a new way to tap the power of environment and baby steps.

Creating positive habits is the place to start, and creating *tiny* positive habits is the path to developing much bigger ones. Once you know how Tiny Habits works—and *why* it works—you can make big one-time changes. You can disrupt unwanted habits. You can work up to bucket-list behaviors like running a marathon.

I'll help guide you through each of the different behavior-change scenarios that you might encounter.

The essence of Tiny Habits is this: Take a behavior you want, make it tiny, find where it fits naturally in your life, and nurture its growth. If you want to create long-term change, it's best to start small. Here's why.

TINY IS FAST

Time. There's never enough of it, and we always want more of it. We eat drippy hamburgers in our cars and take conference calls while we're at the beach with our kids because we feel so pressed for time. This pressure leads to a scarcity mindset—we believe that there will never be enough time, so we say no to changes because we feel like we don't have the hours to cultivate new positive habits. Thirty minutes of exercise a day? Cooking a healthy dinner every night? Writing daily in a gratitude journal? Forget it. Who. Has. The. Time.

You could scold yourself down the path of change. Or you could make your life a lot easier.

You could start tiny.

With the Tiny Habits method, you focus on small actions that you can do in less than thirty seconds. You will quickly wire in new habits, and then they will grow naturally. Starting tiny means you can begin creating a big change without worrying about the time involved. With Tiny Habits, I advise people to start with three very small behaviors or even just one. The more stressed you are and the less time you have, the more appropriate this method is for you. No matter how much you want to cultivate a healthy habit, you won't be able to do it reliably if you start big. When you go big, the new habit probably won't stick. In many people's lives, tiny isn't just the best option, it might be the only option.

TINY CAN START NOW

Tiny allows you to get real with yourself and your life. Tiny allows you to start *right now*. It meets you where you are—whether your life is in a desperate spiral or you are stressed out but otherwise fortunate. We all have our own life circumstances to contend with, ways of thinking that aren't ideal, and quirks of psychology that hold us back. We could feel bummed and ashamed about it, or we could use the Tiny Habits method to hack the system.

I won't prescribe exact habits in this book. I'm sharing a method for wiring in *any* habit you want. You pick the habits. But right here, right now, I'm making an exception. I invite you to start practicing a new habit first thing each and every morning. It's simple. And it takes about three seconds. I call it the Maui Habit.

After you put your feet on the floor in the morning, immediately say this phrase, "It's going to be a great day." As you say these seven words, try to feel optimistic and positive.

The recipe in Tiny Habits format looks like this.

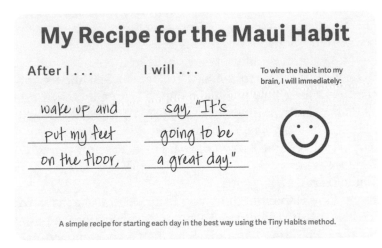

My Recipe for the Maui Habit

After I . . .   I will . . .   To wire the habit into my brain, I will immediately:

wake up and   _say, "It's_
put my feet   _going to be_   ☺
on the floor,   _a great day."_

A simple recipe for starting each day in the best way using the Tiny Habits method.

Over the years, I've helped thousands of people bring the Maui Habit into their lives, and the results have been excellent. It's certainly been effective in my own life. With the Maui Habit, you can start immediately —and almost effortlessly—toward a better future.

Here are a few variations on this habit to consider.

Some people say a slightly different phrase each morning such as "Today is going to be awesome." If that phrase or some variation works better for you, adjust as needed.

A few people have changed the timing. Some say this phrase when they look in the mirror in the morning. I'm quite sure that wouldn't work for me. (I avoid looking in the mirror first thing. Yikes!) But if this spot in your routine works best for you, then go for it.

I suggest you start with the classic version as written on the recipe card, then modify it if needed.

When I do the Maui Habit each morning, I pause for two or three seconds after I say the phrase. I'm still waking up at that point, and I want the idea to sink in.

If you do the Maui Habit and feel that it won't be a great day, I advise you to still say this phrase. I say it even on mornings when I feel exhausted or overwhelmed or anxious about the day ahead. In that moment, sitting on the edge of my bed, I try to feel optimistic. But if this feels phony, then I adjust the phrase and my intonation as I say, "It's going to be a great day—somehow."

I find this oddly helpful even on my worst days. When I'm worried about the day ahead, this statement—even when I say it with a question in my voice—seems to open the door just a crack to actually having a good day. And that's exactly what happens most days.

Think of the Maui Habit as a simple practice you do each morning in about three seconds. This will show you how easy it is to get started, *and* it will help you learn the single most important skill in behavior change —feeling successful.

TINY IS SAFE

A friend of mine has an eighteen-month-old baby named Willa who is new to the whole walking thing. The other day Willa was running around our driveway chasing my dog, Millie, and I watched Willa trip and fall about a half-dozen times. Scaling curbs and negotiating sewer grates is tricky business for a toddler, but she kept popping right back up. Willa would squawk a little bit here and there, but she wasn't actually getting hurt, so why not keep going? If I were the one learning to walk and crashing down on hard pavement, I'd be pretty banged up. At my height—I'm over six feet tall—falling would hurt more.

The same concept applies to starting a new behavior or habit. If you have never done yoga before, there are multiple places to start—but they all have different levels of risk. You could decide to do one sun salutation or buy a month of unlimited classes at your local studio or hop on a plane for a week-long retreat in India. The investment of time and money and expectation is wildly different with each option. Very few people would take off to India without having stepped foot on a yoga mat. Why? Something in our lizard brains inherently understands how high these stakes would be, which is why it can feel hard to start something new if it is too big. If I can barely surf the gentle waves at Cove Park in Maui, I wouldn't dare surf the massive swells at Jaws on the other side of Maui. I would likely get hurt, and I might lose all my confidence in surfing, even on small waves. Why would I do that to myself? It doesn't sound fun. Better stick to Cove Park.

With Tiny Habits, risk doesn't have to factor into the equation. Tiny can also be undercover. You can start to change without making a big scene. No one will sabotage you. This reduces the pressure on you.

Because these behaviors are so small and the program so flexible, emotional risk is eliminated. There is no real failure in Tiny Habits. There are little stumbles, but if you get up again, that's not failure — that's a habit in the making.

TINY CAN GROW BIG

Over the last twenty years, I've found that the only consistent, sustainable way to grow big is to start small. Amy, a former student of mine, was a stay-at-home mom who was trying to get an educational-media company off the ground. The idea of being her own boss and doing something she loved was thrilling. But there was so much to think about: hiring new employees, shopping around for office space, deciphering tax codes. She would procrastinate the important stuff, like legal agreements, and chose to work on tasks she loved, like designing her logo. But she was running out of time to build her business plan, and the thought of the venture falling apart in her hands paralyzed her. Amy wanted to get her business off the ground, and she kept making promises to herself that she'd tackle the big stuff soon — but months after the talking, she still hadn't done any walking.

A change myth was holding Amy back — the pervasive idea that you've got to go big or go home. We live in an aspiration-driven culture that is rooted in instant gratification. We find it difficult to enact or even accept incremental progress. Which is exactly what you need to cultivate meaningful long-term change. People get frustrated and demoralized when things don't happen quickly. It's natural. It's normal. But it's another way we're set up to fail.

When Amy found the Tiny Habits method, she discovered that the best way to eat a monstrous whale — as little Melinda Mae did in Shel Silverstein's poem — was to take one bite at a time. Amy ditched go big or go home and decided to go tiny. Every morning after dropping her daughter off at kindergarten, she pulled over on the side of the road and wrote one to-do on a sticky note. Just one. Each one was something she could accomplish right away: send out one sales e-mail, schedule a project meeting, draft a quick introduction to a patient guide. The simple act of focusing her energy on writing down one task led to a chain reaction that propelled her entire day and eventually led to the successful launch of her company. The feeling of success stuck with her as she drove home with her Post-it fluttering on the dashboard. And when she pulled into her driveway and grabbed the bright-pink sticky note, she took it inside to achieve a quick success.

One tiny action, one small bite, might feel insignificant at first, but it allows you to gain the momentum you need to ramp up to bigger challenges and faster progress. The next thing you know, you've eaten the whole whale.

TINY DOESN'T RELY ON MOTIVATION OR WILLPOWER

When it comes to chatter about behavior change, a lot of what you hear will mislead you. Be careful. Even highly cited academic theories often fail to transform people's lives in the real world.

As you know, motivation and willpower get a lot of airtime. People are always looking for ways to ramp them up and sustain them over time. The problem is that both motivation and willpower are shape-shifters by nature, which makes them unreliable.

Case in point: Juni from Chicago, who had more motivation to make a change than anyone I've met. Her addiction to sugar was threatening her health, her family, and her job. An early morning radio show host with an insanely busy schedule, Juni was always on the move. Instead of sitting down for lunch, she'd drink a caramel macchiato from Starbucks. The pace of life on the air was intense, and she thought she needed the sugar to keep up. Juni believed that having that type of energy required stimulants, and ice cream was Juni's drug of choice—bubblegum and cookie dough, to be exact. She'd crash hard when she got home, her two children playing video games as she lay zonked out on the couch.

A few years before I met Juni, her mother died from diabetes. It should have been a wake-up call—all the motivation Juni would ever need. But she tried to numb the pain with more and more bubblegum ice cream. Juni gained fifteen pounds that summer. Soon after, both of her sisters were diagnosed with diabetes. Then her grandmother, who also had diabetes, died. The disease was picking off members of her family one by one. After years of writing off her sugar addiction as a "sweet tooth," Juni recognized that it was dangerous. She had lost control.

At this point, her motivation spiked. She tried going cold turkey a number of times, which worked—for about a day. Maybe two. Then she'd get down on herself, feel bad, resume the sugarfest, and watch the scale creep up.

Juni thought that conquering sugar was a matter of willpower, that she wasn't strong enough to say no. This was frustrating and confusing for her because she always identified herself as someone who was incredibly strong-willed and determined—you don't make it to a major market radio show any other way. But the idea that stopping a habit is a matter of willpower couldn't have been further from the truth. Soon after Juni joined one of my Behavior Design Boot Camps for business reasons, she looked closely at her personal life and realized that her sugar addiction was a design issue, not a character flaw. The fact that her motivation would seesaw wasn't her fault; it wasn't a moral failing.

Once Juni understood a key maxim of Behavior Design—*simplicity changes behavior*—she refocused her personal efforts to create a constellation of habits, tiny in size but big on impact, that helped her to kick her sugar habit for good. She redesigned her environment and swapped out all her go-to sugary snacks with snacks containing less sugar that she still liked to eat, not unappealing substitutes like celery sticks and carrots. She cultivated a series of exercise and eating habits that crowded out and undermined her desire for sugar. Juni also discovered that her unresolved grief was prompting many of her sugar-bingeing behaviors —so she created a few more habits, always starting tiny, to help her process her feelings in a more positive way. When a wave of grief welled up and threatened to overtake her, Juni took that as a prompt to journal or reach out to a friend instead of reaching for the nearest candy bar. Perhaps most important of all, Juni was able to approach every new habit with a mindset of openness and self-compassion. There were moments when she fell off the wagon with sugar, but she didn't look at this as a failure of character but as a design insight she could use to improve what she did in the future.

Keeping changes small and expectations low is how you design around fair-weather friends like motivation and willpower. When something is tiny, it's easy to do—which means you don't need to rely on the unreliable nature of motivation.

TINY IS TRANSFORMATIVE

With the Tiny Habits method, you celebrate successes no matter how small they are. This is how we take advantage of our neurochemistry and quickly turn deliberate actions into automatic habits. Feeling successful helps us wire in new habits, and it motivates us to do more. I see these results week after week in my Tiny Habits data. But there's more: With Tiny Habits, you also learn *how to feel good* in your life. The ability to pat yourself on the back instead of beat yourself up grows solid, life-changing roots.

Linda planted her first Tiny Habit seed in the middle of what I would call a hurricane-strength life storm. About ten years ago, before she became a Tiny Habits coach, things fell apart tragically. In the course of only a few years, her son died of a drug overdose, her daughter was diagnosed with bipolar disorder, and the family business was circling the drain. In the middle of this already overwhelming time in her life, Linda found out that her husband had been living with undiagnosed early-onset Alzheimer's disease. As she began to take the reins of their business, she discovered another consequence of his illness: a decline in judgment. Bad business decisions coupled with a recession meant that they would be headed to bankruptcy court within months. They lost all their savings, their house, and the horse ranch that had been Linda's dream. This was a series of catastrophes that few of us will ever face. And there wasn't time for despair or shock. Linda had kids to raise and a business to save from bankruptcy. She was grief stricken with no time to grieve, and she quickly fell into a depression.

How to start digging out of such a hole? When Linda first started Tiny Habits, she told me that every morning she would find herself on the edge of her bed praying for strength. She wanted to feel better. She wanted to get out of bed. She wanted to be there for her kids. But she had trouble even putting her feet on the ground in the morning. When Tiny Habits came into her life, she could focus on only one thing: the morning challenge. She wanted to start the day off in hope, not despair. After experimenting with several habits, she finally found one—the Maui Habit—that she says "literally saved my life." It turned out that this tiny tweak, this pivotal behavior, was a fulcrum. Every morning, she woke up, put her feet on the floor, and said seven words out loud: "It's going to be a great day."

Things soon started to feel different. *Very* different.

For Linda, tiny was the *only* option. She needed to start small to grow big, and she needed to feel good about something. This new habit led to others that helped her feel successful. They helped her to be more productive and get healthy and stay strong for her kids. But most important, her new habits were tiny seeds of positivity that she planted in the cracks of her life. And they grew and grew. Even as new cracks kept appearing, Linda could look around her and be reminded that she had the ability to feel successful. She *was* successful. The evidence was blooming around her. She just had to keep watering.

Six years later, Linda has coached thousands of people in the Tiny Habits method. She loves her work. She'll be the first to say that her life is still a struggle. But she no longer hesitates when she wakes up in the morning. She knows that tiny is transformative, so she sits up and puts her feet on the floor and says those seven little words.

"It's going to be a great day."

The Anatomy of Tiny Habits

1. ANCHOR MOMENT

An existing routine (like brushing your teeth) or an event that happens (like a phone ringing). **The Anchor Moment reminds you to do the new Tiny Behavior.**

2. NEW TINY BEHAVIOR

A simple version of the new habit you want, such as flossing one tooth or doing two push-ups. **You do the Tiny Behavior immediately after the Anchor Moment.**

3. INSTANT CELEBRATION

Something you do to create positive emotions, such as saying, "I did a good job!" **You celebrate immediately after doing the new Tiny Behavior.**

Anchor

Behavior

Celebration

TINY STARTS WITH A KEY

I didn't wake up one day and decide to take the idea of baby steps to an extreme. First I discovered how human behavior really works.

It took me ten years of researching human behavior to find the key that unlocked the mystery, but in 2007 I did. The answer is surprisingly simple. At first, it was hard to believe no one had discovered this before, but I now see that some mysteries are like riddles. When you don't know the answers, riddles seem hard to solve. But once you see the answer, the solution seems obvious.

With the answer I discovered, you can decode behavior.

All behavior.

Putting your toothbrush in a new place. Unloading the dishwasher every morning before breakfast. Watering the garden in the evening. Doing two squats while your morning coffee brews. Taking the trash out on Wednesday. Smoking. Not smoking. Checking your watch for the time. Checking your phone for the time. Instagramming at three a.m. Kissing your husband when you get home from work. Making the bed. Not making the bed. Eating chocolate. Not eating chocolate. Reading this book. Not reading this book. That habit you have tried for years to cultivate. That habit you have tried for years to stop.

Some of these behaviors are positive habits. Some are not.

What I discovered is that all of these behaviors emerge from the same components. Their relationship drives our every action and reaction—they are the basic ingredients of human behavior.

In this book I share my Behavior Design models, which will help you think clearly about behavior. I also explain my methods, which will guide you in designing habits. To see a chart of all the models and methods in this book, please go to the appendix "Behavior Design: Models, Methods, and Maxims" on page 277.

My models and methods are supported by research in behavior science and evidence from related domains. You can find a large set of references at TinyHabits.com/references.

In the chapters that follow I give you all the exercises you need to redesign your habits. If you want more, you can find worksheets and other resources at TinyHabits.com/resources.

When you know how to adjust the components of human behavior, you can begin to tackle any behavior-change challenge in your life. Which means there is no feeling stuck. Which means you can be the person you want to be. If this sounds awesome and crazy and a little overwhelming, don't worry. I'll be right there with you, sharing what I've learned from helping thousands of people change their lives.

So where do we start? With the key that unlocks the mystery.

The Fogg Behavior Model.

Tiny Exercises to
Start Practicing Tiny Habits

The best way to learn the Tiny Habits method is to start practicing immediately. Don't wait. Get started with the Maui Habit, as I explained earlier. In addition, do the exercises below. In all of this, don't try to be perfect. Instead, adopt the mindset of a Habiteer (someone who practices Tiny Habits). That means you dive in and learn as you go. Along the way, don't get stressed or uptight. Be flexible and have fun!

EXERCISE #1: THE FLOSSING HABIT

You already know how to floss your teeth — all of them. But if you're like most people, you don't make a habit of flossing. It's not automatic in your life. This exercise can help you change that by focusing on the automaticity of the habit, not the size.

My Recipe — Tiny Habits Method

After I . . .   I will . . .   To wire the habit into my
                                                brain, I will immediately:

brush my teeth,   floss one tooth.

                                                      ☺

Step 1: Find a type of floss you like. You might need to try a few different styles to see what feels best for you.

Step 2: Set the floss on your bathroom counter, ideally right by your toothbrush.

Step 3: After you set down your toothbrush, pick up the floss container and tear off some floss.

Step 4: Floss one tooth.

Step 5: Smile at yourself in the mirror and feel good about creating a new habit.

Note: In the days ahead, you can floss more than one tooth if you want, but view anything more than one tooth as extra credit. You are going above and beyond.

EXERCISE #2: QUICK STARTS

I wrote this book to share the Tiny Habits method in depth. As you read the chapters ahead you'll learn how behavior works and how to create habits quickly and easily, step by step.

You may want to start building habits right away — like right now. That's what this optional exercise is all about.

Below are three "quick start" options for Tiny Habits. You can do any one of these, or all of them. The choice is yours.

- Go to the back of this book (pages 291 to 305) where I share over 300 recipes for Tiny Habits. Choose three recipes that inspire you. If needed, revise each recipe so it fits your life better. Then dive in and start practicing.

- Go online to TinyHabits.com/recipes. At that web page you'll find an easy-to-use tool that helps you design recipes for Tiny Habits. Once you have a few habits designed, you can start practicing immediately.

- Go online to TinyHabits.com/join. At that page you can join my free 5-day program. You'll receive personal guidance from a Tiny Habits coach I've trained (a real human!) who is both kind and supportive.

EXERCISE #3: REMIND YOURSELF THAT YOU CHANGE BEST BY FEELING GOOD

If there's one concept from my book I hope you embrace, it's this: *People change best by feeling good, not by feeling bad.* For that purpose, I have created this exercise for you.

Step 1: Write this phrase on a small piece of paper: *I change best by feeling good, not by feeling bad.*

Step 2: Tape the paper to your bathroom mirror or anywhere you will frequently see it.

Step 3: Read the phrase often.

Step 4: Notice how this insight works in your life (and for the people around you).

THE
ELEMENTS
OF BEHAVIOR

You can change your life by changing your behaviors. You know that. But what you may not know is that only three variables drive those behaviors.

The Fogg Behavior Model is the key to unlocking that mystery. It represents the three universal elements of behavior and their relationship to one another. These elements work together to drive our every action—from flossing one tooth to running a marathon. Once you understand the Behavior Model, you can analyze why a behavior happened, which means you can stop blaming your behavior on the wrong things (like character and self-discipline, for starters). And you can use my model to design for a change in behavior in yourself or in other people.

B = MAP

Behavior   happens when   Motivation & Ability & Prompt

converge at the same moment

A behavior happens when the three elements of MAP—Motivation, Ability, and Prompt—come together at the same moment. Motivation is your desire to do the behavior. Ability is your capacity to do the behavior. And Prompt is your cue to do the behavior.

I'll give you an example.

In 2010, when I was at the gym (rocking out to Janet Jackson on the elliptical strider), I performed a strange behavior for people with pulse rates of more than 120 beats per minute: I donated to the Red Cross. I did it in response to a text message inviting me to do so.

Here's what my one-time behavior looks like when you break it down.

Behavior (B): Donating via text to the Red Cross.

Motivation (M): I wanted to help the victims of a devastating disaster.

Ability (A): It was easy to reply to a text message.

Prompt (P): I was prompted by a text message from the Red Cross.

In this case, the three elements (M, A, and P) converged, so I did the behavior; I made a donation. But if one of the three elements hadn't been sufficient, there's a good chance that I wouldn't have.

My motivation for this action was high. The earthquake effects were well publicized and genuinely heart-wrenching. But what about ability? What if the Red Cross had called me and asked for a credit card number instead? I was striding on the elliptical machine, with my wallet in the car, so that would have made it very hard for me to do the behavior. What about the prompt? What if the fundraisers didn't use the phone at all? What if they sent me something in the mail and I threw it away without reading it, thinking it was junk mail? Then I wouldn't see the request. No prompt, no behavior. Luckily, the Red Cross did me a favor. I already wanted to donate, and they made it easy. Whether the organizers knew it or not, they designed M, A, and P perfectly for the behavior they were trying to encourage. And it's not just me. The texting campaign was very successful, raising more than $3 million in the first twenty-four hours and more than $21 million by the end of the week. Well done, Red Cross!

Behavior Design

Models	Methods
How to think clearly about behavior	How to design for behavior
Fogg Behavior Model B = MAP	Tiny Habits

B=MAP APPLIES TO *ALL* HUMAN BEHAVIOR

When I first teach people my Behavior Model, they are sometimes a little dubious when I tell them this is a universal model. They wonder how one model with just four letters could possibly account for every kind of behavior in every culture. After all, there are "good" behaviors and "bad" behaviors—are they really equivalent? Many people have a hard time understanding how their online shopping diversion has anything to do with their workout regimen. People think that there must be something fundamentally more complex about the fitness regimen because it's a challenge. On the flip side, if a change is easy, like hanging your coat in the closet instead of on the banister, there must be something fundamentally different about that action.

There isn't.

Behaviors are like bicycles. They can look different, but the core mechanisms are the same. Wheels. Brakes. Pedals.

That being said, just because the building blocks of behavior are the same doesn't mean that those behaviors feel the same, look the same, or act the same. Adding to the disconnect, the emotions people have about pleasurable behaviors differ drastically from the ones they have about behaviors they deem challenging. Sometimes it feels more like the difference between a unicycle and a road bike. At first, some people can't see how the two categories of behavior are even related. This concept is important for anyone trying to change *any* behavior.

Every month or so, I hold Behavior Design Boot Camp—a hands-on training where I help professionals create business solutions for wellness, financial security, environmental sustainability, and so on.

My boot campers almost always take what they learn and translate it to their personal lives. That's why I often kick off boot camp with an exercise that uses a personal example. I ask people to tell me about one positive habit they created without much effort and a "bad" habit they feel terrible about and want to stop. Boot campers come up with great stories about their habits, but at one of my events, a woman named Katie nailed how different two behaviors can *seem*.

Katie was a talented executive overseeing dozens of employees and a $10 million budget, and her "good" habit was tied to her productivity. Katie had a rock-solid habit of tidying her desk each day before leaving work. After she shuts down her computer for the day, she neatly stacks her papers and sorts the stickies on her whiteboard into To Do, Done, and In Progress columns. After her desk looks good, Katie pushes her chair in and leaves the office. When she walks in the next morning and looks at her desk, Katie always feels a little punch of energy. She's reminded that she's ready to start the day and that she's all set up to make sure it's a good one. When I asked if acquiring this habit was a conscious choice or not, she said no—she had just started doing it one day.

Katie hadn't thought much about her desk-tidying habit. It even took a while for her to identify this as a positive habit. But when I asked about a habit she *didn't* want, she practically leaped out of her chair.

"Scrolling in bed! I hate it, but I can't stop doing it. Sometimes I lie in bed looking at Facebook for so long that I miss my workout," she added.

Katie told me that it all starts because her phone is her alarm clock. When it goes off, she plucks it off the nightstand, rolls over on her side, and starts tapping and scrolling. I asked when her alarm is set to wake her.

Four thirty a.m.

"Whoa," I said.

At the beginning of the year, Katie had made a resolution to work out every day. Some days she did, but most days she didn't. It wasn't because she'd decided not to; it was because she got sucked into the digital vortex despite her early wake-up time. Those red notification numbers demanded attention. One click would lead to a video, which would lead to a feed from someone she didn't even know, then to another video, and then to the five thirty alarm going off.

Another day had begun by not doing the workout she had promised herself she would do. Cue the self-criticism and guilt. She didn't like the pattern that she'd fallen into, but she told herself that she was on top of her life in so many ways that maybe this was where her "togetherness" ran out.

Let's consider both of Katie's habits together: desk tidying and binge scrolling.

Two behaviors, two wildly different feelings.

One behavior makes Katie feel good and helps her to achieve her larger aspiration of being productive. This tidiness habit has become so automatic that she hardly even thinks about it. In contrast, the scrolling habit is enjoyable in the moment but makes her feel disappointed in herself afterward. Scrolling in bed drives her crazy, but she often can't resist doing it.

These behaviors *feel* very different to Katie. Yet the components aren't. *All* behavior is driven by the same three elements. I wanted Katie to know that she hadn't run out of "togetherness," or willpower. She merely had a third habit—a scrolling habit—that was getting in the way of a *poorly designed* exercise habit.

Remember, for a behavior (B) to occur, three elements must converge at the same moment: Motivation, Ability, and Prompt.

It's a model that has profound implications. Each person's motivation, ability, and prompt will be different in any given situation. The specifics of motivation or ability may differ by culture or age. And that's okay. The universe is unendingly complex, yet we can observe a phenomenon and break it down using some basic principles that apply to *every* circumstance.

Consider this visual representation of B=MAP, which shows how motivation and ability work in relationship to each other.

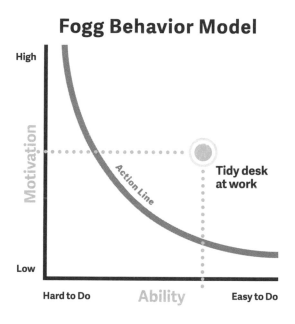

The first thing to notice is the big dot. That's Katie's habit of tidying her desk. The dot's location tells us where her motivation and ability are when she is prompted to act. You can see that her motivation is in the middle and that her ability to tidy her desk is on the easy-to-do side of the spectrum.

Now take a look at the curved Action Line.

True to its smiling shape, the Action Line is our buddy. If I were to have only one thing engraved on my headstone, it would be this happy little curve.

When a behavior is prompted above the Action Line, it happens. Suppose you have high motivation but no ability (you weigh 120 pounds, but you want to bench-press 500 pounds). You're going to fall below the Action Line and feel frustrated when you are prompted. On the other hand, if you are capable of the behavior but have zero motivation, a prompt won't get you to do the behavior; it will only be an annoyance. What causes the behavior to be above or below the line is a combination of motivation pushing you up and ability moving you to the right. Here's a key insight: Behaviors that ultimately become habits will reliably fall above the Action Line.

Let's plot Katie's scrolling behavior.

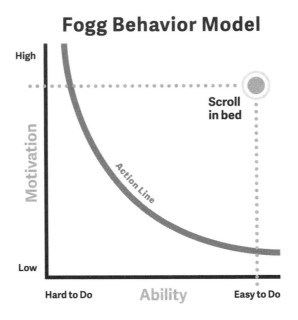

Fogg Behavior Model

Yikes! Look at that big dot. Sky-high motivation and high ability—easy to do. On top of that, you know that Katie's prompt is reliable. Her phone blasts an alarm every morning at four thirty a.m.

When you see it on the model, it makes sense why Katie, a successful, accomplished, and capable person, is having a hard time kicking this scrolling habit. You can see why it's wired in. Unless something changes, she's likely to keep scrolling and not exercising.

We have to do two things: redesign her scrolling habit, then redesign her exercise habit. The first thing to remember is that there is no *one* solution for every behavior challenge. Our job is to adjust the components—M, A, and P—and find out what combination works best in each circumstance to get the behavior we want. We have to make her scrolling hard to do or change her motivation to scroll, then we can look at her exercise habit. There are two core principles that we can rely on when we analyze behavior by turning the dials of motivation, ability, and prompt.

MOTIVATION AND ABILITY HAVE A COMPENSATORY RELATIONSHIP

Once you understand how this principle works, you can design for almost any behavior you want.

The curved Action Line on our graphs visually represents this principle, but here's the explanation in plain English.

1. The *more motivated* you are to do a behavior, the *more likely* you are to do the behavior

Fogg Behavior Model

When motivation is high, people not only take action when prompted, they can also do difficult things. If you've ever read about a mother fighting off a bear to save her child or an ordinary person pulling someone out of the path of an oncoming subway car, you get the point.

Adrenaline races, stakes are high, hard things get done.

When motivation is middling, people will do a behavior only if it's fairly easy—like Katie's desk tidying.

2. The *harder* a behavior is to do, the *less likely* you are to do it

If someone asked you to show them the cover of the book you're reading right now, would you do it? Probably. It requires a flick of the wrist and an interruption of your reading, which is a minor annoyance but no big deal. It's easy to do. However, if someone asked you to read this entire book aloud to them, then your response would probably be different. You would need a lot of motivation to do this behavior. Perhaps the person asking is visually impaired. Perhaps you are offered one thousand dollars to do it. Those things could work. My point: You need serious motivation to do something difficult.

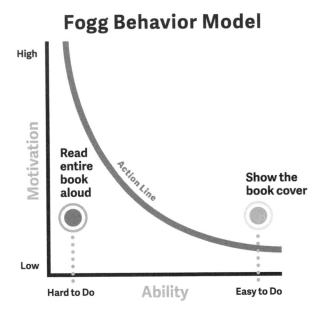

Fogg Behavior Model

Here's a related insight that might begin to transform your life (it transformed mine): The *easier* a behavior is to do, the *more likely* the behavior will become habit.

This applies to habits we consider "good" and "bad." It doesn't matter. Behavior is behavior. It all works the same way.

Consider Katie's scrolling-in-bed habit. She already has her phone in hand, thanks to her alarm. So scrolling, as a next step, is really easy to do.

3. Motivation and ability work together like teammates

You need to have both motivation and ability for a behavior to land above the Action Line, but motivation and ability can work together like teammates. If one is weak, the other needs to be strong to get you above the curve. In other words: *The amount you have of one affects the amount you need of the other.* Understanding the relationship of motivation and ability opens the door to new ways of analyzing and designing behaviors. If you have only a little bit of one, then you need more of the other —i.e., they compensate each other.

In Katie's case, her desk-tidying habit is fairly motivated but also easy to do. She told me that it takes less than three minutes for her to complete her tidying routine, which means it's not something that is going to make her late for picking up her kids. Her ability to do this behavior started out in the easy zone, and the more she does it, the more streamlined her process becomes. In general, the more you do a behavior, the easier it gets.

The Fogg Behavior Model describes a snapshot in time: one specific behavior at a specific moment. But I've also used this model to show how behavior happens over time: Behavior 1 ⟶ Behavior 2 ⟶ Behavior 3. That's a powerful extension of this model. But here I simply want to point out how most behaviors become easier to do when repeated.

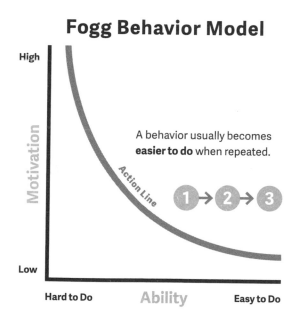

Fogg Behavior Model

*A behavior usually becomes **easier to do** when repeated.*

Even on days when Katie's motivation dips, the tidying task is still easy enough to make up the difference. An important point: if she had started by cleaning her *whole* office she wouldn't have developed this behavior into a habit. When she felt rushed, she'd skip it.

4. No behavior happens without a *prompt*

If you don't have a prompt, your levels of motivation and ability don't matter. Either you are prompted to act or you're not. No prompt, no behavior. Simple yet powerful.

Motivation and ability are continuous variables. You always have some level of motivation and ability for any given behavior. When the phone rings, your motivation and ability to answer it are always there in the background. But a prompt is like lightning. It comes and goes. If you don't hear the phone ring, you don't answer it.

You can disrupt a behavior you don't want by removing the prompt. This isn't always easy, but removing the prompt is your best first move to stop a behavior from happening.

A few years ago I went to the South by Southwest conference in Austin, Texas. I walked into my hotel room and threw my bag on the bed. When I scanned the room, I saw something on the bureau.

"Oh nooooo," I said out loud to absolutely no one.

There was an overflowing basket of goodies. Pringles. Blue chips. A giant lollipop. A granola bar. Peanuts. I try to eat healthy foods, but salty snacks are delicious. I knew the goody bin would be a problem for me at the end of every long day. It would serve as a prompt: Eat me! I knew that if the basket sat there I would eventually cave. The blue chips would be the first to go. Then I would eat those peanuts. So I asked myself what I had to do to stop this behavior from happening. Could I demotivate myself? No way, I love salty snacks. Can I make it harder to do? Maybe. I could ask the front desk to raise the price on the snacks or remove them from the room. But that might be slightly awkward. So what I did was remove the prompt. I put the beautiful basket of temptations on the lowest shelf in the TV cabinet and shut the door. I knew the basket was still in the room, but the treats were no longer screaming EAT ME at full volume. By the next morning, I had forgotten about those salty snacks. I'm happy to report that I survived three days in Austin without opening the cabinet again.

Notice that my one-time action disrupted the behavior by removing the prompt. If that hadn't worked, there were other dials I could have adjusted—but prompts are the low-hanging fruit of Behavior Design.

Teaching the Behavior Model

Now that you've seen how my Behavior Model applies to various types of behavior, I'll show you more ways to use this model in the pages that follow. When I work with students at Stanford or train industry innovators, I teach them how to explain my Behavior Model in two minutes or less. I first give a demonstration, drawing on the whiteboard as I explain each part. After I finish the two-minute demo, I outline the steps that work best, including some specific phrases to use. Finally, I have each person step up to a whiteboard or get out a piece of paper and explain the model to someone else while sketching it out in real time. Learning to explain the Behavior Model quickly and clearly is one of the most useful skills in Behavior Design.

I'm not with you in person to teach this skill so I've created a tiny exercise at the end of this chapter for your benefit. If you need more guidance, you can go online to get the exact script and watch how other people teach the model. The few minutes it takes to learn to teach the Behavior Model is a terrific investment of your time.

Once you've learned the Behavior Model, you can apply this in many practical ways, including stopping or troubleshooting a behavior. And that's what I want to explain next.

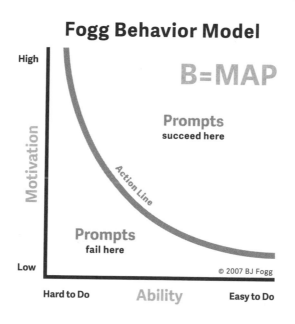

Fogg Behavior Model

B=MAP

High

Motivation

Prompts
succeed here

Action Line

Prompts
fail here

Low

© 2007 BJ Fogg

Hard to Do   Ability   Easy to Do

Using the Behavior Model to Disrupt a Habit

Now that you know how motivation and ability work together and how prompts are vital to behavior, let's go back to Katie. How can she break her scrolling habit? Her motivation is high. The behavior is very easy. That puts her habit far above the Action Line.

Fogg Behavior Model

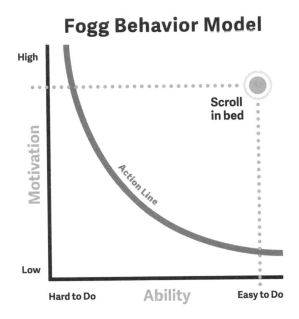

What could she change?

Motivation?

Unlikely. Those happy feelings she gets when she sees that someone liked her post aren't going anywhere; they're baked into the app. Katie wants to stay updated on friends, and Facebook is doing that for her. Motivation is likely to remain high with this one.

What about ability?

This is where we find a big opportunity for change.

Katie could delete her Facebook account to make scrolling her newsfeed impossible to do. But perhaps that's too extreme—she still might want to check it at other times throughout the day. Luckily, there are plenty of other ways to make it harder for Katie to look at her phone while in bed. She could delete the Facebook app from her phone. She could put her phone across the room on the bureau. She could put her phone outside her daughter's door to ensure that she'd spring out of bed to shut off the alarm before her daughter woke up, or she could leave her phone in the car. Because Katie's motivation for scrolling was so high, she had to experiment with a bunch of different options before she finally found this two-pronged solution: She put her phone in the kitchen at night and got an old-fashioned alarm clock for her bedroom. Putting some physical distance between her and the phone made her scrolling behavior harder to do, and having the alarm clock wake her removed the prompt altogether.

If you can't change one component of the Behavior Model (motivation in this case), then you focus on changing the others (ability and prompt).

What about her exercise habit? As it turned out, she didn't need any adjustment. Once Katie removed the distraction of scrolling, she started working out with the plans and tools she already had in place.

With enough tinkering, you can design for almost any behavior you want and short-circuit most behaviors you don't. Katie did it fairly easily and successfully, but first she had to know the ins and outs of what was driving her scrolling-in-bed habit.

Months after Behavior Design Boot Camp, Katie told me how happy she was to finally have a solid workout habit in her life. She still got sucked into her phone on occasion over breakfast or while waiting in line, but it didn't have the same iron grip on her. Most days, she was the master of her mornings. She felt physically stronger than ever, but most important, she was learning that Behavior Design could improve any area of her life.

One Model to Understand All Behavior

If you want to be highly effective at changing your own behavior—or anyone else's—mastering the Behavior Model is the key. Once you have a clear view of how behavior works, you'll be able to decode other people's behavior as well as your own—a powerful skill. You can begin to foster positive habits and disrupt the ones you don't like, and you'll have more compassion for other people's less-than-ideal behaviors.

I was getting on a flight a few years ago, and I saw an active kid seated behind me. As we settled in, I felt his little feet kicking my seat over and over. Ugh. I knew that he'd likely be kicking my seat during the entire flight. He's a kid, after all. So before the plane took off, I asked myself what I could do to stop or reduce the kicking behavior.

I put my Behavior Model to work.

First the prompt. Could I remove it? Nope. I had no control over his internal desire, boredom, or whatever was prompting him to kick the seat. Then ability: Could I make his kicking harder to do? No. So I was left with one final option: motivation. How could I, in a calm and playful way, motivate this little guy to kick the seat less?

I decided to use the rule of reciprocity.

When someone gives you a gift, you naturally want to return the favor in some way. This dynamic helps humans get along with one another. It's also one way we can gracefully influence motivation. I decided to give it a try.

I had a yellow smiley-face button in my computer bag. (Yes, I am practically Mister Rogers, let's get that out of the way right now.) I got it out of my bag and showed it to the little passenger and his parents. "Hey," I said. "I want to give you this smiley-face button. I'm hoping this will help you remember not to kick my seat during the flight."

The kid said, "Yes!" and the parents thanked me with genuine smiles.

The flight went great—no seat kicking—and I made a few friends in the process. We waved good-bye at baggage claim.

By using the Behavior Model at home, you can help people in your household help you. As anyone in a long-term relationship can attest, tension over housework can be corrosive. My partner, Denny, and I have different views about household cleaning because I am more of a "tidy enough" person and Denny is more of a "disinfect everything" person. Over the years, cleaning the shower became an issue. Denny is hypervigilant about mold, but our shower doesn't drain well, which leads to—you guessed it—mold, so he had been asking me to wipe out the shower after I used it. But I didn't do it most of the time. In fact, I rarely did.

One day Denny invited me to look at the shower with him, and he put Behavior Design into action.

"We both want a clean shower," he said.

I agreed.

He saw that I had some level of motivation.

Then he asked me about ability. What seemed hard about wiping out the shower? I told him that I didn't know what his request meant. Did he want me to use my towel or a squeegee? Should I wipe down the walls? This was Denny's aha moment. He hadn't been specific about what he wanted, so the abstract behavior felt hard to do for me. What he did next was brilliant and simple. He showed me what to do. He walked me into the shower, and said, "Okay, when you turn off the shower [prompt], you grab the shower towel off the rack like this, then you put it on the floor and shuffle around on it like this. Then you throw the towel in the dirty laundry and you're done." What Denny showed me was so easy, it almost made me feel silly for not doing it in the first place. It took about ten seconds. Once he showed me what to do, my *perception* of the difficulty of the task changed—it suddenly seemed easy to do.

I have wiped out the shower every day since Denny's theatrical demonstration. Why? First of all, I wanted a clean shower, and I wanted to please him. So I had at least some motivation. But the behavior seemed difficult. Once he showed me exactly what to do, I saw it was easy, and I zoomed above the Action Line. Fast-forward to today: When it comes to household tasks, an area where I'm not an expert, I know to say, "Show me exactly what you want me to do." I watch him, and my ability increases.

These are a couple of small examples of how you can use the Behavior Model with other people. We'll devote a whole chapter to this when we have more tools in our change toolbox.

Three Steps for Troubleshooting a Behavior

We often want to do a behavior—or want someone else to do a behavior—and are met with little or no success. For those situations, I have good news: Behavior Design gives us a specific set of steps for troubleshooting this common problem. And it's not what you'd expect. Let's say you want your employees to show up to your weekly team meeting on time, but they consistently arrive a few minutes late. Many managers would get upset, impose a penalty, or shoot dirty looks at the people arriving late. All those are attempts to use motivation to get the behavior of arriving on time to happen. And all of those are mistakes. You don't start with motivation when you troubleshoot.

You follow these steps instead. Try each step in order. If you don't get results, move to the next step.

1. Check to see if there's a *prompt* to do the behavior.
2. See if the person has the *ability* to do the behavior.
3. See if the person is *motivated* to do the behavior.

To do an expert job of troubleshooting a behavior for yourself or others, start with the prompt. Is the person being prompted to do the behavior? You might ask your tardy employees, *Do you have a reminder to come to the meeting on time?* If they don't, have them find a good prompt. And that might solve the problem. No drama. No dirty looks. Just design a good *prompt*.

If that doesn't work, then you move to the next step. See if people have the ability to do the behavior. Ask your tardy employees what is making it difficult for them to arrive at your meeting on time. (I'll explain a comprehensive approach in chapter 3, but this question is good for now.)

You might learn that the tardy employees have a previous meeting that ends at the top of the hour and that they can't arrive at your meeting on time.

With that, you've found your answer. It's an *ability* problem, not a motivation problem.

But let's pretend that they have a prompt and the ability, and that it is a *motivation* issue. In this case, you'd then try to find a way to motivate punctuality. (And there are lots of ways to do this, both good and bad.)

Notice that fussing around with motivation is the last step in the troubleshooting order. Most people assume that to get a behavior to happen you need to focus on motivation first.

This process of troubleshooting can save you some grief both at work and at home. Let's suppose you've asked your teenage daughter to stop on her way home from school to buy some poster board you need for a church lesson. She has your car, and you think that this is a fair request.

She gets home from school that day, and she doesn't have your poster board. You get upset and explain how much you need that poster board. (Both of those are motivation strategies.) Your daughter says, "Sorry. I'll do it tomorrow."

But there's no poster board the next day.

At this point, you might stomp around the living room, threaten to take away her driving privileges, and make a comment about how unreliable she is. (All three are motivation strategies.)

As you know, this is not a good situation.

Now let's rewind this story and imagine that you know how to troubleshoot. You don't get upset when your daughter arrives home without the poster board on the first day. You go into troubleshooting mode: "Did you have anything to remind you to get the poster board?"

"No. I just thought I'd remember. But I forgot."

So you design a prompt for the next day by asking, "What do you think would be a good reminder for you tomorrow?"

And she says that she is putting a to-do note on her phone.

Guess what? She hands you the poster board with a smile the next day.

When you apply this troubleshooting method to your own behavior, you'll find that it stops you from blaming yourself. Let's say you don't meditate in the mornings as you'd hoped. Instead of blaming yourself for a lack of willpower or motivation, walk yourself through the steps: Did you have something to prompt you? What is making this hard to do?

In many cases, you'll find your lack of doing a behavior is not a motivation issue at all. You can solve for the behavior by finding a good prompt or by making the behavior easier to do.

See the World through the Behavior Model Lens

I want you to practice observing the world through the lens of the Behavior Model. It will serve two purposes. One, it's fun. Two, it will help you break things down along the lines of motivation, ability, and prompt so you can identify what's driving your own behavior — or anyone else's. At the end of this chapter, you'll find some tiny exercises that will help you apply the Behavior Model in practical ways.

Many people who use the Behavior Model for step-by-step troubleshooting, report that this method helps them see the machinery of human behavior. You will be able to deconstruct your efforts at change and know how they are being undermined or supported. You'll be able to better understand why you do some behaviors that you later regret.

We all do things that we don't like.

Eat popcorn for dinner.

Yell at the kids.

Binge-watch Netflix.

But we don't have to be blind to these behaviors or frustrated by them. And we really, *really* don't have to blame ourselves.

No one reminds me of this more than Jennifer, a talented graphic artist and an awesome mom. Before she signed up for Tiny Habits online and learned about the Behavior Model, she was frustrated that she couldn't get herself to exercise. Jennifer used to work out all the time. She was an avid runner in college and even ran a half marathon with a friend a few years before she had kids. Things changed, and these days doing the dishes and the laundry was the most physical activity Jennifer engaged in. She really wanted to work out. But she was out of shape. She knew she had to start slow and steady.

Jennifer began doing yoga in her home office for fifteen minutes once in a while and occasionally ran to the end of the street. All things she was capable of doing. Nothing too strenuous. But she couldn't get herself to do this with any regularity. Days that she exercised became "good" days and days she didn't became "extra glass of wine" days. She told me later that this made her feel like a failure. This thing that used to be so easy for her was a daily struggle. Most days she couldn't get herself to run to the mailbox, let alone run five miles, an achievement that used to bring her much joy. She felt like something was wrong with her. Why couldn't she get herself to do it?

Jennifer was describing something common—a feeling of blockage or resistance. Every day she told herself that she should lift weights or go for a run. But she often came up with reasons not to   online shopping for the kids, research for work—then she felt like a failure at the end of the day. She knew she was making excuses for not doing something that was good for her. Was she depressed? Self-loathing? Weak-willed? What was going on?

When I e-mailed Jennifer in the weeks following her Tiny Habits experience, she told me how she had solved the puzzle of her exercise habit. First, she looked at what was going on with motivation, ability, and prompt. She broke her behavior down step by step and zeroed in on motivation. It was almost nonexistent. Most days she simply didn't *want* to do yoga in the office by herself. Jennifer set aside her idea of solitary yoga to find a better match. By listing different exercises that appealed to her, she stumbled on solid gold. The exercises she enjoyed had one thing in common—they were done as part of a group. The more she thought about it, the more Jennifer realized that working out by herself wasn't fun. It felt like an obligation, and she didn't have enough motivation to get herself over the Action Line. In the end, Jennifer gave up on the idea of working out alone and she matched herself with group exercises: She joined a weekly spin class, then a weekly yoga class, then a mom's running group, and before she knew it, she was back in the habit of working out.

This was a huge victory for Jennifer, but figuring out the behavior puzzle wasn't what she was most excited about. The real life-changer was that she had broken the self–trash talk spell. Before she knew how behavior worked, she felt nagged by why she couldn't exercise as she used to. It was a narrative running on repeat—"You can't do what you used to; what's wrong with you?" At the end of the day, she'd chew on this before having her self-prescribed glass of wine. She'd rack her brain for answers. Maybe she was getting old, maybe she needed to be on anti-depressants, maybe she should see a personal trainer. She'd eventually get so frustrated and down that she had to busy herself with making dinner and picking up toys. It wasn't until she mapped out her behavior that she realized it wasn't all about her. It was about the behaviors. Once she broke them down into their component parts, she realized where the design flaws were. She had the ability, but she was not sufficiently motivated to work out by herself. To make matters worse, she didn't have a reliable prompt for office yoga time.

Lucky for Jennifer (and the rest of us), the Behavior Model doesn't have a "lazy" axis or a "weak" axis. It didn't fit her blame narrative. It's a model, not a referendum on character. Once Jennifer realized that she was not her behavior, everything changed. She started to think about her habits as if they were recipes. If the result wasn't to her liking, she needed to change the ratios and fiddle with the ingredients, not beat herself up or give up.

From now on, I want you to look at your behavior the way a scientist looks at what's growing in a petri dish—with curiosity and objective distance. This is going to be a different mindset than the ones in many of the change books you might have read. I'm not dwelling on willpower or rigidly prescribing something that is going to set you up for feeling bad. I want you to treat your life as your own personal "change lab"—a place to experiment with the person you want to be. A place where you not only feel safe but also feel like anything is possible.

For the next four chapters, we'll learn about the Behavior Design process and use it to start our experiments. We'll focus on the Tiny Habits method because it's the foundation for creating positive habits and it contains all the key principles you'll need to design for other behaviors down the road. You'll use the same process to achieve a specific outcome over time, do a big one-time behavior, or disrupt unwanted behaviors. And the first step to creating a pack of positive habits is to decide which ones to cultivate.

But before you can do that, you've got to take a closer look at what's been tripping you up all these years. If you're reading this book, there's a good chance you have some things you want to change but haven't yet. So what has booby-trapped your attempts at change?

The Motivation Monkey.

The Motivation Monkey tricks us into setting unreasonable goals. He can sometimes help us reach amazing heights, but he will often abandon us when we need him most.

Tiny Exercises to Practice the Fogg Behavior Model

The first exercise is easy. The second exercise will take a bit more work, but don't skip it. I guarantee that your investment of time and effort will pay off.

EXERCISE #1: EXPLORE WAYS TO STOP A HABIT

The Fogg Behavior Model applies to all types of behavior change. In this exercise, you'll explore simple ways to stop a habit.

Step 1: Write down three habits that you'd like to stop. Try to be specific. For instance, write "Stop buying soda for lunch" rather than "Stop drinking soda."

Step 2: For each habit, think of ways you might remove (or avoid) the prompt. If you can't think of anything, that's okay. Move on to the next step.

Step 3: For each habit, think of ways to make it harder to do (ability).

Step 4: For each habit, think of ways to reduce your motivation.

Step 5: For each habit, select your best solution from steps 2, 3, and 4.

Extra Credit: Put your solution into practice.

EXERCISE #2: LEARN THE FOGG BEHAVIOR MODEL BY TEACHING IT TO SOMEONE ELSE

One great way to learn something is to teach it to someone else.

Step 1: See the appendix on page 279 for the script to teach the Fogg Behavior Model.

Step 2: Draw the elements of the Behavior Model as you read the script. Practice this until you can explain the model without reading the script.

Step 3: Find someone you can teach.

Step 4: Explain the Behavior Model using your drawing of the elements. (Or, even better, draw the model as you explain it.)

Step 5: After you are done with the two-minute explanation, ask your learner, "What surprised you?" This is my favorite teaching question because it can lead to a conversation that makes the learning experience better for everyone.

CHAPTER

MOTIVATION— FOCUS ON MATCHING

Sandra and Adrian had just bought their first home. At the first showing, they had stood on the back deck with their agent and surveyed the only downside to the property — the backyard.

It was a mess. A crumbling rock wall, knee-high grass, and a scary-looking compost pile huddled against the back of the garage. At that point, Sandra and Adrian didn't care. They were riding high on the American Dream. All they saw was possibility. A veggie garden and flower beds. A hammock strung between two scraggly oak trees. A rare bird alighting on a lemon tree.

On the day they took down the sold sign, they were excited. They made their checklist of must-do items and jumped in. They started indoors, sanding, painting, and scrubbing every square inch of the place. A couple of weeks later, they had crossed everything off their list except the backyard. They stood side by side on the back deck to check things out. They felt very different this time. Their verve for home improvement had fallen off a cliff. They were overwhelmed. Where should they start? Sandra grew up mowing her parents' lawn, but that was the extent of her experience with landscaping. Adrian grew up in an apartment, so he knew even less. They didn't have any garden tools. Would a lemon tree even grow in New Hampshire? They knew what they wanted —a beautiful backyard where they could enjoy time with friends and watch their future children run through sprinklers and build forts. But now this felt like a fantasy. And a ton of work.

This is where most people turn around, go back inside, and tell themselves they'll get to it later. Or they dive in full-bore and exhaust themselves. Three hours of backbreaking work later, they give up and don't return. Either way, the dream is deferred, replaced by feelings of guilt, disappointment, or failure.

So what happened here?

When it came to their backyard dreams, the problem is that Sandra and Adrian put all their eggs into the motivation basket.

Motivation Is Unreliable

Motivation is often unreliable when it comes to home improvement. And it's also unreliable with diets, exercise routines, creative projects, filing taxes, opening businesses, searching for jobs, planning conferences —self-improvement of all types. The Motivation Monkey's traps are stealthy and numerous. They catch you whether you're facing a big project or attempting to change your habits.

Here's the unfortunate thing—most people believe motivation is the true engine of behavior change. Words like "rewards" and "incentives" get thrown around with such regularity that most people think you can create whatever habits you want if you find the right carrot to dangle in front of yourself. This kind of thinking is understandable, but it also happens to be wrong.

Yes, motivation *is* one of three elements that drives behavior. The problem is that *motivation is often fickle,* and this chapter digs deeper into the challenges it presents.

Motivation is like a party-animal friend. Great for a night out, but not someone you would rely on to pick you up from the airport. You must understand its role and its limitations, then pick behaviors that don't rely on such a fickle friend.

In order to do that, we first have to break down the Motivation Monkey's game trap by trap. Then we'll learn how to navigate around them to get what we really want. No dangling of carrots or self-imposed guilt trips necessary.

1. MOTIVATION IS COMPLEX

Let's start with the basics.

What is motivation?

Motivation is a desire to do a specific behavior (eat spinach tonight) or a general class of behaviors (eat vegetables and other healthy foods each night). Some psychologists talk about extrinsic and intrinsic motivation. No offense to all those psychologists, but I've found this to be a weak distinction that is not very helpful in the real world. In my own work, I focus on three sources of motivation: yourself (what you already want), a benefit or punishment you would receive by doing the action (the carrot and stick), and your context (e.g., all your friends are doing it). To help you visualize this, I created a model called the PAC Person. You'll see him pop up again and again—it turns out that Person, Action, and Context are fundamental for understanding human behavior.

PERSON

Person already wants to do action

ACTION

An external benefit or punishment for doing the action

Motivation caused by a person's context

CONTEXT

As the PAC Person graphics show, motivation can come from one of three places. First, motivation can come from inside a person: You already want to do the behavior. For example, most of us are motivated to look attractive. This is built into us as humans. Motivation can also come from a benefit or punishment associated with a behavior. Let's talk about taxes. Most of us don't wake up in the morning wanting to pay taxes, but there are punishments for not paying. That motivates us. Finally, motivation can come from our context (our current environment). Suppose you are at an art auction that supports a charity. If the cause is worthy and if people are drinking and if the auctioneer creates a lot of energy, all of this—the context (which is carefully designed)—will motivate you to pay a lot for a simple painting.

There also could be more than one source of motivation for doing a behavior. I look at these different motivations as forces pushing you toward or away from an action. Maybe it's the desire to be accepted by a group, or maybe it's the fear of physical pain. Maybe your motivations are moving you toward an action, or maybe they are moving you away. But motivations are always there, pushing you up and down—above the Action Line or below—depending on their strength at any given moment.

Sometimes the complexity of our motivations amounts to a psychological tug-of-war. For instance, Sandra and Adrian may have had *competing* motivations. They wanted to take a rest and enjoy their newly scrubbed house, but they also wanted to tackle the backyard and cross that project off their list. These competing motivations were driving them toward *different* behaviors.

I want to rest   I want to work

Competing Motivations

Our friends may have also had *conflicting* motivations, which are opposing drives related to the *same* behavior. Conflicting motivations can be a source of psychic pain—"I want to eliminate refined sugar from my diet but, man, I want that chocolate cupcake." These conflicts can seesaw depending on what's happening around us.

Conflicting Motivations

I don't want to eat refined sugar.

Action Line

I want to eat that cupcake.

Motivation — High / Low

Ability — Hard to Do / Easy to Do

Even more problematic is the fact that we're blind to at least some of our motivation much of the time. We may not fully understand where the desire to eat a certain food is coming from. Do I *really* love the salty taste of popcorn, or does my daily popcorn habit stem from nostalgia for the days when my family and I used to eat it during movie night? Changing, invisible, competing, and conflicting motivations make this element of behavior hard to pin down and control. This makes us even more frustrated when we fail in our efforts to motivate ourselves or others to make lasting change.

2. THE MOTIVATION WAVE

Big spikes of motivation are awesome for doing really hard things — once.

Rescuing your child.

Quitting your job.

Throwing away all the junk food in your house.

Sprinting through the airport to catch a flight.

Attending your first AA meeting.

Writing a letter to the editor.

Keeping all ten of your New Year's resolutions . . . for a day.

When motivation surges, you can do hard behaviors.

Motivation · High · Low

Action Line

Hard to Do · Ability · Easy to Do

But high levels of motivation are both scattershot and unsustainable. Sandra and Adrian don't buy a house every day. With the keys in their hands that first day, they had a lot of motivation for home improvement, and they felt capable of doing hard behaviors. And they *were* capable right then. In fact, motivation helped them for a while. It allowed them to fix up the inside of their home, which was hard and time-consuming. But when they made their checklist, they didn't account for how they would feel the next day, or the next week, or the next month. At some point, their motivation would sag.

In Behavior Design, we've named this temporary surge in motivation the Motivation Wave. I'm sure you've experienced this before: Your motivation crested, then came crashing down. And maybe you blamed yourself for not sustaining it. You're not to blame. This is how motivation works in our lives.

Each year almost one hundred million people enroll in an online course, but the vast majority drop out. Most studies show that less than 10 percent cross the finish line. These students started out excited and dedicated, but then their motivation waned. Even the prospect of having to pay regardless of the outcome wasn't enough motivation to get students to complete the course. You see the same thing happen all around you. If you've ever bought a shoulder massager (as seen on TV!), I'm sorry to say that there is a good chance you can't remember the last time you used it. And remember that vegetable juicer the incredibly fit guy sold you at the mall? Yep, that juicer got used only a couple of times after you got it home. In these and other cases, you got caught in a common trap of the human mind—you overestimated future motivation. It happens to the best of us. You are not dumb or frivolous or easily hoodwinked. You are human.

So why do we get thrashed by the Motivation Wave even though we *know* we're being overly optimistic? When you are prompted to act in a way that seems like a good idea, even a *necessary* one, you feel something. Whether you feel desire, excitement, or fear, it doesn't matter —whatever is motivating the behavior will be quickly rationalized by your brain. It suddenly feels totally logical to do this thing that might be costly, time-consuming, physically demanding, or disruptive to our everyday lives. We start from emotion, then find the rationale to act. Back in our prehistoric past on the savannah, this was a good thing. Motivating emotions evolved to help us succeed and survive. After all, you'd better have an automatic spike of fear that will make you run fast when you suddenly spot a lion. If we were wired to start with rationality, we would be more like Mr. Spock from *Star Trek*. Do you think Spock has a juicer hanging out in his basement collecting dust? No. Spock doesn't get washed away by the Motivation Wave. He sees it rising, then he swims under it. He reasons that his enthusiasm for fresh juice will likely wane when he sees how much time it takes to clean the darn thing.

3. MOTIVATION FLUCTUATION

You also need to recognize that motivation changes on a smaller scale. It fluctuates day to day, even minute to minute, and you probably already know some of your own predictable motivation shifts. When was the last time you bought a Santa hat on December 26?

Retailers know how this works, and they adapt by selling Santa hats for cheap the week following the holiday when motivation is low and shoppers won't pay a lot of money for Santa hats. But here are some more subtle and predictable shifts: Willpower decreases from morning to evening. Complex decisions get harder by late in the day. Motivation for self-improvement can vanish on Friday nights. These shifts are among the reasons why you cannot take full control of your motivation.

People in the health and wellness industry are particularly tuned into these fluctuations. Years ago, I taught Behavior Design to the product team at Weight Watchers so they could streamline their global program and focus their members on the best ways to change. Then-CEO David Kirchhoff explained the seasonality of their business. The company saw predictable surges in online signups and keyword searches during certain times of the year. Signups were way above average in January—hello, New Year's resolutions. Weight Watchers also saw a spike in enrollments after Labor Day when people were looking to get back on track after a summer of hot dogs and ice cream. The company could also see where the Motivation Wave left people high and dry. Weight loss efforts plummeted in early November when people realized that they couldn't refuse Aunt Bev's pecan pie at Thanksgiving *and* Christmas. November and December are the weight-loss equivalent of a becalmed sea—no Motivation Waves in sight—which is why it's not a good idea to rely on them.

Predictable waves are not the only way motivation shifts. Some waves are unpredictable. The same teenager who bugged you for a week to let her go to the Ariana Grande concert will declare the day before the show that she definitely does *not* want to go anymore. Little did you realize that her best friend cancelled at the last minute, tanking your teenager's motivation.

Shifts in motivation can also happen quickly. You are motivated to eat lunch at 12:15 so you have a big lunch. When someone tells you there is pizza in the conference room at 1:30, you aren't so motivated because you just ate.

That said, there's a special situation in which motivation can be enduring. Consider a grandmother who is always motivated to spend quality time with her grandkids. Or the teenager who always wants to look good to her friends. These enduring motivations I call aspirations, and that's exactly what I will explain next.

4. MOTIVATING TOWARD AN ABSTRACTION DOESN'T YIELD RESULTS

We all want to be healthy. We all want to have more patience with our kids. We all want to feel fulfilled by our work. And our desire to achieve these aspirations is enduring. (Or at least it doesn't change quickly.) This seems like a good thing, right? Yes, it is. An aspiration is an excellent starting point for changing your life.

Millions of people genuinely aspire to live healthier, less stressful, and more fulfilling lives. But here's the problem: People often believe that motivating themselves toward an aspiration will lead to lasting change. So people focus on aspirations. And they focus on motivation. And that combo doesn't produce results.

This misleading idea is pervasive. You've probably seen a well-meaning public-health poster in the doctor's office that shows lots of colorful vegetables with the headline: EAT THE RAINBOW!

At first glance, you think: *Yes, I need to eat better food.* But then you're not sure what practical steps to take. How much green and how much red? That means salad and apples, right? It can't mean mint ice cream and red licorice, can it? You are motivated to "eat the rainbow," but maybe you don't know how. You may feel frustrated and end up being a little hard on yourself.

Dreams and aspirations are good things. So are public-health campaigns. But investing time and energy to motivate ourselves—or other people—toward an abstraction is the wrong move.

5. MOTIVATION IS *NOT* THE WINNING TICKET FOR LONG-TERM CHANGE

When it comes to changing their behavior for the better, people largely believe it's mostly about personal agency and choice. People think that if they could only find the right motivator they would do the thing that they *should* do (which is usually an abstraction).

This unfortunate way of thinking puts the blame squarely on you and your ability or inability to motivate yourself. I want to change all that.

I want people to know that if they focus only on motivation they are ignoring two key components of what actually drives behavior—ability and prompt. Let's say someone offers you a million dollars if you can immediately reduce your blood glucose to normal levels. A million dollars is pretty darn motivating, right? But can you reach this outcome immediately? Probably not. Motivation alone doesn't get you there.

You can't achieve outcomes or aspirations solely through high levels of motivation, which is the least predictable and reliable of the three components in my Behavior Model.

You're not alone if you previously focused entirely on motivation. But now I hope you see that you can't rely on motivation alone to create lasting change because you probably can't sustain it and you might not be able to manipulate or design for it reliably. And I hope you see that this is not a character flaw. It's human nature. You have to *work around* the Motivation Monkey's traps instead, not stumble into them.

Outsmarting Motivation

Before we see how to outsmart the Motivation Monkey, let's get one thing straight. I'm here to tell you that you *should* shoot the moon, daydream, or create a vision board. The more vividly you can picture what you want, the better. You usually have to know where you're going in order to get there. Sandra and Adrian were not wrong to be excited and ambitious about their backyard. That was good. Same goes for you if you're coming to this book with aspirations of starting your own business, saving for an early retirement, or winning a lifelong struggle with obesity.

Humans are dreamers by nature, so we've all got a few moon shots tucked into our back pocket at all times. But that's often where they stay —in part because of the way we are tripped up by fickle motivation. So how do we pull our aspirations out of our pockets and start making them happen without relying on motivation?

First, let's get clear on the difference between three things: aspirations, outcomes, and behaviors. When I teach boot camps and workshops on Behavior Design, one of the first things I ask people is what new *behavior* they wish to bring into their lives. This is what I hear.

+ "I want to reduce screen time."

+ "I want to sleep better!"

+ "I want to lose 12 percent body fat."

+ "I want to have more patience with my son."

+ "I want to be more productive."

And I say, "Great—I can show you how to make those wishes a reality. But those aren't behaviors. Those are the aspirations you have or the outcomes you want to get."

Aspirations are abstract desires, like wanting your kids to succeed in school. Outcomes are more measurable, like getting straight As second semester. Both of these are great places to start the process of Behavior Design.

But aspirations and outcomes are not behaviors.

Here's an easy way to differentiate behaviors from aspirations and outcomes: A *behavior* is something you can do *right now* or at another specific point in time. You can turn off your phone. You can eat a carrot. You can open a textbook and read five pages. These are actions that you can do at any given moment. In contrast, you can't achieve an aspiration or outcome at any given moment. You cannot suddenly get better sleep. You cannot lose twelve pounds at dinner tonight. You can only achieve aspirations and outcomes over time if you execute the right specific behaviors.

I've found that people don't naturally think in terms of specific behaviors, and this tendency trips up almost everyone.

People use the word "goal" when they are talking about aspirations or outcomes. If someone says "goal," you can't be sure what they are talking about since the word is ambiguous. For that reason, "goal" is not part of the vocabulary in Behavior Design. Use either "aspiration" or "outcome" for precision.

I once worked with a major bank on a savings initiative. The objective was to encourage customers to have an emergency fund of five hundred dollars. The bank's web pages had articles, experts, and data that made it clear that if you didn't have money for emergencies then you would get into financial trouble when you got a flat tire or clogged toilet that required a plumber.

"So what *behavior* are you asking your customer to do?" I asked.

"Save five hundred dollars for emergencies," the project leader said.

To this group of highly educated, intelligent, and wonderful people, that seemed pretty specific. But notice that they were talking about an outcome, not a behavior.

I wanted to make this point, so I challenged the team in a playful way: "Each of you, save five hundred dollars right now."

They laughed. And they got my point.

Then we went to work. I focused our session on finding *specific behaviors* their customers could do in order to create an emergency fund, and these are a few of the ones we came up with.

+ Call your cable company and scale back your service to the lowest level

+ Empty your pocket change into an emergency-fund jar every evening

* Announce a garage sale, then put all the revenue into an emergency fund

In the end, we came up with more than thirty different specific behaviors. Some were better than others, but all of those behaviors had a shot at helping the bank's customers take concrete steps toward reaching the savings outcome.

The bank leaders realized that motivation wasn't the missing piece in their puzzle. Instead, they needed to match their customers with specific behaviors that were easy and effective. They learned that their web pages should focus less on the "why" and focus more on the "how to."

Healthcare providers also need to shift their focus in this way. If you've ever been to the doctor and been told that you need to eat better and exercise more, you've probably wondered what "eating better" entails and how you do that.

I start professionals in the same place where I start people who do Tiny Habits. And it's exactly where you can start.

STEP 1: GET CLEAR ON YOUR ASPIRATIONS

Steps in Behavior Design

 Step 1: Clarify the Aspiration

The first step in Behavior Design is to get clear on your aspirations (or outcomes). What do you want? What is your dream? What result do you want to achieve?

Write down your aspirations or outcomes and consider whatever you write as something you will probably revise.

If you wrote down "lose weight," ask yourself, "Is that really what I want?" Maybe it is. Or maybe it's that you want to feel better in your clothes. Or you want to control your diabetes. Or you want to start paddleboarding, but you feel like you're carrying too much weight.

Getting clear on your aspiration allows you to design efficiently for what you really want. You might assume your aspiration is to be more mindful. But when you think about this, you decide that what you really want is to reduce stress in your life. And reducing stress will be easier than being more mindful. You could take a daily walk outside, play a musical instrument for ten minutes, or cut back on watching TV news. In this step, revise your aspiration or outcome so it taps into what really matters to you.

(A note on starting with aspirations versus starting with outcomes: You can start with either. However, I like aspirations as a starting point because they are more flexible and less intimidating than specific outcomes.)

STEP 2: EXPLORE BEHAVIOR OPTIONS

Steps in Behavior Design

 Step 1: Clarify the Aspiration

 Step 2: Explore Behavior Options

You get down to specifics in step 2. You select one of your aspirations, then come up with a bunch of specific behaviors that can help you achieve your aspiration.

You are not making any decisions or commitments in this step. You are exploring your options. The more behaviors you list, the better. You can tap into your creativity or maybe ask friends for their ideas.

I created a way to help people explore behavior options. This tool is called the Swarm of Behaviors (or Swarm of Bs). Here's how it works: Write your aspiration inside the cloudlike shape shown in the graphic. Then start filling in the boxes with specific behaviors.

Swarm of Behaviors

Let's say I'm guiding my friend Mark through this process, and he is clear about his big aspiration. He writes "reduce my stress" inside the cloud.

Next, I would say, "Mark, if you could wave a magic wand and get yourself to do any behavior that would reduce your stress, what would it be?"

After Mark comes up with his first behavior—getting a massage each week—I'd say, "Great. What else?"

We don't stop and we don't explore his idea in depth. Mark continues to write things down and I continue to say, "Great. What else?"

When guiding people in this process, I like to remind them that for now they have magical powers. They can get themselves to do *any* behavior. *Move to Maui. Bring a dog to work. Get a management job that pays 30 percent more.* It's important to explore in this step—and be wildly optimistic. I call this method Magic Wanding.

Even with a magic wand in hand and my encouraging them to use those superpowers, people sometimes wish for practical behaviors (which is fine). Some wishes are behaviors you do one time: download a meditation app. Some wishes are for new habits: stretching for two minutes after every conference call. And some wishes are to stop doing a behavior: stop checking e-mail after seven p.m.

To generate lots of behavior options, you can use the following categories during your own Magic Wanding sessions.

- What behaviors would you do one time?
- What new habits would you create?
- What habit would you stop?

After you come up with each behavior wish, think to yourself, *Great. What else?* and keep going. Eventually, you will have a Swarm of Behaviors that will range from wacky to logical to surprising. And that's a good thing.

As you come up with behavior options, you'll see that there are lots of ways to reach your aspiration. In a later step, you'll sort through these options and get realistic. But for now, you want to explore widely, and the fantasy of having magical powers helps you get there.

Many different behaviors can lead to your aspiration

If you haven't gotten started, you can do that now.

Write your chosen aspiration in the cloud. Next, imagine you have a magic wand that can get you to do any behavior. What would you wish for?

The Swarm of Behaviors tool has boxes for ten behaviors. But don't stop there. The more ideas, the more breadth, the more variety, the better results you will have in the later steps of Behavior Design.

If you're having a hard time coming up with fresh ideas, enlist other people. Ask a partner, your kids, even your social media friends if they can suggest any behaviors that will help you achieve your aspiration. You could say (or write), *"If you could get me to do any behavior that would help me ____, what would it be?"*

You might be surprised at what you hear. And don't worry if some behavior wishes are totally unrealistic. I'll show you how to select the best ones—and how to make those a reality. For now, getting creative and coming up with new behaviors will help you have more fun *and* be more successful.

Once you've exhausted the powers of your magic wand, look over your behavior wishes and try to make each one more specific. If you've written down "play with my dog" as a way to reduce stress, you could make that wish more specific by revising it to this: "Play fetch with my dog each evening at home." After you revise your behavior wishes to be super specific (what I call "crispy"), move on to the next step in the Behavior Design process and get analytical and practical.

How to Find Your Best New Habit

Before I give you the next official step in Behavior Design, I want you to understand the larger context of designing for change.

A major flaw in the way people typically approach change is how they decide what behavior to put into practice. How people decide to get from point A (the start) to point B (reaching their aspiration or outcome) varies widely, and here are some of the most common but flawed ways they do this.

Wrong way #1: Just guessing, no methodology

Let's say you're riding the bus to work. While stuck in traffic, you look out the window and see a guy on a bike whiz by. You think, *Now that is the way to commute. I should do that! I used to bike. I love biking!* Unfortunately, you were twelve the last time you rode a bike, and your current commute is fifteen miles. But you really want to do it (in that moment!), so you buy a bunch of gear at a bike shop. You put on all the gear the next day, and as you step out the door, you discover that it's cold and raining. You didn't buy gear for that, so you feel a flash of annoyance and disappointment, and you walk to the bus stop instead. In the end, biking to work turns out to be a poor match for you.

The problem with this approach is its haphazard nature. It's like playing roulette. Maybe you'll buy the right stuff that will help you do the behavior, maybe you won't. Your behavior is too big of a leap, or it's not. Maybe it's realistic for your life, maybe it's not.

With Behavior Design, you don't guess.

Okay, next problem.

Wrong way #2: Inspiration from the Internet

Many of us watch talks online and get inspired. Lots of speakers have amazing stories and do awesome things. Let's say you watch a video featuring a Buddhist monk who is a meditation master. He's speaking with wisdom and grace. He doesn't seem stressed out or even slightly grumpy. He's telling you about his blood pressure (awesome) and his resting heart rate (even more awesome), and he presents the brain scans to prove it. You think, *Oh, my gosh. I see the power of meditation. People have been doing this for thousands of years.* At the end of the talk, he says that thirty minutes a day is all you need to substantially improve your life in these scientifically irrefutable ways. You're blown away. You have to do this. You're going to do this.

That same day you actually do sit for thirty minutes as the monk suggested. You struggle to quiet your mind, but you feel pretty good . . . until you get bored. The next day you try fifteen minutes. You feel okay for a while. But some days you don't do it, and on others you can't quiet your mind. You tried and you failed, and you feel bad about it. Eventually you stop.

Why didn't it work?

For starters, you're not a Buddhist monk. But it's mostly because this behavior was probably too hard for you. Not to mention that you probably started with unrealistic expectations about meditation. The Buddhist monk meant well, but he was talking about what worked for him. Meditating might not work for you the way it works for him.

The other thing to consider is that the videos you're watching and the articles you're reading and the bloggers you're following may or may not be credible sources of information. While this approach to choosing behaviors is better than mere guessing, it's still risky because it wasn't chosen according to any criteria other than what excited you in that moment.

Wrong way #3: Doing what worked for a friend

Advice from a friend or family member is the most well-meaning of all, but it's not the best way to match yourself with a new habit. While hot yoga may have changed your friend's life, does that mean it's the right practice for you? We all have friends who *swear* their new habit of getting up at four thirty a.m. changed their lives and that we have to do it. I don't doubt that getting up super early changes people's lives, sometimes in good ways and sometimes not. But be cautious: You don't know if this habit will actually make your life better, especially if it means you get less sleep. So yes, you can try what worked for your friend, but don't beat yourself up if your friend's answer doesn't change you in the same way.

* * *

All of these approaches involve guessing and chance. And that's not a good way to design for change in your life. Having systematic criteria for *how* to choose behaviors for *yourself* will make you effective in getting results, and the next step in Behavior Design will save you from guessing.

THE RIGHT WAY: MATCH YOURSELF WITH SPECIFIC BEHAVIORS

Steps in Behavior Design

 Step 1: Clarify the Aspiration

 Step 2: Explore Behavior Options

 Step 3: Match with Specific Behaviors

Once you have a wide range of behavior options thanks to Magic Wanding and your Swarm of Behaviors, shift gears and get practical. In this step, you will match yourself with specific behaviors, and there's no guessing in this systematic approach.

This concept is important enough that I gave it a name: Behavior Matching. And this is the most important step in Behavior Design. No matter what kind of change you want to make, matching yourself with the right behaviors is the key to changing your life for good. In Behavior Design we have a name for the best matches: Golden Behaviors.

A Golden Behavior has three criteria.

+ The behavior is effective in realizing your aspiration (impact)

+ You want to do the behavior (motivation)

+ You can do the behavior (ability)

There are a few good ways to behavior match. Getting help from a coach is a great way if you have someone in your life who can skillfully match you with Golden Behaviors. You might be working with a trainer, a doctor, a dietician, or a person who has either the training or the intuition to know what will work for you. For example, a coach trained in *Tiny Habits for Weight Loss* can match you with the tiniest behaviors that lead to the most weight loss. If you've found an expert like this, consider yourself fortunate. For everyone else, I offer you a method I designed called Focus Mapping.

You'll use the Swarm of Behaviors you created earlier. Doing a Focus Map should take you less than ten minutes start to finish. At the end, you'll have two or three behaviors that rise to the top. Those are your Golden Behaviors. And that's what you design for while setting aside all the other options.

A Golden Behavior can be a one-time action. Canceling your cable subscription is a task done one time that will probably lead to watching TV less. Other Golden Behaviors will be habits you repeat day after day, such as charging your phone in the kitchen instead of next to your bed.

Focus Mapping

Focus Mapping is my favorite method in Behavior Design. I created this during ten years of working on Stanford projects, changing my own life, and helping business leaders to design new products and services. Over the years, I've worked hard to improve Focus Mapping, and today I believe this is the best method for matching yourself with Golden Behaviors.

This is the landscape for a Focus Map.

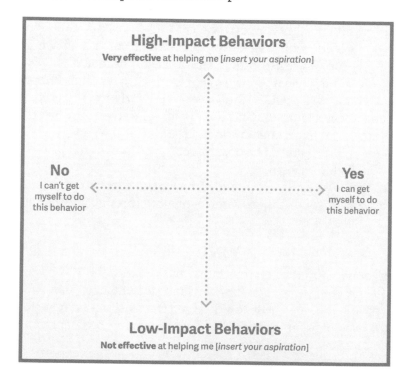

You're eventually going to plot each behavior in your swarm on this landscape. First, I'll show you how it works using our buddy Mark, who is trying to reduce his stress.

Mark writes each behavior from his Swarm of Behaviors on its own index card, then he goes through the stack of behavior cards one by one.

ROUND ONE

In the first round of Focus Mapping, Mark thinks about only the impact of the behavior—how much it helps him to reduce his stress—and he doesn't consider the feasibility or practicality of each behavior in this round.

For each behavior card, he asks himself: *How effective is this behavior in helping me to reduce my stress?*

The first behavior Mark picks up is *playing the guitar for ten minutes every day*. This is straightforward—Mark loves the guitar, and he's always in a good mood after even a short strumming session. He knows this will have a big impact on him so he places the card close to the top of the map near the High-Impact Behaviors end of the spectrum. The next behavior he picks up is *leaving work fifteen minutes early every day*. That seems like a good idea at first, but later he thinks that it might have the opposite effect—especially if he is on deadline. He puts that behavior toward the bottom near Low-Impact Behaviors.

You continue in this way, card by card. If you're not sure about the impact a behavior will have, do your best and put it somewhere that seems right. You can revise later in the process if needed.

If Mark had mistakenly put *leaving work early* as High Impact—no big deal. Worst-case scenario, he leaves work early for a couple of days and realizes that rushing out the door is actually stressing him out *more*. Mark knows that experimentation is the name of the game, and he's loving his new guitar habit so he doesn't get too bummed that leaving work early didn't reduce his stress.

Once you've plotted your potential new behaviors on the impact spectrum, it's time to look at those same behaviors through another lens.

ROUND TWO

In this round you focus on feasibility and practicality. You become the real you, not the fantasy version. In round two you don't move cards up or down; you slide them side to side along the feasibility dimension.

Mark eyes his guitar-playing and work-leaving behaviors and asks himself: *Can I get myself to do this?*

The phrasing of the question is important. It brings together both motivation and ability at the same time. With this one question, you are addressing two components of my Behavior Model.

Most people can answer the feasibility question pretty easily. When Mark asks himself, *Can I get myself to play the guitar every day?* the answer is obvious to him—yes. However, when he asks himself, *Can I get myself to leave work early every day?* he grimaces a little and starts arguing with himself in his head. That's a sign that he can't get himself to do this.

It's this simple for a lot of behaviors. But for others, it helps to know what's causing us to hem and haw.

To do this, ask yourself, *Do I want to do this behavior?*

Motivation, in other words.

You can't get yourself to do what you don't want to do. At least not reliably. You might do the behavior once or twice, but it's unlikely to become a habit. When we match ourselves with behaviors that we already *want* to do, not what we think we *should* do, there is no need to fuss with motivational tricks or techniques later. We take the Motivation Monkey out of commission.

Let's say you want to make eating ice cream a daily habit. No problem, right? Why? Because there's no need to motivate yourself to dig into that chocolate chip ice cream after a long day at work. If you were Focus Mapping that behavior, you'd think, *Sure, I can get myself to do that behavior.* And you'd slide that card far to the right side of the chart.

As you slide the cards side to side, remember that there's no judgment here. Imagine yourself doing the behavior. Do you feel a little pop of dread? Or do you feel excited about doing the behavior? There is plenty of room in between these feelings, but the important distinction here is between "want" and "should."

Behavior Design recognizes this reality: A key to lasting change is matching yourself with behaviors that you *want* to do. In your quest to exercise daily, for example, you'll find plenty of options. If streaming Beyoncé and dancing for five minutes while you make breakfast is the exercise you *want* to do, then make dancing a daily habit. And forget about the treadmill at the gym.

One big difference in Behavior Design versus other approaches is that with my methods you focus on habits you already have motivation to do. You don't pick a habit and try to bolt on motivation later. In Behavior Design, motivation is already embedded in the new habit. In other approaches you will struggle to maintain a habit you think you *should* do. And that doesn't work very well.

Matching people with behaviors they want to do is so important for lasting change that I've given this concept special status in Behavior Design.

This maxim has been a game changer for many of the professionals I've trained in Behavior Design. And this maxim can change the game for you when you help yourself do what you already want to do. I've designed the Focus Mapping method to adhere to this maxim.

But there's more. The round two question—*Can I get myself to do this behavior?*—is also about ability.

Perhaps you're motivated to eat fresh peaches every morning, but if you live in Maine and there are no peaches to be found in the winter, eating a daily peach is not going to happen consistently. You don't have the ability to do this behavior reliably, and you would slide this card toward the left-hand side.

As you sort your cards, imagine yourself doing the behavior in the context of your day-to-day life. Let's say your aspiration is to eat more fruit, and the behavior you brainstormed is to put blueberries in your oatmeal. Don't imagine the Fantasy-You getting up early to fix oatmeal each day. Instead, think of Real-You rolling out of bed twenty minutes before dashing out the door. Daily blueberries in oatmeal is probably not realistic. How about putting an apple in your purse instead?

The purpose of a Focus Map is to match yourself with easy behaviors that you want to do and that are effective in getting you to your aspiration. When you start with the easiest, most motivating thing, you can ladder up naturally to bigger behaviors—perhaps eventually eating blueberries in your oatmeal.

In Behavior Design we match ourselves with new habits we can do even when we are at our most hurried, unmotivated, and beautifully imperfect. If you can imagine yourself doing the behavior on your hardest day of the week, it's probably a good match. It's probably a Golden Behavior.

Finding Your Golden Behaviors Easily

When I first started researching and experimenting with Behavior Matching, I bought a lot of index cards. With practice, I learned to Magic Wand a Swarm of Behaviors very quickly. I'd set a timer for five minutes and see if I could write down twenty-five behaviors on the cards. (Easier than you think.) Then I'd sort the behavior cards and plot them on a Focus Map on the kitchen counter. It was like solving puzzles. My Behavior Design process always started with an abstraction—either an aspiration or outcome. About twenty minutes later, after taking the steps in Behavior Design, I would discover specific behaviors that I could readily turn into a reality. Twenty minutes and I was done.

I still do this all the time. It's so fast and effective.

I'm going to walk you through an early Focus Map that worked for me. It came at a time when I was pretty stressed by having to organize a big conference at Stanford, and I wasn't sleeping well. I wasn't my usual optimistic self, and I was seriously worried about the conference being a disaster.

But I felt that getting more sleep would help me be optimistic and get more done. With that as my aspiration, I sat at my kitchen counter with my favorite black Sharpie and a stack of index cards. I started Magic Wanding behaviors that would help me get better sleep.

+ Put phone on airplane mode after seven p.m.

+ Eat dinner an hour earlier

+ Turn on my white-noise machine each night

+ Install blackout blinds

+ Purchase better bedding

+ Do a fifteen-minute wind-down ritual in the evening

+ Make a list of all my anxieties before bed

+ Put Millie in her crate at night

This was about a quarter of the behaviors I came up with, but you get the idea.

With a stack of potential behaviors in hand, I started placing them on my Focus Map according to impact. The ones that I knew would have lots of impact were putting my phone on airplane mode, turning on the white-noise machine at night, and installing blackout blinds, so I put them close to the high-impact end of the spectrum. I also knew that putting Millie in her crate would definitely make a difference because the older she gets the more she wanders at night. Eating dinner earlier would mean that I was able to go to bed earlier, but I wasn't sure that I would be able to fall asleep earlier. So I put this behavior in the middle of the spectrum. Making a list of my anxieties seemed like it might work, but I wasn't sure.

I then moved on to round two and asked myself if I could get myself to do each behavior.

I knew right away that eating dinner earlier was too hard to do, so I put that all the way to the left. But installing blackout blinds was an easy one-time behavior (because I could hire someone to do it). I put that all the way to the right. Same with the white-noise machine—it would be easy for me to switch on each night. Turning my phone to airplane mode would take multiple steps (turn on the phone, swipe up, etc.), so I edited the card: "Put my phone on silent mode." Easier. And then that card went way to the right along with the card for putting Millie in her crate every night.

When you complete a Focus Map, you'll have behaviors distributed on the chart. It might look like this.

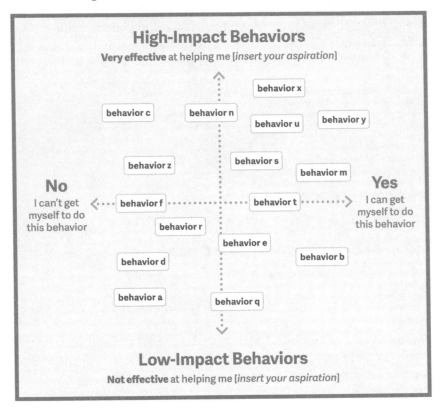

This whole process of Focus Mapping took only a few minutes, and suddenly I had my Golden Behaviors: a one-time behavior (installing blackout shades) and three behaviors I could turn into habits (putting my phone on silent, turning on my white-noise machine, and crating Millie).

The last step in the Focus Mapping method is to select which behaviors you will design for. What's in and what's out? You will almost always select a handful of behaviors that are in the upper-right corner. You design for these Golden Behaviors, and you forget the rest.

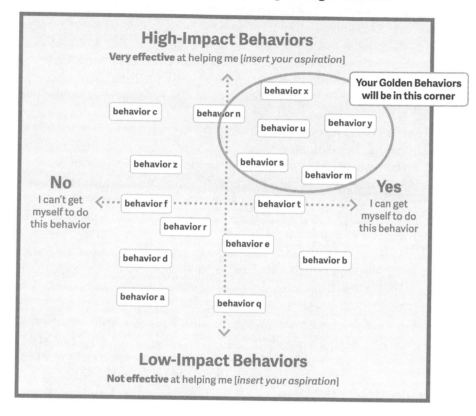

When I saw my Golden Behaviors in the upper right-hand corner, what struck me was not the speed of my process but how *right* it felt. For weeks I had been thinking about how I could get better sleep, and this problem seemed overwhelming. In the modern world, sleep is *hard* sometimes. But by moving from the aspiration to the practical, I suddenly had concrete, easy behaviors I could do. They weren't terribly creative or wildly inventive, but they were mine. I knew *I* could do them —me, BJ, in my real life. When I looked at my Golden Behaviors, I felt something like recognition. I thought, *Of course I can do that,* and *Why didn't I think of that before?*

I'm not alone in reacting this way to the matching process. Whenever I do Focus Mapping with students and clients, there are plenty of aha moments.

After completing my one-time behavior and locking in my new sleep habits, I saw a huge improvement in my sleep after a week or so. Before this, I had slept terribly most nights when I was worrying about the conference. I hated going to bed — it felt like gearing up for a battle. But I was able to change that. I got more sleep, I regained my optimism, and I completed what seemed like a bajillion tasks to make the conference a success. I have my Focus Map — and the Behavior Design process — to thank.

(Update: I have since stopped putting Millie in her crate at night. Imagining what it was like to be locked up in a crate made me feel guilty. And I don't like feeling that way, so I ended this habit. And that was the right thing to do: You should feel free to revise whenever a new habit ends up being not what you wanted.)

If you're like most people, when you're done sorting your Focus Map, you'll look at the Golden Behaviors and feel optimistic and energized. What you *want* to do and what you *can* do will converge into what you most likely *will do*, and that's the most fertile ground for growing habits.

In the Tiny Habits method, I teach people to think about their new habits as small seeds. If you plant a good seed in the right spot, it will grow without coaxing. Starting with behaviors that you can and want to do makes for a good seed. Choosing behaviors that set you up for success increases your confidence and mastery as you go, thus increasing your natural motivation to do bigger and bigger behaviors. But it all starts small and honest and specific.

We should be dreamy about aspirations but not about the behaviors that will get us there. Behaviors are grounded. Concrete. They are the handholds and footholds that get you up the rock face. Your path to the top is your own, and you choose your behaviors according to the particular rock you are climbing.

Matching yourself with the right behaviors is the most critical step in the Behavior Design process and an important place to return to when troubleshooting.

To review: Clarify your aspiration or outcome, generate a big set of behavior options, and match yourself with specific Golden Behaviors. That's

Steps in Behavior Design

 Step 1: Clarify the Aspiration

 Step 2: Explore Behavior Options

 Step 3: Match with Specific Behaviors

how you put Behavior Design into practice in your own life. And it's also how you match yourself with the best habits for doing Tiny Habits.

You can use Behavior Design at work to design a wellness program, recruit the best talent, and create habits for productivity. These methods I'm sharing are the most practical, powerful, and reliable way to succeed on your professional projects. The concepts can be applied broadly: *Tiny Habits for Better Meetings*, *Tiny Habits for Working Parents*, *Tiny Habits for Effective Teamwork*, and many more.

The next step in the process of Behavior Design is to make things *as simple as possible.* The kind of simplicity I'm talking about may surprise you. Everyone has heard of taking baby steps, but I realized years ago that no one was taking this approach quite far enough in the world of behavior change. So I did. And that created breakthroughs. In the next chapter, I'll help you see what tiny *really* means and how to make your Golden Behaviors a reality by starting intentionally, purposefully, and *radically* small.

Tiny Exercises to Practice Behavior Design

In the first exercise, I'm going to define the aspiration for you: Get better sleep. In the second exercise, you'll come up with your own aspiration.

EXERCISE #1: A SHORTCUT FOR BEHAVIOR MATCHING

Step 1: Draw a cloud on a piece of paper.

Step 2: Write the aspiration "Get better sleep" inside the cloud.

Step 3: Come up with ten or more behaviors that would lead you to your aspiration of getting better sleep. Write each behavior outside the cloud with arrows pointing toward the cloud. You've now created your Swarm of Behaviors.

Step 4: Put a star by four or five behaviors that you believe would be highly effective in reaching your aspiration.

Step 5: Circle any effective behavior that you can easily get yourself to do. Be realistic.

Step 6: Find the behaviors that have both a star and a circle. Those are your Golden Behaviors.

Step 7: Design a way to make your Golden Behaviors a reality in your life. Do your best with this step. I haven't yet explained how to systematically design a solution, so use your intuition for now.

EXERCISE #2: FOCUS MAPPING TO FIND GOLDEN BEHAVIORS

Pick your own aspiration this time and use Focus Mapping (not stars and circles) to match yourself with the Golden Behaviors.

Step 1: Draw a cloud on a piece of paper.

Step 2: Write your aspiration inside the cloud. (If you can't think of anything, write "Reduce my stress.")

Step 3: Come up with ten or more behaviors that would lead you to your aspiration. Write each behavior outside the cloud with arrows pointing toward the cloud.

Step 4: Write each of the ten behaviors on a card or a small piece of paper. This is the first step in using Focus Mapping.

Step 5: Sort the behavior cards up and down along the impact dimension. Don't think about feasibility. Focus on the impact that the behaviors could have. (For guidance, refer to the Focus Mapping graphic a few pages back.)

Step 6: Slide the behavior cards side to side along the feasibility dimension. Be realistic. Can you really get yourself to do these behaviors?

Step 7: Look in the upper right-hand corner. Those are your Golden Behaviors. (If nothing is in this corner, go back to Step 3.)

Step 8: Design a way to make your Golden Behaviors a reality in your life using your intuition for now. I'll share a systematic way to do this in a later chapter.

3

ABILITY—EASY
DOES IT

What's the difference between Yahoo! and Google? Between Blogger and Twitter? Why does one innovation fade and another take over the world? Talent? Vision? Money? Luck?

All of those things and plenty more. But the biggest one is perhaps the most overlooked.

Simplicity.

When Mike Krieger and Kevin Systrom started talking about creating a new app in 2009, they began by examining the previous year's failure—a location-sharing app called Burbn. They did a thorough digital autopsy, analyzing not only what went wrong but also what went right. Inside the analytics of failure, they found a multibillion-dollar seed: photo sharing.

Even though few people had liked the check-in part of Burbn (the app shared your whereabouts in real time with your friends), they *had* loved the sharing pictures part of the app. So the partners decided they would create an app that allowed people to capitalize on the iPhone cameras conveniently stashed in their pockets. Photo sharing was the Golden Behavior for Systrom and Krieger—their potential customers already *wanted* to do it. Sharing pictures with other people is fun, and everyone likes positive feedback. Another important Golden Behavior for the duo was allowing people to add filters to make their pictures of food and sunsets and puppies look much better. This would make users feel good about the pictures they were sharing, which encouraged them to do it more often. Notice that Krieger and Systrom nailed the motivation component by choosing a behavior that people already wanted to do. According to the Behavior Model, they were already in good shape. That alone might have brought them some success. But what they did next catapulted them into the pantheon of Silicon Valley demigods— they made their Golden Behaviors easy to do.

Krieger was fresh out of one of my classes at Stanford. He knew how human behavior worked and how important it was to make things easy to do if you wanted people to do them. This was another place where Burbn had fallen short. There were a lot of features that people didn't need or couldn't figure out how to use. This realization reinforced Krieger and Systrom's desire to make the new photo-sharing app simple. So that's what they did.

When Instagram launched in 2010, it took only three clicks to post a photo. According to the original description in the app store, Instagram was as "easy as pie," which is notable when you look at their early competition. Krieger and Systrom weren't the first people to understand that people love photos and might want to share them. Their biggest competitors when they launched were Flickr, Facebook, and Hipstamatic. All three offered users great full-feature experiences, and Facebook and Flickr had the advantage of money and infrastructure. Instagram, on the other hand, was a free app built by a couple of dudes in a coffee shop. All you could do was take a picture, put a filter on it, and share it with people. That kind of simplicity was not (and still isn't) the norm. While all of Instagram's competitors had features that people wanted, none of them cracked the code on photo sharing. Less than eighteen months after the app's launch, Facebook bought Instagram for a billion dollars. (At the time, the behemoth social network was openly mocked for overpaying. Today, Instagram's estimated value is more than $100 billion.)

So why was Instagram's simple approach so successful? Why doesn't every app developer do that? It seems pretty obvious. Right?

Not exactly.

Most people operate under the assumption that they've got to go big or go home. They think that in order to kick a bad habit, destress, or make a pile of money they've got to do something radical. Go cold turkey. Sell their house and move to the beach. Put all their chips on the table. Go all in. Those who take these extreme measures and succeed are lionized. If you've ever watched a special about an Olympic athlete who's been training twelve hours a day since she was three or a successful businessperson who sold everything and moved to Italy to find true happiness, you know what I'm talking about. There's nothing wrong with taking bold action. Life and happiness occasionally demand it. But remember that you hear about people making big changes because this is the *exception*, not the rule. Narrative drama comes from bold action, not from the incremental progress that leads to sustainable success. Which is why I don't have a camera crew following me around while I do my two post-pee push-ups. (Okay, maybe that's not the only reason.) My point is that big bold actions on the balance are not as effective as many of us are led to believe.

While small might not be sexy, it *is* successful and sustainable. When it comes to most life changes that people want to make, big bold moves actually don't work as well as small stealthy ones. Applying go big or go home to everything you do is a recipe for self-criticism and disappointment. We already know that the Motivation Monkey loves to help us make big moves, then slips away from us when the going gets tough. And doing big things can be painful. We often push ourselves beyond our physical, emotional, or mental capabilities. And while we might be able to keep up this effort for a while, humans don't do things that are painful for very long. As you can imagine, this isn't a good recipe for creating successful habits.

Despite all this, go big or go home is the way many people approach change. As a result, most people don't know how to think tiny. Designing simple behaviors is not a skill everyone has. If they do break things down into steps, those steps are often too big or complicated. The result is that people become overwhelmed and find themselves without a way to correct their course when they get caught in bursts and busts of motivation because their ebbing Motivation Wave leaves them high and dry.

Sarika, a project manager for a Fortune 500 company based in Bangalore, experienced this motivation cycle for years. Before she started Tiny Habits, Sarika had tried to get in the habit of cooking for herself and exercising to keep herself healthy. She lives with bipolar disorder, which means she experiences extreme highs and lows in mood and energy. In the past, Sarika had used medication to manage her condition, but she hated the side effects. Her doctors told her it was possible to treat her symptoms with meditation, exercise, and therapy, but that maintaining a routine was critical to making this approach work. A routine would help her identify the severity of her symptoms early on so she could take action before they negatively affected her life. Sarika couldn't always tell if a manic high or a depressive low was sneaking up on her. So it made sense to her that daily habits would be a great way for her to gauge how she was feeling. If she started watering the jade plant in her hallway every morning, she would know what it feels like to complete that action. On good days she does it without thinking. But if she feels the urge to ignore the watering jug she placed by the doorway as a reminder, she knows something is up and that she should pay closer attention to how she feels doing all of her other habits.

There was only one problem. Sarika could not maintain a routine no matter how hard she tried.

Before she found Tiny Habits, nothing was routine in Sarika's life except going to work—and even then she rarely got to work at a consistent time. Breakfast was grabbed from a food truck, and lunch, if it happened at all, was takeout. She didn't clean her kitchen until the mess got really bad, then she'd make like a whirling dervish and do it in an hour. Sarika loves to meditate but would go weeks without sitting on her cushion. Without medication and without these habits as a steady baseline, she often felt out of control. She was short-tempered at home and down in the dumps at work. And she felt like she was being asked to build a spaceship to Mars when her doctors told her to create habits.

Sarika was caught in a "burst and bust" cycle. One of the most problematic issues in Sarika's life was physical therapy. After months of only occasionally doing a prescribed thirty-minute exercise routine, Sarika found that her injured knee wasn't getting any better. She needed to do the exercises, but she couldn't get herself to get out those elastic bands. When she couldn't take the pain anymore, Sarika would hit a motivational high—a burst—and only then would she do what she had been putting off. But because she hadn't been doing the exercises regularly, they felt even more painful than usual, and she would hit the "bust" part of the cycle and wouldn't do her exercises for several days. She repeated this cycle with most every habit she tried to undertake.

What Sarika was going through is common. Many people get stuck in a burst and bust cycle that makes us anxious and disappointed whether they are trying to quit drinking soda, get up before the sun rises, cook dinner at home every night, track each penny earned or invest time each day in finding new prospects. Like most people locked in this cycle, Sarika's emotions were all over the map—some days she'd feel fine and some days she felt bad about not being able to establish healthy habits. Her confidence was nearly zero, and she was worried that she wasn't capable of making permanent changes.

Sarika finally found a simple method for designing her habits that didn't feel like she had to master astrophysics. She began building her routine the Tiny Habits way, small and steady. Instead of aiming for twenty minutes of meditation each day, she started with three breaths on a pillow strategically placed in the middle of her living room. Instead of cooking an entire breakfast, Sarika committed to turning on the stovetop burner right after she entered the kitchen. Instead of thirty minutes of physical therapy exercises, she started with thirty seconds of stretching on her favorite blue yoga mat. From there, Sarika built skills and confidence and wired in these Tiny Behaviors until they took root as habits. Then they grew. She mastered the daily routine that she chased for all those years, and her health has improved now that she makes herself meals, cleans the kitchen, exercises, meditates, and waters her plants every day. Sarika told me that she feels a sense of resilience that she's never had before.

According to Sarika, the most important part of this was not just the creation of her healthy habits and symptom management but also the confidence it gave her. She knows now that she can do almost anything she wants to—as long as she starts small.

Even if there are times when she can't do her habits because she isn't feeling well, she doesn't go into a shame spiral anymore. Sarika recently sprained her ankle and was bedridden for a few days. Because she lives in a building with no elevator, she told me that in the past she would have cried and thought, *Why do these things always happen to me?* But this time she accepted the pain without a downward emotional spiral. She took it one day at a time, knowing that she could get back to her healthy routine as soon as she healed. The reason she felt this way is that it's easier to pick things up again when they are small. There is no mountain to climb, only a little hill. Simple. Easy to do. And that makes all the difference—not just with Sarika's ability to act but also how she feels day to day. She doesn't beat herself up on the days when she's not feeling well because she knows she can resume her bigger routine tomorrow. On the days her motivation is high, she climbs her little habit hills and finds she has the mental and emotional space to experiment and be curious about what other good things she can bring into her life. Things feel lighter and more doable. If she wants to start a new habit, she gets excited and curious instead of overwhelmed. That mindset shift is something that has rippled throughout her life.

Sarika and the founders of Instagram were able to overcome a fundamental change myth and find success because they capitalized on the most reliable way to drive behavior—fiddling with the ability dial and making things easy. While I'm primarily focusing on habits in this book, making things easy to do will help you with almost *any* behavior. I'll talk specifically about how to solve for those one-time actions you've been putting off and also give you more tools to help you design the life you want. You'll be able to use these new skills to tackle big long-term goals. With Behavior Design, you have enormous potential. Whether the change you're aiming for is big or small, tiny is where we start.

Steps in Behavior Design

 Step 1: Clarify the Aspiration

 Step 2: Explore Behavior Options

 Step 3: Match with Specific Behaviors

☺ **Step 4: Start Tiny**

Using Ability to Create Habits

The reason we want to make a behavior easy to do—which often means starting tiny—is so the unpredictability of the Motivation Monkey doesn't mess up our future success. In order to do a behavior, motivation and ability have to exist in sufficient amounts to put you above the Action Line in the Behavior Model. We've already established that motivation is unreliable. Luckily, ability is not. By looking at where our ability lands on the Behavior Model, we get a good idea of what behaviors are more or less likely to become habit. Let's say you want to do twenty push-ups every day. Here's what that behavior looks like mapped on the Behavior Model.

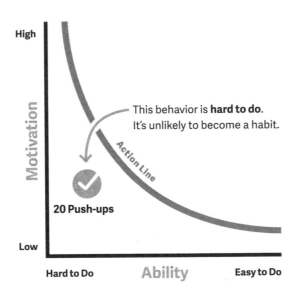

At most times of the day, your motivation to do twenty push-ups is probably on the low end, which pushes you to the bottom half of the vertical axis. On the horizontal axis, this behavior is located almost all the way to the left because this is hard for you. Both of these inputs place the behavior well beneath the Action Line. This tells us that doing twenty push-ups at a time is unlikely to become a habit for most people. Because your ability is so low, you'll only do this behavior on days when you're riding the Motivation Wave. (And that's not very often.)

But here's what it would look like if your new habit was to do two push-ups against a wall.

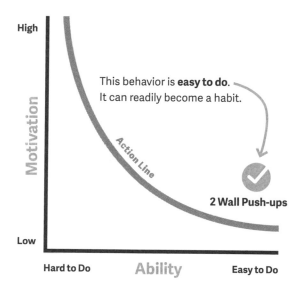

When we look at the vertical motivation axis, we see that it's similar to the twenty-push-ups version. But there's an important difference: Two push-ups against a wall has moved you all the way to the right on the horizontal axis. Notice that if you make a behavior easy to do your motivation can still be low but you will be above the Action Line. This is one of the hacks in the Tiny Habits method: Make the behavior so tiny that you don't need much motivation. Doing two push-ups against a wall is easy to accomplish so you're much more likely to keep it as a habit.

When you are designing a new habit, you are really designing for consistency. And for that result, you'll find that simplicity is the key. Or as I like to teach my students: Simplicity changes behavior.

If you want to do a habit consistently, you've got to adjust the most reliable thing in the B=MAP model—ability. That's where we have the most power to stack the deck in our favor. If a behavior is hard, make it easier to do. You'll see that over time your motivation will vary, but your ability will improve the more you do your new habit. And that increase in ability helps your habit grow.

Here's a model showing how it would look if you consistently did two push-ups against a wall for a couple of weeks.

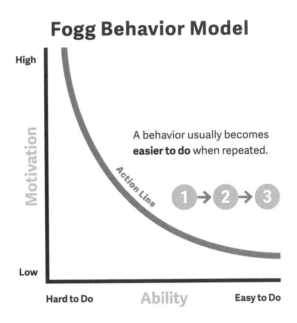

Every day you do the behavior, you build a bit more muscle strength, flexibility, and skill. This makes the behavior easier and easier to do, moving the behavior farther and farther to the right on the horizontal axis. (And if you feel successful, your motivation will also increase. More on that in the next chapter.)

When you set motivation aside and design your habits by manipulating ability, you might be surprised at how quickly your habits take hold and grow. I learned this early on when I was experimenting with creating my own habits before I had named this method Tiny Habits. I had already figured out the Behavior Model, and I knew that the ability component of B=MAP was critical to making a behavior happen consistently over time. But I had used this only in my research at Stanford and when I was helping professionals to design new products and services. I hadn't shifted to the arena of personal change.

Until one day.

I was in the dentist's chair being gently chastised (again) for not flossing my teeth.

Embarrassing, right? There I was, a behavior scientist, and I couldn't get myself to floss daily. Some days I was motivated (like the day after a dentist visit), but other times I didn't care so much. The Motivation Monkey was winning.

But I was pretty sure I could make flossing a daily habit if I focused on the ability component of my Behavior Model.

As the hygienist went to get the dentist for a final check, I asked myself: *How can I make flossing easier to do?*

I came up with an answer though I didn't dare tell my hygienist. She would have been horrified.

I decided to floss just one tooth.

Seriously.

After I brushed my teeth in the morning, I would floss one tooth.

My Recipe — Tiny Habits Method

After I . . .   **I will . . .**   To wire the habit into my brain, I will immediately:

<u>brush my teeth,</u>   <u>floss one tooth.</u>   ☺

That's it.

Despite how silly this might seem, it worked. For the first few days I flossed only one tooth just to keep things simple. But I made a rule: I got extra credit for flossing more teeth even though one tooth was all I had to do. After about two weeks, I was flossing all my teeth twice a day. I've been doing that ever since.

Once I figured out my plan of action, regularly flossing my teeth was easy. But there is an underlying and beautiful complexity that made this all possible. I got to my solution by making flossing my teeth ridiculously easy to do, but first I had to understand what makes something hard to do. That's why you should always start with this question: What is making this behavior hard to do?

What I've found in my research and years of experience is that your answer will involve at least one of five factors. I call them the Ability Factors. Here's how they break down.

- Do you have enough **time** to do the behavior?

- Do you have enough **money** to do the behavior?

- Are you **physically capable** of doing the behavior?

- Does the behavior require a lot of creative or **mental energy**?

- Does the behavior fit into your current **routine** or does it require you to make adjustments?

Your Ability Chain is only as strong as its weakest Ability Factor link.

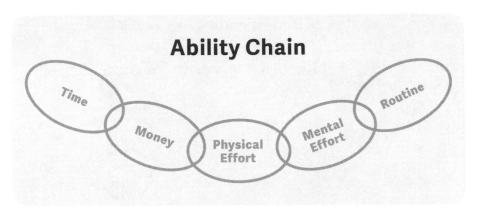

Ability Chain

Time • Money • Physical Effort • Mental Effort • Routine

By asking what I call the **Discovery Question,** *What is making this behavior hard to do?* we are lasering in on which factor is likely to cause us the most trouble. And when I say "hard to do," keep in mind that I don't just mean *very hard.* I mean any amount of hard to do that would keep you from doing the behavior.

You'll see what I mean with this next example.

Let's take a look at the habit of doing a seven-minute workout—something that most people would say sounds easy. But is it? Let's break things down by using the Ability Chain. Time is probably the strongest link; seven minutes is easy for most people to fit into their day. At least it is when compared to the expectation that one should exercise thirty minutes a day. Money? You can do this in your own home so this behavior is free. Physical effort? Aha. Here we go. For some people, doing a seven-minute workout sounds easy. However, most apps for this workout urge you to push yourself as you cycle through the exercises. And that's not easy. So for people who follow directions, the physical-effort link is probably weak. That alone could be enough to derail your efforts at making the seven-minute workout a habit.

Which brings me back to my tiny flossing behavior.

Flossing takes only a few seconds (time). It cost almost nothing (money). I already knew how to do it (mental effort). It slotted nicely into my life (routine). So those factors were all strong links. But when I thought about the physical-effort factor, I was surprised.

Flossing was hard to do physically.

This may sound strange because flossing isn't like digging a ditch or lifting up a car, but for me, it was hard enough to derail my habit. The important overshare here is that flossing is hard for me because my teeth are very close together. My hygienist calls this phenomenon "close contacts," which means that it is a struggle for me to get the floss between my teeth. I have to wrestle with the floss to get it in there, then I feel like I am pulling my tooth out to wrestle it back out again. Then the floss would shred and get stuck, and I'd have to start again with a new piece. This wobbly little link in my Ability Chain was weak enough for me to blow off flossing for months at a time. The behavior was just hard enough and my motivation just weak enough that flossing was never going to become a habit the way I was doing it.

So what did I do to make flossing easy to do? I searched for floss that would fit between my teeth. After buying and sampling about fifteen types, I found the perfect floss for me.

Almost everyone I meet has habits like this that elude them. Think about all the things you don't do for your health, your productivity, and your sanity that you want to do. So why can't you?

You can — with the right approach.

Ask the Discovery Question and identify the weak links in your Ability Chain. Then zero in on the right problem to solve. This is what makes the Ability Chain such a transformative tool. It allows you to shift into action without confusion, irritation, or exasperation. When it came to my flossing transformation, I didn't blame myself for lacking motivation to floss. Instead, I set out to make it easier to do by starting with one tooth and using thinner floss. Once I had shored up that Ability Factor, I did the behavior repeatedly. I cultivated a habit that I had been chasing for years. Once I had taken the first step, it felt easy to do the rest. I already had my hands in my mouth, right? Plus, the more I did it, the more skilled I became. This feeling of success motivated me to floss again the next day.

By keeping the behavior tiny, I helped this habit root itself into my routine. Here's how to think about it: Imagine a big plant with small roots. When a powerful wind kicks up, the big plant might topple over because it's not held firmly in place. And that's how habit formation works. If you start with a big behavior that's hard to do, the design is unstable; it's like a large plant with shallow roots. When a storm comes into your life, your big habit is at risk. However, a habit that is easy to do can weather a storm like flexible sprouts, and it can then grow deeper and stronger roots.

So if you haven't gotten off the couch in a year, don't start with seven minutes of strenuous activity. Start tiny instead. Shore up the weakest link in your Ability Chain by making your new workout habit radically easy to do. Scale back to doing one wall push-up. Just one. When you run into a setback—a cold, for instance—you can still manage to do one wall push-up, stuffy nose and all. By going tiny, you create consistency; by staying tiny, you get your new habit firmly rooted.

Which leads us to the second critical question we should ask about any behavior or habit we want to cultivate: *How can I make this behavior easier to do?* I call this the **Breakthrough Question,** and it turns out that there are only three answers.

Let's return to the PAC Person graphic to see how we can make a behavior easier to do.

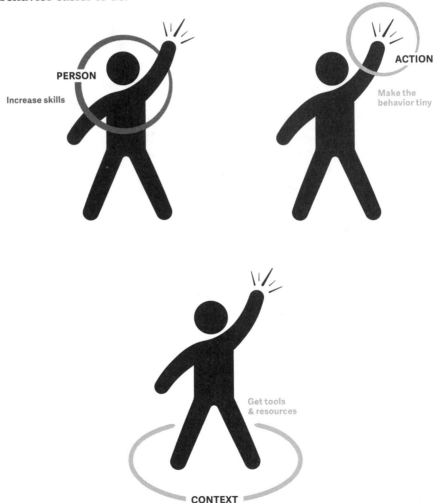

All three approaches manipulate the ability element of B=MAP to move you above the Action Line and increase the likelihood that you will actually do a behavior. Regardless of what your aspiration is, increasing your skills, getting tools and resources, and making the behavior tiny are what makes things easier to do.

But it's important to remember that designing for behaviors can take different paths. Sometimes all you'll need is the right tool to make a new habit easier to do, like using skinny floss, and other times all you have to do is scale the behavior back to its tiniest version, such as flossing just one tooth. Think of making something easy to do as a pond with three different ways to enter the water. Whether you jump off the dock, wade in at the beach, or drop in from a rope swing, you'll soon be swimming in the same water.

Now let's break down each approach.

The Three Approaches to Making a Behavior Easier to Do

1. INCREASE YOUR SKILLS

When you are better at something, it's easier to do. By gaining skills, you're turning up the volume on ability. How you increase your skills depends on the behavior. It could mean doing online research, asking a friend for tips, or taking a class. And you can increase your skills by doing the behavior over and over. I increased my flossing skills by watching some videos on the Internet (if you can think of a behavior, there is a video showing you how to do it). Marie Kondo's book *The Life-Changing Magic of Tidying Up* is a global best seller not because her book focused on motivating people to keep their houses clean but because it focused on teaching them the block-and-tackle steps of *how* to tidy up.

Increasing your skills could mean hiring a voice coach, taking a knife-skills class at your local grocery store, or practicing your push-up form. The act of "skilling up" feels natural when you are riding a Motivation Wave because you are using this energy crest to your advantage. They are one-time actions that make future behaviors easier to do, so why not do them when you're bursting with energy at the outset? Let's say you finish this chapter and are feeling jazzed about doing push-ups. This would be a good time to look up a video on the Internet about the proper push-up form while your motivation is still high.

You may not always have the energy for skilling up, and that's fine. There are other ways to make your behavior easier.

2. GET TOOLS AND RESOURCES

Something as small as unwashed lettuce or mismatched Tupperware lids can be the difference between bringing a salad to work and grabbing a burger. If a behavior frustrates you, it will not become a habit. Getting the right tools to make a behavior easier could mean anything from getting a better set of kitchen knives to finding more comfortable walking shoes. If you want to make the Tiny Habits method easier to do, this book is a terrific first step. Getting personal guidance from a coach I've trained is also a great option.

Tools were crucial to making flossing easier for me. I had to find the right floss—thin and slippery. I became such a fan that I got myself a special tour of the floss factory when I traveled to Dublin for work. I know it seems weird (Denny thought I was nuts at first). But for a floss geek like me, a tour didn't feel weird at all.

My former boot camper Molly is another example of how tools and resources can catalyze change. Molly had struggled with maintaining a healthy weight ever since she was ten years old. As an adult, her biggest habit hurdle was meal preparation. She couldn't do it consistently even though she knew how much better she felt when she made her own food ahead of time instead of being cornered into making poor choices—vending-machine lunches or leftover meeting pizzas. Without a healthy prepared meal in her bag, she'd find herself with an anxiety-provoking dilemma at noon. "Am I going to eat? Where should I go? Will it be healthy enough?" Molly called this "decision fatigue"—the burden of making a choice when she was least equipped for it (hungry and busy)—and it not only created unnecessary mental spinning, it often led her to eat out of alignment with her healthy aspirations. As a busy professional, she was not only pressed for time, but she was also deeply ambivalent about cooking.

From a B=MAP standpoint, Molly's motivation for meal prep was low but not nonexistent—she really *did* want the energy, good health, and confidence that came along with eating well. Ability was where Molly had the most room for improvement. As luck would have it, she met a resource—a good-looking one at that. Ryan, Molly's future husband, was into Olympic weightlifting and paid close attention to nutrition. He was methodical about preparing meals for the week and didn't seem to mind doing this as much as Molly did. She observed and adopted some of his techniques—using Tupperware and cooking massive amounts of sweet potatoes for low blood sugar moments. Soon they got into a habit of cooking and prepping every Sunday for the week ahead. While she loved spending the time with her husband, Molly was less enthused about spending five hours in the kitchen. Sunday would roll around and she'd make other plans so she could avoid the kitchen, promising herself she'd pick up a salad on the way to work every day. But she rarely would. Then she'd find herself in the middle of the workday staring down the leftover pizza in the conference room, knowing what she would choose and already disappointed in herself.

After attending my two-day boot camp, Molly knew this was a Behavior Design problem, not a character flaw or a matter of willpower. Instead of getting down on herself about skipping out on a Sunday in the kitchen with her future husband, she started thinking more strategically about how she could make meal prep easier. She joked that since meal prep was so fun for him maybe he could just do hers as well. She said that suggestion got her a raised eyebrow and a hearty laugh but not much else.

One day Molly went to a friend's house and watched her use an unfamiliar device with a flat frame and an adjustable blade. Her friend sliced an entire carrot into a salad bowl in about ten seconds with no wobbly cutting board and no dull knife. This seemed like magic to Molly. She asked her friend, "Wow! What is that thing?" It was a mandoline—the first of many time-saving kitchen tools that Molly would later acquire (warning: mandoline slicers are great but also dangerous—be careful). Using her future husband as a resource and key tools like her handy mandoline, Molly reduced her Sunday food prep time from five hours to two and a half. Now she mandolines carrots, cucumbers, and peppers into Tupperware containers lined up for each day of the week. Cutting the time in half and making the process more enjoyable was all she needed to move her above the Action Line.

Months after she redesigned her behavior, Molly and Ryan were consistently prepping ten meals per week, which covered all their lunches and dinners on workdays. Ditching decision fatigue meant Molly could make room during her day for exercise, which helped her increase her energy and overall wellness even more. She found herself better able to keep up with Ryan on their trail runs, and she even proposed that they keep their healthy eating going while on vacation. The night before their honeymoon, Molly dragged Ryan to the bulk section of the supermarket to stock up on nuts and blueberries for the plane ride. A year later, she told me she is happier, more energetic, and more productive than ever before. Most important, she now asks, "How can I make this easier?" when she lacks the motivation to do something she wants to do.

Not everyone should buy a mandoline or fancy kitchen equipment to make their behavior easier to do, but in Molly's case, she had experimented with other ways (buying precooked food, prepping meals every evening) and nothing had worked. She knew tools and resources were one Behavior Design strategy that she hadn't tried, so she went for it. By cutting her time in half, she crossed the line from too hard to easy to do. In the end, I'd say that a flexible, experimental mindset for problem-solving was perhaps Molly's most handy tool of all.

EASY-TO-DO ANALYSIS

Meal Prep Habit — What is making this behavior hard to do?

The problem: The weakest links in Molly's Ability Chain were time (five hours was too much) and physical effort (chopping and cutting with bad equipment is laborious).

Meal Prep Habit — How can I make this behavior easier to do?

The solution: Molly used tools to help her eliminate the time and physical effort factors that were hampering her ability to act. She also leaned on Ryan as a resource to guide her in what to prepare for the week and how to do it.

3. MAKE THE BEHAVIOR TINY

Making a behavior radically tiny is the cornerstone of the Tiny Habits method for a reason — it's a foolproof way to make something easier to do, which means it's often a good place to start regardless of your motivation levels.

We have already looked at several examples of how to make things tiny. They fall into two categories: Starter Step and Scaling Back.

Starter Step

This is exactly what it sounds like: one small move toward the desired behavior. If you want to make a habit out of walking three miles every day, your Starter Step might be putting your walking shoes on. That Starter Step becomes your Tiny Behavior and the only action you need to do at the start of your new habit. The objective here is to begin with a crucial step in the process of doing the desired behavior. Tell yourself: *I don't have to walk. I just have to make sure I put on my shoes each day.*

Putting those shoes on will shift your perception. Walking suddenly won't seem so hard. Most days you'll head out the door and take a spin around the block after putting your shoes on. This is one way Starter Steps can turn into bigger habits. However, I want to share an important part of the Tiny Habits mindset: Do not raise the bar prematurely. Don't rush to make the behavior bigger. It's *always* okay to not walk after putting on your shoes if that's all you want to do for the day. By keeping the bar low, you keep the habit alive. You'll ensure that you're always capable of doing the behavior no matter how your motivation fluctuates.

One of Sarika's biggest victories was cooking herself breakfast. This was a task that she had felt was both insurmountable and defeating. People cooked breakfast every day; why did this feel so hard for her to do? After taking a Tiny Habits course and learning about Starter Steps, Sarika was determined to play around with habits to see if she could design her way out of the problem. So Sarika decided that she'd turn the stovetop burner on first thing in the morning. That was her new habit. Oh, so tiny. It was a Starter Step to cooking breakfast. And that's all she did the first few days. She'd leave the burner on for a few seconds, then turn it off. But she soon built on that Starter Step and put a pot on top of the burner. Then once the pot was there, she thought, *Why not boil water for porridge?* Once the water was boiling, it seemed silly not to put the porridge in, and she wound up making herself breakfast most days, amazed at how much easier it felt than what she'd built it up to be in her head. But if she ever felt rushed or distracted, it was okay if she just turned the burner on and off because the Starter Step is the behavior that needs to become hardwired into her routine.

The Starter Step is a kind of mental jujitsu—it has a surprising impact for such a small move because the momentum it creates often propels you to the next steps with less friction. The key is not to raise the bar. Doing the Starter Step *is* success. Every time you do it, you are keeping that habit alive and cultivating the possibility of growth.

Sarika was surprised by how quickly her burner habit blossomed into multiple habits that led to a full-blown breakfast habit. Buoyed by her success, she enlisted her mom as a resource, and she also began skilling up. Within a few months, she'd moved beyond porridge and was whipping up morning *dosas* with chutney.

EASY-TO-DO ANALYSIS

Discovery Question
Breakfast Habit—What is making this behavior hard to do?

The problem: The weakest link in Sarika's Ability Chain was mental effort. She didn't have a plan for what to cook, and the dishes were piled up on the counter so she had nowhere to assemble a meal, and this felt too complicated for her to handle.

Breakthrough Question
Breakfast Habit—How can I make this behavior easier to do?

The solution: Sarika made it easier to do by using a Starter Step to break down an otherwise overwhelming process into discrete steps.

Lighting the burner was easy to do, and this simple behavior gave her a sense of success that caused her habit to grow.

Scaling Back

Now we come to the second way to make a behavior tiny: Scaling Back.

This means taking the behavior you want and shrinking it. As a result, your Tiny Habit will be a much smaller version of your desired behavior. Consider my flossing habit: I wanted to floss *all* my teeth but began with just one. I scaled it back.

If your desired behavior is to walk a mile every day, you can scale back by walking to the mailbox. Nothing more. As with the Starter Step, the scaled-back version *is* your Tiny Habit—it's your baseline behavior, the only thing you have to do every day to cultivate the walking habit that will eventually grow to full size.

EASY-TO-DO ANALYSIS

Discovery Question
Flossing Habit—What is making this behavior hard to do?

The problem: The weakest link in my Ability Chain was physical effort. The thick floss I used was difficult to get between my teeth, and this took effort and frustrated me as I struggled to get the floss between each close contact.

Breakthrough Question
Flossing Habit—How can I make this behavior easier to do?

The solution: I made flossing easier to do by acquiring the right tool —I found floss that glided smoothly between my teeth. No effort. No strain. But the key was this: I scaled the behavior back from all my teeth to just one tooth. Without scaling back, flossing would not have become a habit for me. I needed to start tiny.

Designing Your Tiny Habits

Take your Golden Behaviors from chapter 2 and see if you can make them tiny. Find a Starter Step or scale back—either way is fine.

Let's look at some examples.

Habit to Make Tiny	Starter Step	Scale Back
Read every day	Open my book	Read one paragraph
Drink more water	Put water bottle in purse	Drink a sip of water
Meditate for ten minutes	Take my meditation pillow out of the closet	Meditate for three breaths
Clean the kitchen after every meal	Open the dishwasher	Clear the table after every meal
Take vitamins daily	Put vitamins in a small bowl	Take one vitamin
Eat blueberries for a snack	Pack blueberries in my work bag	Eat two or three blueberries
Pay my bills online	Visit one bill payment website	Pay one bill

Where Do I Start?
Skills, Tools, or Tiny?

Because Behavior Design is a system with various pathways, there is no single right answer. However, I can guide you in making that determination for yourself. Even though you don't *have* to do all three things to make something easier to do, using all three options is a great way to set yourself up for success by making sure your behavior is as simple as it can be.

To decide which jumping-off point is best for you, look at your motivation level. Acquiring skills and tools are often one-time actions best done when your motivation is high. When our motivation is high, we can do more difficult things; but when it's on the low side, we need to compensate by making the behavior tiny. Gauging our motivation for completing each behavior helps us determine our next step on the road to making it a habit. It's like checking the pressure in your car tires. Do you need to add more air or can you drive away without doing that?

Because I'm someone who loves systems, I've created a flowchart that tells you how to make any behavior easier to do. You'll find it in the appendixes, but we'll walk through an example here to help you conceptualize how this works in real life.

Let's say you want a habit of doing twenty push-ups every day. Here are the steps to make that behavior easier to do, with questions to guide you.

ANALYSIS PHASE

Ask the Discovery Question: *What makes doing twenty push-ups hard to do?*

The Ability Chain will give you your answer. In this case, it will most likely be physical effort. That is the link you are solving for.

DESIGN PHASE

Ask the Breakthrough Question: *How can I make push-ups easier to do?*

Knowing that physical effort is the weakest link, ask yourself which of the ways to make a behavior easier to do will work for you. For the design phase, we turn to the three parts of the PAC model.

Will improving my push-up skills make it easier to do?

Not the full solution, but probably a good idea if you have the motivation.

Will getting the right tools or resources help me to make it easier?

Not really. There are videos that can guide you in the right way to do push-ups, but they don't make this exercise any easier. And a trainer can't actually *do* the push-ups for you.

Can I make twenty push-ups tinier so the new habit is easier to do?

Yes. Doing twenty push-ups requires a lot of physical effort so the best option is to make this habit tinier. There are a few ways to do this. Cutting it down to one push-up, doing a few push-ups on your knees, or doing push-ups against a wall.

No matter what new habit you want to create, these questions and three approaches will guide you through the process of designing your new habit to be easier to do. And these questions will become second nature with practice.

Are you feeling motivated enough to learn a new skill?

Yes? Great — do it. And now go to the next question.

No? Next question.

Are you feeling motivated enough to find a tool or resource?

Yes? Excellent, make it happen. And now go to the next question.

No? Next question.

Can you scale back the behavior to make it tiny?

Yes? Fantastic. You're done. You can start practicing your new habit.

No? Next question.

Can you find a Starter Step for your behavior?

Yes? Great. Make the Starter Step your initial habit, then do more later when you feel like it.

No? Uh-oh. If you said no to all of these questions, you might need to go back and match yourself with a different behavior from your Swarm of Behaviors.

Keep the Habit Alive

Making your behavior easy to do not only helps it take root so it can grow big, but it also helps you hang on to it as a habit when the going gets tough. Think of it this way: You can keep many tiny plants alive by giving them a few drops of water a day. It's the same with habits. There are still days when my motivation is unusually low for flossing. On those days, I floss only one tooth. The key is that I never feel bad about it because I've done my habit — I know one tooth is enough to keep the habit alive. Most days I do all of them, so I'm not about to sweat a day or two here and there. Stuff happens. People get sick, take vacations, and have emergencies. We're not aiming for perfection here, only consistency. Keeping the habit alive means keeping it rooted in your routine no matter how tiny it is.

The Winning Pattern: Simplicity Changes Behavior

When it comes to habit formation, simplicity wins. And not just in our personal lives.

I've seen a clear pattern in the digital products that millions of people use every day: Everything big started small.

Look at Google, Instagram, Amazon, and Slack. When they first launched, each company started with something small and focused. Because they were simple to use, these products became firmly rooted in people's lives. The companies added more features only when these products became solid habits. (Most products that launch with lots of features and complexity spiral down in flames.)

I'm urging you to apply this pattern of success to your own life: If you want a habit to grow big, you need to start small and simple. Once the habit wires in, you can grow it naturally.

Before Sarika and Molly started using the Tiny Habits method, both women felt overwhelmed. They were experiencing dread, a lack of confidence, and a mysterious feeling of resistance. Going tiny changed all that. They got started easily, and they quickly enjoyed feeling successful. With each success, their fears diminished. The change process started feeling less like work and more like fun.

You can apply the Tiny Habits approach to everything, not just habits. So many frustrating family dynamics and workplace dramas erupt because of the misplaced belief that manipulation motivation is the key to changing behavior. But now you know that simplicity is what reliably changes behavior.

A note on one-time behaviors

Starter steps can also work magic on things that don't need to be habitual. Not long ago I had to call the oral surgeon to schedule a follow-up appointment (not fun), so I was procrastinating even though this doesn't sound like a hard behavior to execute. But it's a good example of those things that we feel silly for putting off but avoid nonetheless. The important thing to remember about procrastination is that the perception of difficulty can be just as important as the actual difficulty. In addition, every day you don't do the task, it grows in your head, which makes the task seem more and more difficult. Before I sank too deeply into the hole, I came up with a Starter Step: Write the doctor's number on a Post-it and put it on my phone. I told myself that writing down the number was all I had to do, so I did it.

By lowering the bar, I was able to hack my brain. Writing the number down wasn't intimidating—I felt I could do it. Once I did, I had already taken a step toward completing the full behavior, so I picked up the phone and dialed. Think about how many of these tiny to-dos that you don't want to do are clogging your brain every day. It can get mentally exhausting. Taking the first step, no matter how small, can generate a sense of momentum that our brains love. Completing tasks gives us a boost of confidence, and this increases our motivation to do the entire behavior.

In the next chapter, we'll talk about prompts. The last component of the Behavior Model is also the next step in the process of cultivating successful habits. We know that no behavior happens without a prompt. Prompts are the cues that remind us to act. They are the spark that lights the fire. So why not make the prompt easy, too? What if you designed a prompt that was already built into your day? Something that takes no time, effort, or money to construct? Now *that* sounds simple.

Tiny Exercises for Making a Habit Easier to Do

There are two parts to this exercise. The first focuses on analysis, the second on design.

PART A: ANALYSIS OF A DIFFICULT HABIT

Step 1: Write down one difficult habit that you tried to create in the past but couldn't make stick. If you can't think of anything from your own life, then use this: Eat more vegetables every day.

Step 2: Ask yourself the Discovery Question: What made that habit hard for you to do? Consider the links in your Ability Chain: Did this desired habit require too much time? Money? Mental or physical effort? Did it disrupt your routine?

PART B: DESIGN TO MAKE YOUR HABIT EASIER TO DO

Step 3: For each weak link that you found in step 2, ask yourself the Breakthrough Question: How can you make this habit easier to do? For example, you might consider how you can make this habit require less time. But make sure to come up with a variety of ideas for each weak link.

Step 4: Select your top three ideas from step 3.

Step 5: Imagine yourself taking action on your top three ideas to make the habit easier to do. Explore in detail how you would do that.

Extra credit: Put your insight into action and see what happens.

To help you with this exercise, I brought back our friendly PAC Person to remind you of the three ways to make a behavior easier to do.

PROMPTS—THE POWER OF AFTER

Prompts are the invisible drivers of our lives.

We experience hundreds of prompts each day, yet we barely notice most of them. More often than not, we simply act. The stoplight turns green—you hit the gas. You're offered a cheese sample at the grocery store—you eat it. A notification pops up on your computer screen letting you know you have a new e-mail—you click to open it. Some prompts exist naturally—you feel a few drops of rain on your arm so you open your umbrella. Some prompts are designed—the smoke alarm blares so you open a few windows and rescue that forgotten pizza in the oven. Whether natural or designed, a prompt says, "Do this behavior now."

But this is the crucial nugget: *No behavior happens without a prompt.*

People respond reliably to prompts when they are motivated and able, which is exactly what makes well-timed prompts so powerful. The writers who create clickbait headlines and the designers who craft the apps on our phones know this. There's a reason many of us can't resist clicking on an app with a little red number on it—that feature has been designed to grab our attention and get us to act. Internet advertisers know that if you can combine a prompt with a motivator (Click here to win a prize!), people will respond in even higher percentages.

On the flip side, if there is no prompt, there is no behavior even if you have high levels of motivation and ability. Maybe you wanted to use the meditation app that you downloaded last week, but since there was no prompt, you forgot.

Life is filled with an overwhelming number of prompts that we don't want, but there are plenty that we *do* want. But most people soar on autopilot at the behest of invisible prompts while desperately trying to remind themselves to do things they keep forgetting to do. If your desk is covered with sticky notes and your phone is pestering you with notifications and you are still not doing the things you want to do, it's time to take the power of prompts back.

In this chapter, I'll teach you how to design prompts *in* or *out* of your life. Once you've matched yourself to the right behavior and made it easier to do, you're ready for the next step: Designing a good prompt for the behavior you want. This is important. Don't leave prompts to chance.

Steps in Behavior Design

 Step 1: Clarify the Aspiration

 Step 2: Explore Behavior Options

 Step 3: Match with Specific Behaviors

 Step 4: Start Tiny

(!) **Step 5: Find a Good Prompt**

In the Behavior Model, motivation and ability exist on a continuum, but prompts are black-and-white. You either notice the prompt or you don't. And if you don't notice the prompt, or if the prompt happens at the wrong time, then the behavior won't happen. That makes prompts a crucial component to get right. Designing a good prompt is a key part of Fogg Maxim #1: *Help yourself do what you already want to do.*

One person who learned to design prompts effectively was my friend and colleague Amy, whose decision to go tiny was detailed in the beginning of this book. About seven years ago, Amy was busy caring for her three kids and trying to grow her business as a freelance educational-media writer. She loved her work developing patient-education materials for doctors and hospitals, but she wasn't doing the necessary behaviors to grow her business. Usually an optimist, Amy found that she was overwhelmed by worry about the future. She wasn't sleeping well and carried a sense of foreboding that she couldn't shake. Every business owner worries about keeping on top of things, but Amy's dread was driven by something far worse than falling behind or losing clients— her real fear was losing her kids.

Amy and her husband hadn't been happy for years, but things had become unbearable lately. The fighting had escalated, and she knew it wasn't a healthy environment for her kids. She wanted to get out, and she suspected that he did, too. Separating their lives would be painful, but more worrisome to Amy was what would come next. For years, she had chosen to focus on her husband's good qualities—he was quick to laugh and generous, and he always supported her professionally. But now she felt backed into a corner with no healthy way to resolve the hostility, contempt, and growing lack of transparency between them. These were sides of her husband that she hadn't wanted to see that now kept her up at night. Divorce can bring out the worst in people, and she feared what he might do if she got on the wrong side of him. Amy sensed that she was about to be on the very wrong side of him. She knew that there was a real possibility that her husband would bring their kids into the fight, and without a solid income, Amy faced the threat that she might lose custody of them.

More than anything else, Amy loved her kids. The idea of not being always available for them was shattering. But if she couldn't make ends meet financially, her worst fears could be realized. Amy worried that her husband might resort to using every move available and that she would be stripped of her options and stuck in a never-ending conflict with the children in the middle. The only thing she could think to do was hire a lawyer and get her finances in order before beginning divorce proceedings. But she was stuck on how to create more business.

The anxiety over her crumbling marriage and the day-to-day stress of raising three kids made it difficult for Amy to concentrate. She had every reason in the world to knock things off her to-do list—return phone calls, hustle for work, and write her butt off—but she couldn't get herself to take action on things that mattered. She'd try to get down to business every morning, but on most days Amy would end up folding clothes, cleaning the kitchen, or rewriting and reordering her to-do list instead of taking actions that would bring income to support her family. She would do a few tasks on her list, but they were usually easy and not very essential. She was either overthinking or underacting, but either way she wasn't getting the work done. She wasn't putting money in the bank and getting any closer to securing a future with her kids.

After learning about Behavior Design and Tiny Habits, Amy discovered her solution: Every day she would write down one thing—the *most important* thing—that she needed to get done that day on a Post-it. That was it. That would be her new habit. Amy felt confident and optimistic that she could do this each day. After all, she didn't actually have to *do* the item on the Post-it; she just had to write it down. Simple. Ability was dialed in. But what made this habit a success wasn't motivation or ability; it was designing a good prompt.

For some habits, it's all about finding out where a new habit fits into your day.

Where a habit is located in your daily routine can make the difference between action and inaction, success and failure. Fortunately for

Amy, she got it right on the first try; she planted her new habit seed in just the right spot.

Here's how it worked: Amy would drop her daughter Rachel off at kindergarten every morning, and Rachel would wave good-bye and shut the car door. The door shutting was Amy's prompt. She would immediately drive to a nearby parking space at the school, then she'd do her habit—writing down her most important task on a Post-it. Once she was done, Amy would stick the note to her dashboard, clap once for herself, and say, "Done!"

After the first week of doing her new habit, Amy said it felt effortless and automatic. She had found a natural place for it in her routine. Until she dropped off her daughter, Amy was thinking about what everyone needed to get out the door. Because she made her Post-it habit the *first* work-related thing she did, there was no time to overthink or get distracted. She also did herself a favor by designing this Starter Step to be laser-focused. Car door shuts. Mindset switches to business mode: Park the car and figure out the most important thing to do today and write it down. Finito. (And hooray!) It easily became part of her morning because she had anchored it to something that was already part of her routine. She didn't need a text alert or a calendar notification to tell her to take Rachel to school, which meant she didn't need an artificial reminder to write her Post-it. Amy designed a solid prompt, so the new habit formed naturally.

Amy was delighted by the clarity this simple habit lent to her day. Yes, this was a small action, she knew that, but her feelings of focus and success snowballed into much bigger actions. She created other habits that built on that first one. When she got home from dropping off Rachel, Amy would go immediately to her office and put the Post-it on the wall in front of her desk.

Some days Amy didn't do her most important task, but most days she did. A surge of pride and accomplishment motivated her to create a flurry of to-do items, and with her Golden Behavior rooted firmly in place as a habit, Amy became more productive than she could have imagined. Somewhere along the line, her fear started to fade. At one point she said out loud to herself: "Wow, I'm really doing it. I *can* do this."

And she continued on the path.

What had started with one Post-it turned into a productivity avalanche. Amy realized that she had a huge passion and desire to grow her business from a one-woman shop to a multiperson strategy and content-creation agency. Once she found the right prompt, it broke her logjam, and all that pent-up ambition came rushing out as she finished writing projects and completed proposals for new ones. When a large healthcare company asked her to send a proposal in for a million-dollar project, Amy didn't hesitate. It would mean hiring people to help her get everything done, but after months of success, her self-doubt was gone. Amy told me later that what had won the project was the self-confidence she projected in her pitch meeting.

Half a year later, Amy was divorced. She had also quadrupled her income. Most important, she had gained custody of her kids and was sleeping peacefully through the night.

One simple new habit can lead to more habits that ripple out well beyond the initial one. In Amy's case, her success hinged on designing the right prompt. Whether you are designing a habit from scratch or troubleshooting a habit that won't stick, you've got to figure out what will prompt you to do it every time, and Behavior Design provides a system to find the answer that is right for you.

Don't leave prompts to chance!

The good news is that you already have lots of experience designing prompts even if you don't realize it. You've made a checklist. You've asked someone to remind you. You've set up a calendar notification in your work e-mail. In each case, you are adding a prompt to influence your behavior.

But all too often the prompts people think will work are poorly designed. If you're the person who hits the snooze button six times before getting up, you know what I'm talking about. (On some phone alarms, the snooze button is bigger and easier to hit than the off button. Oddly enough, it seems we've been set up to hit snooze by design.)

When designing prompts for ourselves, it doesn't work to put one more Post-it on a computer screen already filled with other Post-its. And writing a reminder on your hand might not look very professional when you're in a business meeting. In any case, there is more to the story about which prompts work and which ones don't. Otherwise we would all be Habit Ninjas.

Designing prompts is a skill you can learn and practice.

A Systematic Approach to Prompts

Let's look at what kinds of prompts are available to us and how they work. Once we figure this out, we can stop leaving prompts to chance or other people and start planting our new habit in fertile soil.

For insight into prompts, we can again turn to the PAC Person model. There are three types of prompts in our lives: Person Prompts, Context Prompts, and Action Prompts.

Let's start with the Person Prompt.

PERSON

Have person
prompt self
to do action

This prompt type relies on something inside of you to do a behavior. Basic bodily urges are the most natural Person Prompts we have. Our bodies remind us to do necessary things like eat and sleep. That pressure in your bladder? Yep, that's a prompt. Grumbling stomach—prompt. Thanks to evolution, these prompts are pretty reliable in getting us to take action.

However, if your survival is not dependent on your behavior, then the Person Prompt isn't a good solution because our memories are notoriously faulty. Sure, there are a few times when you've magically remembered your mom's birthday, but there are probably more times you forgot if you were relying on the Person Prompt.

A few years ago, I met some new neighbors, Bob and Wanda. She was a retired executive at Intel, and he had worked as an engineer. I was glad when they invited Denny and me to dinner. I responded with an enthusiastic yes and promised to be there at six p.m. sharp with a salad.

Two weeks later, my phone rang at 6:42 p.m. I was deeply immersed in work that had a deadline, and I didn't recognize the incoming phone number. I let the call go to voice mail, but I was curious so I listened to the message immediately. As soon as I heard Wanda's voice, I was flooded with regret. "Hey, BJ. The pasta is getting cold and sticky. I made it from scratch so it won't keep. We were expecting you at six p.m. Are you coming? Or I guess we'll plan something else. Bye."

Yep. I blew it.

I called Wanda and apologized profusely. I was mortified. This was a terrible way to say, "Welcome to the neighborhood!"

Not my finest moment, but a great example of why you should be wary of Person Prompts in general and avoid them completely when you are designing behavior. This goes for one-time actions like showing up at a dinner party, but it's even more true for behaviors that you're trying to turn into habits. Relying on yourself to remember to do a new behavior every day is unlikely to lead to meaningful change. Ditto for trying to help someone else cultivate a habit. Let's say you want your daughter to do her homework every night instead of spending an hour on her phone. Asking her to remember to do that isn't the best strategy because Person Prompts are not reliable.

Onward to the Context Prompt!

Something in the person's context prompts action

CONTEXT

This prompt is anything in your environment that cues you to take action: sticky notes, app notifications, your phone ringing, a colleague reminding you to join a meeting.

You can learn to design these Context Prompts effectively. If I had entered our dinner appointment on my calendar with a pop-up reminder, Denny and I would have shown up on our neighbors' doorstep at six p.m. with a fresh salad. Creating this Context Prompt would have taken me about twenty seconds. But if I had put "Go to Wanda and Bob's for dinner" on my to-do list, that design would have probably failed because I don't look at my to-do list when I'm deep into a project.

Effective design of Context Prompts is a skill. And learning this skill takes practice.

About ten years ago, I realized that there were certain behaviors I needed to do only once a week: water plants, pay bills, and restart my computers. I first tried setting alarms on my phone. At ten a.m. on Saturday, the alarm to water plants would go off. Fine. But sometimes I was at the grocery store, so my ability to do the task was zero. I was below the Action Line. Sometimes an alarm would go off for a task that I had already done for the week, so that prompt wasted a bit of my time.

I searched for a solution to this problem and found my answer. I wrote each weekend task on a small plastic sticky about half the size of your typical Post-it. I placed all the stickers on a laminated page that was labeled WEEKEND TASKS. Now my typical routine on Saturday mornings is to get out the laminated sheet and put it on the kitchen counter. Simple. This sheet becomes my checklist for the weekend. As I do each task, I move the sticker to the back of the sheet so I see only the tasks I haven't completed. On Sunday, when I finish the final task, I flip the laminated page over, put the final sticker on the page (victoriously!), and store my laminated sheet of tasks for the next weekend. My weekend checklist was a game changer for me. I finally could reliably do tasks like clean the fridge and water my houseplants.

There are times you will need to design a Context Prompt for yourself or others. This kind of prompt is best suited for a one-time behavior (like making a doctor's appointment), yet it's not a great way to create a habit. When I teach industry innovators, I ask them to share their most effective Context Prompts. Some are common and obvious. Others are surprising. Here are a few of them.

+ Put your ring on the wrong finger.

+ Send yourself a text message.

- Write on your bathroom mirror with a dry-erase marker.

- Rearrange furniture so something is oddly out of place.

- Set an alarm on your voice assistant.

- Put a reminder note inside the fridge.

- Ask your child to remind you.

- Stick a Post-it on the screen of your mobile phone.

Context Prompts can be helpful for one-time actions, like registering to vote. However, using Context Prompts for daily habits can be both stressful and ineffective. Managing our prompt landscape effectively is one of the biggest challenges in our modern lives. When you set up too many Context Prompts, they can actually have the opposite effect — you become desensitized and fail to heed the prompt. You end up not hearing notification dings and not seeing sticky notes. It's like living next to train tracks — at first the noise of a train is deafening, then . . . what train?

I have a huge whiteboard in my home office listing dozens of tasks that are organized by project and coded in different colors. It's . . . a lot. In order to manage this visual and psychological avalanche, I cover up the prompts for the tasks I'm not doing with a movable curtain so I see only the prompts for what I need to do that day. I've learned that covering up all the other prompts makes me calmer — and more focused.

If you've created a Context Prompt and it's not working, you are not doing anything wrong. You probably don't lack motivation or willpower. Do yourself a favor — don't blame yourself. Redesign the prompt instead. Find what prompt works for you.

In today's world, many of our Context Prompts are created by other people or organizations. We get e-mails asking us to do favors. Our digital wristwatch tells us to stand up. A red dot appears on app icons when we get a new message.

The classic prompts we grew up with are relatively easy to manage: We put junk mail in the recycling bin, and we remove ourselves from mailing lists. We change the channel during an infomercial. We tape DO NOT DISTURB on our office door.

However, the prompts coming from digital technology are harder to manage. LinkedIn has invested a lot of time and money to tell you that 233 people have looked at your profile this week and that you should click to see who they were. Do you want to remove that prompt? Maybe. Maybe not. After all, you're curious and the attention is flattering. Spam is a clearer issue. It continues to steal our time every day.

Other than getting off the grid, we may never find a perfect way to stop unwanted prompts from companies with business models that depend on us to click, read, watch, rate, share, or react. This is a difficult problem that pits our human frailties against brilliant designers and powerful computer algorithms.

That said, you can find ways to calm your Context Prompts. I urge you to invest a little effort now to save yourself time and energy later. Sometimes it's simple and fast. An industry innovator recently sent a text message to my mobile phone asking for a business favor: He wanted me to make a presentation to his team. I liked his proposal, and I knew I'd likely say yes. But he asked me using the wrong channel. I texted him back: "Hello! I want to respond to you, but please send me this request in an e-mail. (I use texting only for family and friends.) Thank you!" The next morning I saw his reply via e-mail: "Sorry. I'll use e-mail from now on." In about thirty seconds, I had saved myself from dozens of future prompts on my mobile phone that would interrupt and distract me.

You and I may never have full control over how companies prompt us or how business colleagues and other well-intentioned humans send things our way. Context Prompts are here to stay. But when it comes to designing prompts for ourselves and others, there is a better option than Context Prompts.

The third type of prompts—and my favorite—are what I call Action Prompts.

ACTION

A person's existing
routine prompts
next action

An Action Prompt is *a behavior you already do* that can remind you to do a new habit you want to cultivate. This is a special type of prompt.

The Action Prompt is one way you hack your behavior with the Tiny Habits method.

For example, your existing habit of brushing your teeth can serve as your prompt to floss, a new habit. Starting the coffee maker can be your prompt to do a new stretching habit using the kitchen counter.

You already have a lot of reliable routines, and each of them can serve as an Action Prompt for a new habit. You put your feet on the floor in the morning. You boil water for tea or turn on the coffee maker. You flush the toilet. You drop your kid off at school. You hang your coat up when you walk through the door at the end of the day. You put your head on a pillow every night.

These actions are already embedded in your life so seamlessly and naturally that you don't have to think about them. And because of *that*, they make fantastic prompts. It's an elegant design solution because it's so natural. You already have an entire ecosystem of routines humming along nicely — you just have to tap into it.

Action Prompts are so much more useful than Person Prompts and Context Prompts that I've given them a pet name: Anchors. When talking about Tiny Habits, I use the term Anchor to describe something in your life that is already stable and solid. The concept is pretty simple. If there is a habit you want, find the right Anchor within your current routine to serve as your prompt, your reminder. I selected the term "anchor" because you are attaching your new habit to something solid and reliable.

Using Anchors to remind me to do a new habit came to me like a bolt of lightning after taking a shower many years ago. (Sure, I've heard of people having breakthroughs *in* the shower, but I'm the only person I know who had mine *after*. Which you'll soon see is perfectly fitting.) After showering one evening and thinking about nothing in particular, I stepped out, dried off, wrapped a towel around myself, and walked into the bedroom. As I was opening my underwear drawer, the insight hit me. *The key is "after."*

I suppose my brain was noticing this pattern: After a shower, I *always* dry off. After I dry off, I *always* walk into the bedroom. After I walk to the bedroom, I *always* open my underwear drawer. And so — aha! — to create a new habit, you need to find what behavior it should come after. For example, if I want to always floss my teeth *after* I brush, then brushing my teeth is a great prompt for my new habit of flossing.

With my underwear drawer still open, I realized I'd found my answer: behavior sequencing. You simply need to figure out what comes after what. Eureka!

I now see this like creating computer code. If you get the algorithm correct — this behavior then this behavior then this behavior and then *bam* — you have a reliable outcome.

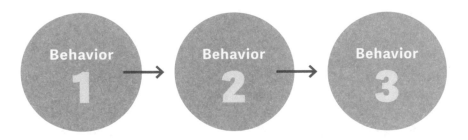

Behaviors happen in sequences, one leading to another.

A reliable *habit*. You just have to "code" things correctly by putting them in the right order.

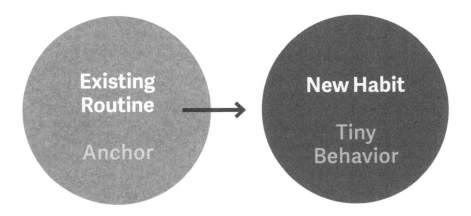

You design the sequence for a new habit.

When I opened the underwear drawer, I recognized that there were plenty of things I already do every day. If I could insert my new behaviors into my existing habits, they would fit into my life without much effort. And this scales beautifully—you can keep folding in new habits as long as you anchor them to existing ones. This method avoids the pitfalls of the Person Prompt and the Context Prompt because you're not relying on yourself or anyone else to remind you. You're not overwhelmed by prompts. Your day-to-day life is the prompt instead. It doesn't get much simpler than that.

I immediately tried it. I took one of the most basic and reliable behaviors humans have—going to the bathroom—and used that as the prompt for a new push-up habit. I decided that after I flushed the toilet I would do two push-ups. This might sound weird, but I worked mostly from home at the time so it was no big deal. It wasn't long before this habit was rock solid. It was like snapping puzzle pieces together. Doing push-ups after I peed soon became something that I did a few times every day. I got stronger pretty quickly, too, which helped me to scale up and do more push-ups. Seven years later, I *still* do this habit. Some days I end up doing fifty push-ups or more (depending on how much water I drink!), but when I'm at home, I always do at least two after I pee. That's my Tiny Habit Recipe: *After I pee, I will do two push-ups.*

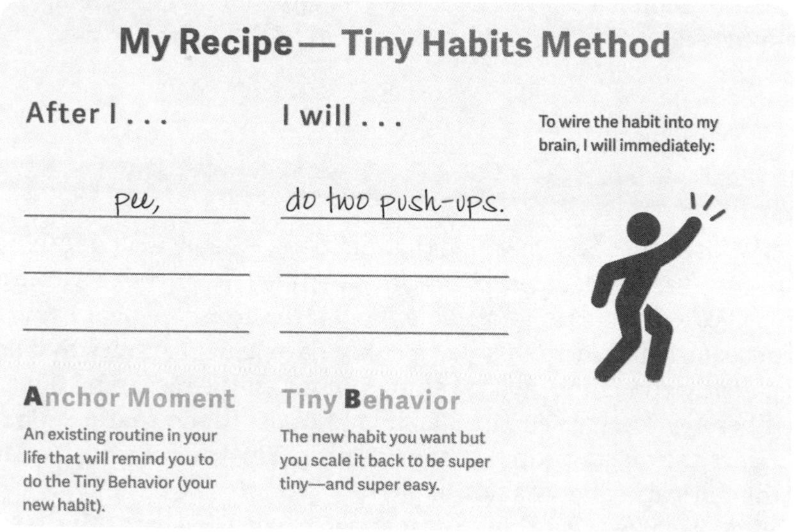

My Recipe — Tiny Habits Method

After I . . .

I will . . .

To wire the habit into my brain, I will immediately:

pee,

do two push-ups.

Anchor Moment

An existing routine in your life that will remind you to do the Tiny Behavior (your new habit).

Tiny Behavior

The new habit you want but you scale it back to be super tiny—and super easy.

Using Anchors is a great approach to designing prompts because anyone can do it. There's no need for fancy watches or whizzy apps to prompt new habits. You can do it yourself more effectively, and you will discover how transformative a simple design hack can be. The power of *after* is not magic, it's closer to chemistry. Combine the right behaviors with the right chronology, and, *poof,* a new habit is created.

The Recipe for Tiny Habits

At this point in the Tiny Habits design process, you have identified at least one new habit you want in your life. You've matched yourself, you've shrunk those behaviors to make them easy to do, and now you're going to add a prompt. After you finish this chapter, you'll have what you need to create a full Tiny Habit Recipe that looks like this.

After I (ANCHOR), I will (NEW HABIT).

- *After I flush the toilet, I will do two push-ups.*

- *After I pull the car over, I will write down the most important task of the day.*

- *After I brush my teeth, I will floss one tooth.*

Finding the right sequence and fit for your new habits takes a little tinkering, but it's ultimately pretty straightforward. If you want to see a long list of sample recipes, check out the appendix where I share three hundred recipes for Tiny Habits. Or see TinyHabits.com/recipes.

Identify Your Anchors

Your Anchor must be something that happens reliably in your life. Some of us lead very scheduled lives that are filled with reliable routines. Other lives are more unpredictable. No matter how haphazard your day might seem, I guarantee that you already have many routines that occur consistently enough to be used as an Anchor. In the research I did a few years before creating the Tiny Habits method, I found that people typically have the most routines in the morning. This makes morning fertile soil for cultivating new habits.

People reported that their routines can easily go awry as the day progresses. And once one routine breaks down, then other routines do, too: Daycare pick-up gets pushed back because of a late meeting. You grab a pizza rather than cook dinner because you're late and exhausted from a trying day. Stuff happens.

So morning is likely our most predictable time, but there is plenty to work with in the afternoon and evening. Here are some examples of common anchors at different times.

Morning routines

- After *my feet hit the ground* in the morning, I will . . .

- After I *sit up in bed*, I will . . .

- After I *turn off my alarm*, I will . . .

- After I *pee*, I will . . .

- After I *flush the toilet*, I will . . .

- After I *turn on the shower*, I will . . .

- After I *brush my teeth*, I will ...
- After I *brush my hair*, I will ...
- After I *make my bed*, I will ...
- After I *tie my shoes*, I will ...
- After I *start the coffee maker*, I will ...
- After I *pour myself a cup of coffee*, I will ...
- After I *put my dish in the dishwasher*, I will ...
- After I *feed the dog*, I will ...
- After I *put the key in the ignition of my car*, I will ...

Midday (or anytime) routines

- After I *hear my phone ring*, I will ...
- After I *hang up the phone*, I will ...
- After I *drink a cup of coffee*, I will ...
- After I *empty my inbox*, I will ...
- After I *use the bathroom*, I will ...

Evening routines

- After I *walk in the door after work*, I will ...
- After I *hang up my keys*, I will ...
- After I *put down my purse*, I will ...
- After I *hang up the dog leash*, I will ...
- After I *sit down to eat*, I will ...
- After I *put my dinner dish in the dishwasher*, I will ...
- After I *start the dishwasher*, I will ...
- After I *turn off the TV*, I will ...
- After I *put my head on my pillow*, I will ...

You can see more examples of Anchors in the appendix where I list three hundred sample recipes for Tiny Habits.

* * *

You'll notice that all these examples are precise events. A fuzzy Anchor ("after dinner" or "whenever I feel stress") doesn't work. Make them precise. One good way to think about Anchors is to call them Anchor Moments, which implies a precise moment in time.

Now that you've got the gist, make a list of unique-to-you Anchors using the Tiny Exercise at the end of this chapter.

Once you have a collection of Anchors to choose from, look closely at the new habits you want to cultivate so you can pair your new habit with the best Anchor.

WHERE CAN THIS NEW HABIT FIT NATURALLY INTO MY DAY?

In teaching thousands of people how to find good Anchors for their new habits, I've learned that you should take three things into account.

Match the physical location

First, consider the physical location of your new habit. Find an Anchor you already do in that location. If the new habit you want is wiping down the kitchen table, look for an existing routine in the kitchen. That could be your Anchor. You want to avoid having the Anchor happen in one location and the new habit in another. My research shows that this rarely works. Location is the most important factor when you pair Anchors and new habits.

Match the frequency

Next, as you look at your existing routine, decide how often you want to do your new habit. If you want to do it once a day, then sequence it after an Anchor that happens once a day. If you want to do your new habit four times a day, then sequence it after an Anchor that happens four times a day. I wanted to do push-ups throughout my day, so placing it after I peed was a good—though quirky—solution.

Match the theme/purpose

Finally—and this element is less vital than the previous two—the best Anchors will have the same theme or purpose as the new habit. If you view coffee and its jolt of caffeine as a way to be more productive, then this might be a good Anchor for a new habit of launching your to-do app. However, if your morning coffee is more about relaxation and "me time," then a to-do app is not a good thematic fit. You might create this recipe instead: "After I pour my coffee, I will open my journal."

Remember Sarika from last chapter? One of the first habits that she incorporated into her new morning routine was to drink a glass of water before she had tea or coffee. The Anchor that she found worked best was "After I water the jade plant in my bathroom, I'll take a drink of water." When I asked her why it worked so well, she told me that she thought about both actions as nourishing. By watering the plant, she was giving it what it needed to thrive, and by "watering herself" she was doing what she needed to do to thrive. The theme here was an act of care, which made it even easier for her to remember. Both habits dovetailed so nicely that they became difficult to separate.

But this recipe — *After I brush my teeth, I will sweep the garage* — will almost certainly fail to create a habit because it doesn't match location, frequency, or theme. If you want to sweep the garage every Saturday, then find an existing routine you already do on Saturday at home (and ideally in the garage) to use as your Anchor.

As you design your new habit, don't worry too much about creating the perfect recipe. If the recipe isn't to your liking, then change it. That's one reason I named this format a "recipe." You should feel free to modify your creations whether they are Anchors and new habits or potatoes and gravy.

I've created a format to help you design recipes in the Tiny Habits way. You can use a blank index card. Or you can go online and use my template. In any case, think about this recipe card as part of a Habit Recipe collection you'll create over time. Maybe you store the cards in a recipe box. In that way, it's easy to review the habits you're practicing. And you can revise as needed, crossing out things and writing a new version directly on the card.

My Recipe — Tiny Habits Method

After I . . .	I will . . .	To wire the habit into my brain, I will immediately:
_____	_____	_____
_____	_____	_____
_____		

Anchor Moment
An existing routine in your life that will remind you to do the Tiny Behavior (your new habit).

Tiny Behavior
The new habit you want but you scale it back to be super tiny—and super easy.

Celebration
Something you do to create a positive feeling inside of yourself (the feeling is called Shine).

Experimentation Is Good

At this point, you've got what it takes to start experimenting with the Tiny Habits method. Because our lives are complex and unique, there will naturally need to be adjustments. Where to put some habits is going to be obvious—what better time to floss your teeth than after you brush them, right?—while others might take a while to dial in. In the first few days or even weeks of experimentation, your new habits might shift a lot, and that's better than okay; that's great. It means you're honing your skills and learning more about pairing Anchors with Tiny Behaviors.

If one habit doesn't hook naturally to an Anchor, you might be inspired to replace it with a different habit that seems like a better fit. The moment my head hit the pillow *seemed* like a good time for me to mindfully take three breaths, so I tried it out. It worked, but I didn't feel like it was doing much for me. It didn't grow naturally, and sometimes it felt pointless. Instead of getting down on myself, I got curious. What else could go there? I'd been wanting to practice more gratitude, so after my head hit the pillow, I thought of one thing that happened that day that I was thankful for. When I did it the first time, I got a happy little *zing* in my brain that told me I had found the right spot.

By playing around with forming habits, we hone our skills. With practice, you'll get better at using these principles to create habits that help you reach your aspirations. Quite often the skill you'll need is finding a good Anchor and pairing it with the right Tiny Behavior. Then you can efficiently design for change in your everyday life.

A few years ago, I was eating at a great restaurant, and I couldn't finish the delicious entrée. It wasn't the first time this had happened. I knew what the problem was: I had chowed down too much bread early in the meal. When servers bring fresh bread to the table, it is oh so tempting, but making an early meal of bread led me to overeat later or not fully enjoy the main course. Both were problems I wanted to address. So I looked to the Tiny Habits method for a solution. And I found what worked for me.

I created a recipe that went like this: *After the server offers bread, I will say, "No bread for me, thank you."* And this tiny statement gave me the results I wanted right away. I no longer fill up on bread, and I enjoy main courses more thoroughly. Yes, I had to practice this new habit a bit to wire it into my life—and navigate any social reaction at the table— but saying this sentence is now automatic.

One tiny statement at the right moment and I can stick to my game plan.

My Recipe — Tiny Habits Method

After I ...	I will ...	To wire the habit into my brain, I will immediately:
<u>hear the server</u> <u>offer bread,</u>	<u>say "no bread,"</u> <u>please."</u>	☺
Anchor Moment	**T**iny **B**ehavior	**C**elebration
An existing routine in your life that will remind you to do the Tiny Behavior (your new habit).	The new habit you want but you scale it back to be super tiny—and super easy.	Something you do to create a positive feeling inside of yourself (the feeling is called Shine).

Refine Your Anchor with the Trailing Edge

It's worth reinforcing how important it is to choose a precise event in your routine—that Anchor Moment. Using the Anchor "after I pee" got me to do two push-ups. I didn't need to get more specific than that. But if it hadn't worked, I could have looked a little closer at the Anchor for a specific moment I call the Trailing Edge. You look for the last action you do in a behavior. The last action of peeing, at least for me, is flushing the toilet. So I could refine my recipe to *After I flush the toilet, I will do two push-ups.*

To find the Trailing Edge, we look at the Anchor under a microscope to see what the end of an action looks like. This is particularly important for Anchors that are rather fuzzy. Here are some examples of how to be more specific and boost the likelihood of your success by using the Trailing Edge in your recipe.

The fuzzy Anchor of "After I eat breakfast" is better when you focus on the Trailing Edge, "After I start the dishwasher." The fuzzy Anchor of "After I get home from work" is better stated as "After I put my backpack on the bench."

One Habiteer (someone who practices Tiny Habits) I taught was trying to create a habit of wiping the kitchen counter. Elena created a recipe with what appeared to be a specific Anchor: *After I put my breakfast dishes in the sink, I will wipe one counter.*

That recipe looks good, right?

Except it didn't work very well. Wiping the counter wouldn't stick. Elena solved the problem by finding the Trailing Edge. She realized that the last action of "put my breakfast dishes in the sink" was turning off the water after she rinsed her cereal bowl. So turning off the water was the terminal point of the Anchor. Her adjusted Habit Recipe then became *After I turn off the water, I will wipe one counter.*

Guess what? Success.

Finding the Trailing Edge was all it took to snap her new habit into place. The feel of shutting off the faucet and the sound of the water abruptly stopping were sensory inputs that made the prompt more concrete and noticeable. Even though wiping a counter sounds like a small thing, Elena told me that it was actually a big point of tension between her and her husband in the morning. (Crumb-strewn counters being his number one pet peeve.) By incorporating that one simple habit into her daily routine, she changed the tone of their mornings together.

Here are some more examples of fuzzy Anchors alongside revised versions using specific Trailing Edges.

Fuzzy Anchor	Trailing Edge of Anchor
Brush my teeth	Put my toothbrush back into the charger
Pour coffee	Put down the coffee carafe
Take a shower	Hang my towel up after a shower
Shave my face	Put my razor back into the charger
Arrive at work	Put down my backpack at work
Comb my hair	Put my comb back on the counter

Power Move: Start with Anchors

Ready for a twist?

You can create successful recipes in Tiny Habits by *starting* with an Anchor. It's basically a flip of what we've been doing. Instead of starting with a habit you want to create and finding a place for it, you begin with the routines you already have and find new habits to plug in. If you empty the dishwasher reliably every morning, what new habit could you put right after that? Folding the dishtowels or tidying the counter? After you buckle your seat belt, what new habit might you insert there? Perhaps you take a deep breath of relaxation. Let's suppose you always put your coffee mug on your office desk. What new habit would fit right in after that reliable routine? Perhaps it's getting out your to-do list.

Starting with your reliable daily routines — your Anchors — you can find what new tiny behavior to insert after them. Some people use this approach as an advanced technique — something to try when they've already created a bunch of new habits but are looking for more opportunities in their day. Others might want to start with it. Either way, you've got more than one strategy at your disposal when it comes to creating recipes for Tiny Habits.

Meanwhile Habits

When you look carefully at your existing routines, you'll find tiny pockets of open time that are ideal places to cultivate a new habit. When I turn on the shower, the water is cold at first. I don't like cold showers, so my typical routine is to wait until the water warms up, which takes about twenty seconds. This waiting period creates an opportunity: *After I turn on the shower (and while I wait), I will . . .*

I call this type of habit a Meanwhile Habit.

As I wait for warm water to emerge, I think of one thing about my body that I'm grateful for. I search for something new to appreciate every day, from the flexibility in my shoulders to my body's ability to heal a scratch.

We all have these tiny pockets of time: after we stop for a red light, after we get in line at the grocery store, after we start watering the plants on the porch. We have a choice. We could use these moments to be annoyed or distracted, or we could use these waiting periods as Anchors for new habits.

These new habits will start tiny and stay tiny — I have twenty seconds to wait for warm water. But don't underestimate the power of Meanwhile Habits. A tiny behavior done consistently can make a big difference. As you find a new way to appreciate your body each day, you'll likely be more motivated to take better care of the magnificent creation that is your physical self.

While most Meanwhile Habits will stay tiny, you may find bigger time pockets for habits you want to grow. Brittany, a working mom with five kids, always seemed to have ten or more books stacked by her bedside. Seeing this pile get bigger and bigger created stress. A certified Tiny Habits coach, she had designed a solid reading habit at night; however, this wasn't enough for all she wanted to learn. Brittany looked for a spot where audiobooks would fit naturally into her life. After some exploration, she created a Meanwhile Habit with this recipe: "After I buckle my seatbelt, I will push 'play' on my audiobook." So now, while she commutes to work, she listens to books. Lots of them. Thanks to her Meanwhile Habit, Brittany gets through at least five books a month, and the reading stack by her bed is no longer a source of stress.

The Best Prompts for Your Customers

Whether you are creating an app or asking people to donate or helping people take magnesium supplements, a well-designed prompt is vital for most businesses. In fact, it's difficult to think of any product or service that doesn't rely on getting customers to take action. No prompt means no action. To succeed with your product or service, you need to figure out what will prompt your customer at the right moment.

In today's world of apps, e-mail, and social media, we are bombarded with Context Prompts from businesses. In addition, we still get postal mail and phone calls that are designed to prompt us. That's not news to you. But I am going to make a prediction right now that will be news to many people. I predict that Context Prompts will be less and less effective over time. Businesses will pay more to get in front of their customers, but they will get a lot less in return. Why? In the future, Context Prompts won't reach customers at the right moment, or they will be filtered out and not noticed. And if Context Prompts *do* reach people, they will increasingly be able to skip them, much like we fast-forwarded through commercials on TiVo. (*What's TiVo?* my students wonder.)

For your business to succeed, I predict that you will need to find a better way to prompt your customer since Context Prompts are losing their effectiveness. The good news is that there are Action Prompts. Businesses rarely employ Action Prompts today, but I believe they will be the gold standard in the future. Many products and services will succeed by helping customers create Action Prompts. Here's how it might work.

Let's suppose your organization needs patients to measure their blood pressure once a day. In the past, you relied on Person Prompts —having the patients remind themselves to do this every day—and you found that this didn't work very well. So you started using Context

Prompts: You sent text messages, your app popped up a red reminder, or you had nurses call patients at home. But these prompts worked less well over time because your patients were bombarded with too many competing prompts. Instead of ramping up on Context Prompts, you turn to Action Prompts.

To discover good Action Prompts, start with a bit of research. Reach out to your two hundred best patients, those people who reliably measure and report their blood pressure. Ask them, "At what point in your daily routine do you typically take your blood pressure?"

Analyze their answers and look for trends. Let's suppose that 26 percent of people say they measure their blood pressure after they sit down with coffee to read the morning newspaper. Another 21 percent report they measure right after feeding their pet. Then you find that 17 percent of patients take a measurement at the start of their favorite morning show on TV. But the remaining 36 percent of patients have a wide variety of answers with no clear trends.

You now have insights about what works with real people; you have data on what daily routines could serve as Anchors for the habit of measuring blood pressure. As you try to increase adherence, explain that many successful patients do this daily habit at one of three times.

Ask them, "Which one of these times would work best for you?"

In this way, you help your patients find where the new habit fits naturally in their lives.

This customizes the prompt for each person's daily routine. You aren't relying on patients to remember to check their blood pressure. You aren't annoying them with notifications. And you aren't hoping that they can figure this out on their own. You are using Behavior Design and the power of Action Prompts to help your patients to be successful.

The scenario above may sound strange to you today, but I predict that this will be commonplace and essential in the future. Businesses that help customers create habits will have a huge advantage over those that don't.

Pearl Habits — Creating Beauty from Irritations

When you learn to design and redesign prompts in your life, you're opening the door to new ways of managing situations that would otherwise distress you.

Getting good sleep has been a challenge for me in the past few decades. I've long understood the importance of quality sleep, but it's probably been my number one health issue. I knew that noise in my bedroom was causing me to wake up in the middle of the night because the wall control for the air-conditioning clicks every time it turns the A/C on and off. I was planning to install some high-tech thermostat gadget, but I found a faster, simpler solution. When I was awake one night and anticipating the next click, I decided to make this noise my Anchor for relaxing my face and neck. So my recipe was *After I hear the click, I will relax my face and neck.*

My Recipe — Tiny Habits Method

After I...	I will...	To wire the habit into my brain, I will immediately:
hear the click of the air-conditioning unit,	relax my face and neck.	☺
Anchor Moment	**Tiny B**ehavior	**C**elebration
An existing routine in your life that will remind you to do the Tiny Behavior (your new habit).	The new habit you want but you scale it back to be super tiny—and super easy.	Something you do to create a positive feeling inside of yourself (the feeling is called Shine).

It worked, and I soon wired in this habit. When I hear the click, I relax. Because of this positive result, I'm actually happy when I hear the click because it's reminding me to relax so I sleep better.

I call these habits Pearl Habits because they use prompts that start out as irritants then turn into something beautiful.

My example isn't exactly earth-shattering, but I recently learned that my friend Amy did something similar by leveraging the power of after in a creative, positive way.

Amy tackled a much trickier problem, and she created a remarkable Pearl Habit along the way.

As she and her husband were separating, the word "acrimonious" was thrown around by everyone from her lawyer to the children's court-appointed therapist. Even when they finally worked out the logistics of custody, her ex-husband was still angry with her, and she wasn't too happy with him. But they couldn't avoid each other.

Amy began to notice a pattern after a few months. She would have an unpleasant exchange with her ex-husband, and she would flash back to that throughout the day and feel upset or angry or guilty all over again.

So she decided to try something.

She couldn't control what her ex-husband said to her or how their interactions unfolded. His verbal assaults were like bad weather—sometimes she could see them coming and other times they came out of nowhere. What *was* predictable was how she felt in the aftermath. So that's what she decided to change. Her objective was to take the focus off him. Using her husband's behavior as her prompt, Amy made a plan: Any time she felt defeated or attacked by her ex, she would immediately decide to do something nice for herself—listen to a new album from her favorite band or the audiobook that she wanted to finish but never had the time to. Sometimes Amy drove straight to Starbucks for a cup of her favorite tea. But whatever she did had to make her feel good. Since Amy had precious little time during the day for herself, she realized that making her new behavior a "self-care" habit gave her double rewards—she could wrestle back some control *and* do something nice for herself. *After I feel insulted, I will think of something nice to do for myself* was her winning Habit Recipe.

My Recipe — Tiny Habits Method

After I . . .	I will . . .	To wire the habit into my brain, I will immediately:
feel insulted,	think of	
	something nice	☺ ♡
	to do for myself.	
Anchor Moment	**Tiny B**ehavior	**C**elebration
An existing routine in your life that will remind you to do the Tiny Behavior (your new habit).	The new habit you want but you scale it back to be super tiny—and super easy.	Something you do to create a positive feeling inside of yourself (the feeling is called Shine).

It worked beautifully. Instead of insulting him back or feeling attacked, she would say to herself, *Oh, look, another insult. Guess it's time to watch that movie I've been wanting to see.* Instead of reacting to him, she'd say good-bye, get on with her business, and formulate her evening plans. Her days didn't get derailed, she didn't find herself replaying the conversation in her head, she . . . let it go. She began to see his insults as inadvertent gifts. After all, *he* was the one prompting her to take good care of herself. She recognizes that this is a funny kind of logic, but thinking about a difficult situation as generously as possible helped her to get through it.

Ideally, Amy wouldn't have had someone in her life who made her feel that way. But we can't always edit all the toxic people and situations out of our lives. Sometimes we have to put up with people who treat us unfairly, get on our nerves, or behave badly. But we can take control of our side of the equation. That's what Amy did with her brilliant use of prompts. Using someone's behavior as a prompt for a healthy response as opposed to a self-defeating one is a great idea that can work for all sorts of situations where we feel powerless. And Amy discovered that the positive impact far exceeded her initial intent. Her kids, who were sometimes caught in the crossfire, seemed less stressed after the weekly handoff. She also noticed that her newfound calm seemed to rub off on her ex. It was as if she'd taken the air out of his anger balloon. He would still make the occasional cutting remark, but his heart didn't seem in it anymore. For the first time in a long time, Amy dared to hope that one day they could actually be friends. Or at least civil coparents. This additional shift rippled out to him, and it wasn't long before he cut out the insults altogether. Amy remembers him cracking a joke one day when she dropped their kids off. They laughed together for the first time in more than two years. It felt surreal. They had reached a kind of unspoken truce that only a year ago had felt like a moon shot.

When I called her recently to ask for her help on a project, she told me that she and her ex-husband had just cohosted their youngest daughter's graduation party. I told her that this was great but also kind of mind-blowing. She laughed a little, and said, "Trust me, BJ, no one is more shocked than we are." I asked her how she thought it happened, and she told me that it had to do with compassion. By using his negative behavior to prompt positive behavior on her part, she became happier and more capable of compassion. When she moved out of that place of shame and discouragement, she was able to think more clearly. She realized that her ex hadn't spent as much time developing his skills for getting along with people as she had. During their marriage, she had been the social buffer for his moods. So he had to figure all that out on his own when they divorced. Amy knew that this was hard for him, and she found compassion for him.

As human beings, we have instincts that tell us how someone feels about us even if they're not being explicit. Amy thinks her husband sensed the attitude shift and the compassion behind it, and started to make his own changes. She also told me that this was totally unintended. When she created her self-care habit, she was simply trying to protect herself and change a terrible situation.

This is what happens when you hone a skill and let yourself experiment with it in new and wonderful ways. Amy's using prompts to problem-solve and flip the script on her husband's behavior was a unique and creative fix. What is not unique about Amy's story is the cascading effect that this initial positive habit had on other people and her own life.

Why it rippled out so positively is the underlying secret to why Tiny Habits works so beautifully: *People change best by feeling good, not by feeling bad.* Amy set herself up for success by thoughtfully using prompts to design changes. Those changes worked because they helped her do what she already wanted to do. And that success? *That* felt good. So she kept chasing that feeling and felt increasingly confident that she could bring good things into her life by designing for them. Her ability to make behaviors easy to do and her willingness to play with prompts increased, which made starting new habits a snap. The ease of that process increased her motivation and made her more likely to try new, seemingly difficult things.

But there is one more reason that Amy was so successful.

She took one last step to dial in the good vibrations. She would create positive emotions, on the spot, by using a technique she had learned from the Tiny Habits method. She celebrated. And that's our next topic.

In the chapter that follows, I will share a technique for hacking your brain to give you the power to create habits quickly and easily.

Tiny Exercises to Find Prompts for Your New Habits

EXERCISE #1: FIND YOUR ANCHORS

A list of habits (or routines) you do each day is a valuable resource. You can use any reliable habit on your list as a prompt —an Anchor—for a new habit.

I broke a full workday into various parts in the steps below to help you create a big list.

Step 1: List all the daily habits you do in the morning, before you arrive at work.

Step 2: List all the daily habits you do before lunch.

Step 3: List all the daily habits you do during lunch.

Step 4: List all the daily habits you do right after lunch. (If you're like most people, you may not have many reliable habits in the afternoon. That's okay.)

Step 5: List all the daily habits you do to wrap up your day at work. (You might have only a few, but they make great Anchors for new habits.)

Step 6: List all the daily habits you do after you leave work (including those at home).

Step 7: List all the daily habits you do just before you go to bed.

Step 8: Save your list. You'll use it in the next exercise.

EXERCISE #2: CREATE TINY HABIT RECIPES BY USING YOUR LIST OF EXISTING HABITS

One fast and effective way to create new habits is to start with your existing daily habits, then find a new habit that would naturally follow. In the previous exercise, you created a big list of daily habits. That's good. *You will use that list now.*

Step 1: Pick one reliable habit from your list of habits that you never forget to do.

Step 2: Think about what new habits could naturally follow this one. Come up with a few ideas.

Step 3: Pick the new habit you like most from step 2. Write out a recipe in the Tiny Habits format: After I _____, I will _____.

Step 4: Repeat steps 1 through 3 for two more reliable habits to create two more recipes for Tiny Habits. (By working on three habits at once, you will learn more.)

Step 5: Start practicing your new habits. (Don't be too serious or uptight about it. Dive in and have fun.)

EXERCISE #3: CREATE PEARL HABITS TO DEAL WITH IRRITANTS IN YOUR LIFE

This exercise is about creating something valuable from an irritant.

Step 1: List at least ten things that often happen to you that irritate you (a long line, a noisy motorcycle, a barking dog next door).

Step 2: Select the most frequent and annoying thing on your list.

Step 3: Explore new, beneficial habits you could do after the annoyance. Come up with at least five options.

Step 4: Select your best option from step 3 and create a Tiny Habit Recipe. For example: *After I realize I must stand in line, I will practice standing on one foot, then the other.*

Step 5: Start practicing your Pearl Habit. (And notice what happens to your irritation level.)

And before we move to the next chapter, here is PAC Person to remind us what we have learned about the sources of prompts.

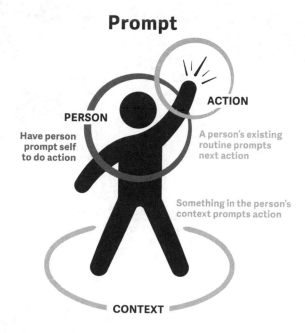

Prompt

PERSON

Have person prompt self to do action

ACTION

A person's existing routine prompts next action

Something in the person's context prompts action

CONTEXT

EMOTIONS
CREATE HABITS

Linda had a postcard taped on her fridge next to her kids' finger-painted masterpieces. It was a black-and-white illustration of a 1950s housewife talking on the phone. Above the woman's perfectly coiffed hair was a talk bubble: "If the kids are alive at five o'clock, I've done my job."

When Linda saw it, she laughed out loud.

It had made her smile, then it made her think. It represented an attitude of self-acceptance that she badly wanted but felt was too difficult to adopt. The idea that you could feel satisfied with what you were doing for your kids made sense to her logically, but it was totally inaccessible emotionally. Which is why she put the postcard on her fridge.

When her husband came home and saw it hanging there, he raised his eyebrows at the irony.

"It's aspirational," Linda said with a sigh.

Back then, Linda was a full-time stay-at-home mom with six kids under the age of thirteen. She loved being home with them and wouldn't have had it any other way, yet she felt constantly underwater and overwhelmed. When she laid her head down at night, every thought was about what she didn't get done that day. Images from the day spun up in her mind: Cheerios littering the backseat of her car (*I should have vacuumed it*); piles of unfolded laundry (*I should have put it away*); her son's face falling after she snapped at him for pushing his sister (*I should be more patient with him*); the dirty plates piling up in her sink (*I should have done all the dishes; my mom would never have left them like that*). What had started out as small deficits on her to-do list ended up amounting to something much worse. Every undone task that paraded through Linda's mind at night morphed into a rumination on all the ways she didn't measure up as a mom or a partner or a human being.

Some evenings, as Linda put the milk back in the fridge for the umpteenth time, even the 1950s housewife seemed disappointed in her. Not only did Linda never knock off mom duty at five o'clock, she also couldn't give herself credit for all of her hard work. Glancing at the woman on her fridge ended up being less of an inspiration and more of a reminder of just how far away she was from that attitude of plucky self-acceptance.

When Linda told me this story years later, it didn't surprise me.

In my research, I've found that adults have many ways to tell themselves, "I did a bad job," and very few ways of saying, "I did a good job." We rarely recognize our successes and feel good about what we've done.

Feeling good about your tiny successes may feel strange to you. Like Linda, you might focus only on your shortcomings as you scamper through your days and trudge through your years. I'm here to tell you that you are not alone. And that's why I'm writing this chapter for you.

In the pages ahead, I will show you how to gain a superpower—the ability to feel good at any given moment. You can use this superpower to transform your habits and, ultimately, your life.

Feeling good is a vital part of the Tiny Habits method. You can create this good feeling by using a technique I call celebration. When you celebrate in the Tiny Habits way, you create a positive feeling inside yourself on demand. This good feeling wires the new habit into your brain. You'll find that celebration is surprisingly effective, and it can be quick and easy, even fun.

Celebration is both a specific technique for behavior change and a psychological frame shift. Imagine how different Linda's nightly ruminations would have been if she'd had a way to make things *feel* a lot less lopsided. Because the truth is that her day was filled with both deficits and surpluses, stressful moments and successful ones. She may not have vacuumed the car, but she got her kids to school, soccer, and violin lessons on time. She may not have folded the laundry perfectly, but she had washed and dried all the dirty clothes. She may not have done all the dishes, but she had fed her kids a healthy meal that they enjoyed together. At the time, Linda didn't understand the importance of embracing those small victories as a way to change her behavior and her life. Those wins were there all along, but Linda, like many people, needed the skills to know how to celebrate them.

A confession: I didn't tell you everything about why my tooth-flossing habit was so successful so quickly.

Sure, I dialed my behavior in from a B=MAP perspective.

I made flossing easy to do. I found a great prompt. *Bam*—it's all looking good, right?

Well, there was one more piece of the puzzle. I stumbled on it during a time when I felt so much stress that I could barely get through each day. A new business I had started was failing, and my young nephew had died tragically. Navigating the personal and day-to-day fallout of those events meant that I hadn't had a good night's sleep in weeks. I was so anxious most nights that I would get up at three a.m. and do the only thing that calmed me down—watch videos of puppies on the Internet. In the morning, I'd stumble out of bed and start the day. As I washed up in the bathroom, I avoided looking in the mirror. I didn't want to be reminded of the reality that I knew would be staring me in the face: I looked terrible, felt terrible, and was scared to face the day.

One early morning, after a particularly bad night, when even the puppy videos didn't calm me, I reluctantly glanced in the mirror and thought to myself, *You know, this could be the day when the wheels totally fall off.* A day of not just setbacks but paralyzing failure.

As I went about my morning routine, I picked up the floss. I thought to myself, *Well, even if everything else goes wrong today, I'm not a total failure. At least I flossed one tooth.*

I smiled in the mirror and said one word to myself: *Victory!*

Then I felt it.

Something changed. It was like a warm space had opened up in my chest where there had been a dark tightness. I felt calmer and even a little energized. And this made me want to feel that way again.

But then I worried that I was losing it. My nephew had just died, my life seemed ready to fall apart, and flossing one tooth had made me feel better? That's nuts. How did *that* make me feel better?

If I hadn't been a behavior scientist and endlessly curious about human nature, I might have laughed at myself and left it alone. But I asked myself, *How* did flossing that tooth make me feel better? Was it the flossing itself? Or was it saying "Victory!" into the mirror? Or was it smiling?

I tried it again that evening. I flossed one tooth, smiled at myself in the mirror, and said, "Victory!" In the days that followed, many of which were still difficult, I continued to floss and proclaim victory. No matter what else was going on, I was able to create a moment in each day when I felt good—and that was remarkable.

My Recipe — Tiny Habits Method

After I...	I will...	To wire the habit into my brain, I will immediately:
brush my teeth,	floss one tooth.	victory!
Anchor Moment	**Tiny Behavior**	**Celebration**
An existing routine in your life that will remind you to do the Tiny Behavior (your new habit).	The new habit you want but you scale it back to be super tiny—and super easy.	Something you do to create a positive feeling inside of yourself (the feeling is called Shine).

At the time, I didn't know why my little celebration worked, but I sensed an important shift. I started using my victory proclamation with other new habits, and I noticed that those seemed to lock in more quickly than the ones that I didn't celebrate. So I tried different ways to celebrate by giving myself a thumbs-up or doing a fist pump and saying, "Awesome!"

I also found ways to celebrate quietly: I could create a feeling of success by simply smiling and saying *Yay!* in my head.

When I started sharing my Tiny Habits method with others in 2011, I made celebration part of the program. I didn't explain why I wanted the Habiteers to do this, I just said, "After you do your new habit, celebrate."

Later, while training and certifying coaches to teach the Tiny Habits method, I learned that using celebration to self-reinforce doesn't come naturally to everyone and that it even makes some people uncomfortable (we'll tackle that later; don't worry).

Despite my instructing them on how to celebrate, some Habiteers blew this off, thinking that celebration was optional or just too hokey to try. Even professionals who were learning my method in depth sometimes didn't take celebration seriously. I started emphasizing this technique more and more because I became increasingly convinced of the power of feeling good as the best way to create habits. I knew that people who embraced celebrations turned out to be the most successful at creating habits quickly. What's more, people who celebrated were telling me how surprised they were that this one little shift made such a difference. People said that they started looking forward to doing their new habits just so they could celebrate. Some would ask me, "Is that crazy?" (No. It's actually a very good sign.)

Steps in Behavior Design

Step 1: Clarify the Aspiration

Step 2: Explore Behavior Options

Step 3: Match with Specific Behaviors

Step 4: Start Tiny

Step 5: Find a Good Prompt

Step 6: Celebrate Successes

Why have I been so adamant about celebration? To answer that, let me rewind to the early days of Tiny Habits.

A few months into my sharing the Tiny Habits method, I had an experience I will never forget. I was reading an e-mail from a woman named Rhonda. She wrote to thank me. She explained that my celebration technique had made a major impact on her life. To her surprise, she felt optimistic that she was finally discovering her potential. Once she started practicing Tiny Habits, she realized that she had endured a "lifetime of self-trash-talk."

This insight from Rhonda galvanized me. It made me even more determined to share Tiny Habits and the powerful technique of celebration. Thanks to Rhonda, I changed course: The project I called Tiny Habits needed to be more than research. It needed to be a global intervention.

To be effective in my quest, I set out to learn more. I wanted to find out why saying one little word like "victory" could make such a huge difference. Why did celebration lock in my own flossing habit so quickly?

To find the answer, I kept teaching celebration to thousands of Habiteers and measured the impact each week. In everyday life I also observed how some people, including world-class athletes, celebrated their success naturally. And I dug into the scientific literature. I learned that no one had studied this phenomenon, but I did find related concepts here and there. After a few years of piecing them together, I had my answer.

When you celebrate effectively, you tap into the reward circuitry of your brain. By feeling good at the right moment, you cause your brain to recognize and encode the sequence of behaviors you just performed. In other words, you can hack your brain to create a habit by celebrating and self-reinforcing. In my research I found that this technique had never before been named, described, or studied. I realized that by studying and teaching celebration I was breaking new ground to help people change for the better.

The time has come to say "hello" to feeling good.

Positive Experiences Reinforce Habits

Every parent remembers the pure, unfettered joy of watching her or his child's first steps. While the setting varies, the plot is the same. Wobbly but determined, the baby pulls herself up on the coffee table and scoots alongside it for a few minutes before spying her mom kneeling a few feet away. Maybe her dad is on the couch recording the moment for posterity. They've been encouraging her for a while now, but today might just be the day. Eventually, the baby gathers her courage and takes one hand off the coffee table. Mom holds out her arms and says, "Come on, honey, you can do it!"

The about-to-be-toddler takes a step, then another, then one more before tumbling into her mother's arms.

"Yay! Good job, baby girl! Look at you, you walked!"

Dad will probably put down his phone and scoop the baby up in a hug. Maybe he even twirls her around while she giggles and grins.

Walking is a behavior that is repeated until it becomes second nature. And parents clap and cheer for their babies. This is a natural reaction from parents around the world, and it serves a purpose: Celebrating at the right moment *helps their babies learn more quickly.*

By learning, I don't mean memorizing multiplication tables. In psychology, learning is the process by which your brain facilitates a change in behavior in response to your environment. The evolutionary aim of these changes is to make us more likely to survive, thrive, and reproduce.

A range of positive experiences can reinforce a new behavior that leads to a habitual response. For example, anything that gives you instant pleasure can reinforce a behavior and make it more likely to happen in the future. Food can be a powerful tool for this reason. Whether you're trying to train your dog to sit or getting students to arrive on time by offering snacks at the start of the first few class periods, treats can both motivate behavior and reinforce a habit.

In my lab at Stanford some years ago, we wanted to see if using humor was an effective way to promote recycling. We rigged a recycling bin so people would hear a funny audio clip from *The Simpsons* every time they put something in. When someone dropped in an empty soda can, the bin would play "Marge, the mail's here!" in Homer's distinctive voice. We secretly deployed the bin at a trade show in San Jose and watched the reactions. When people used this bin, they were surprised and amused. Some people looked for errant scraps of paper to put into the bin to hear more funny clips. Other people removed things from our bin and put them back in. Would a bin like this create a habit of recycling? Maybe. In any case, we were on the right track. A positive feeling from humor can reinforce behavior.

Getting relief from physical, emotional, or psychological discomfort is also a positive experience. It's three a.m. and you are having another bout of insomnia. You're restless and thinking about work. There's a big deadline tomorrow, and everyone is rushing to get a project out the door. You're the manager, so you've got to keep things moving. And as you lie there awake, you're worried that there will be a productivity bottleneck in your inbox tomorrow morning. The thought of it makes you anxious. So you roll over, grab your phone off the nightstand, and check your e-mail. Whew, nothing urgent. No need to respond to anything. You feel relieved. This is a positive experience that you'll seek the next time you wake up in the middle of the night. You check your inbox and once again you feel relief. And then checking your e-mail will start becoming a habit. During some of my corporate speaking events, I've asked audiences if this sounds familiar. At times, well over 30 percent have raised their hands and acknowledged this habit. Little did they know that relief was the cause.

Early levels of some video games make it easy to feel successful. That's by design. It makes you eager to keep playing. *Candy Crush* has been downloaded more than two billion times. It's a simple (and free) matching game that you can play on your mobile device. The first level is ridiculously easy. To help signal that you've been successful, the designers built in all kinds of fun sensory experiences. There are pleasant little dings and satisfying visual cues. The word "sweet" even pops up after you reach a certain score. The result? You feel successful really fast — and you keep firing up that *Candy Crush* app whenever you have a free minute or two. Why? Because you are sweet at this game — and that? That feels great.

While these experiences are different feel-good paths to the land of habit, they all have one thing in common. What happens in your brain when you experience positive reinforcement isn't magic — it's neurochemical. Good feelings spur the production of a neurotransmitter (a chemical messenger in the brain) called dopamine that controls the brain's "reward system" and helps us remember what behavior led to feeling good so we will do it again. With the help of dopamine, the brain encodes the cause-and-effect relationship, and this creates expectations for the future.

You can hack into this reward system by creating an event in your brain that neuroscientists call a "reward prediction error." Here's how it works: Your brain is constantly assessing and reassessing the experiences, sights, sounds, smells, and movements in the world around you. Based on previous experiences, your brain has formed predictions about what you will experience in any given situation. Your brain predicts what will happen when you drop your phone on concrete (oh no!), and your brain predicts the taste of clam chowder at your favorite restaurant (yum). When an experience deviates from the pattern your brain expects (oh, my phone didn't break after all), that's when you get a "reward prediction error," and neurons in your brain adjust the release of dopamine in order to encode an updated expectation.

Suppose you have a habit of writing daily in a journal. One morning you pick up a new pen that has purple ink. As you begin journaling you notice how smoothly the pen flows over the paper; it's effortless, like you have superpowers. Then you notice your handwriting is so much better. You feel unusually successful writing with the purple pen, which is a surprise to your brain — a reward prediction error. The emotions in that moment cause your neurons to release dopamine, which quickly encodes this new behavior as something you should repeat. The same thing happens when a parent squeals with delight as a baby learns to walk. The baby's brain dishes out the dopamine and encodes "walking" as something good, something that she should definitely do again.

Emotions Create Habits

There is a direct connection between what you feel when you do a behavior and the likelihood that you will repeat the behavior in the future. When I unearthed this connection between emotions and habits in my research on the Tiny Habits method, I was surprised I had not seen this truth before. Like an answer to a riddle, it was suddenly so obvious. I wondered why this insight was not already common knowledge.

For too long people have believed the old myth that repetition creates habits, focusing on the number of days it requires. Some of today's popular habit bloggers still talk about repetition or frequency as the key. Just know this: They are recycling old ideas. They have not done groundbreaking research.

In my own research, I found that habits can form very quickly, often in just a few days, as long as people have a strong positive emotion connected to the behavior. In fact, some habits seem to get wired in immediately: You do the behavior once, and then you don't consider other options again. You've created an instant habit. For example, if you give your teenage daughter a mobile phone, her emotional response to using the device will wire in a habit very quickly. No need for repetition.

When I teach people about human behavior, I boil it down to three words to make the point crystal clear: **Emotions create habits.** Not repetition. Not frequency. Not fairy dust. Emotions.

When you are designing for habit formation—for yourself or for someone else—you are really designing for emotions.

Consider how Instagram, for better or worse, taps into this dynamic. Once you take a picture, the app makes it easy to apply filters. As you try out different filters, you see your photo transform before your eyes like magic, and your photo isn't merely a photo anymore. You feel like you are sharing a unique artistic creation. You might even be surprised or impressed by your skills. When that happens, your brain releases dopamine, and you seek opportunities to use Instagram again because it feels good.

When it comes to behavior, decision and habit are opposites. Decisions require deliberation, habits do not. You probably decide what to wear to work every morning. But most people don't decide if they will take their phone when they leave the house. They just take it with them, without deliberating. It's autopilot.

I've created a simple model to explain the difference between decisions and habits. I call this the Spectrum of Automaticity.

How automatic is the behavior?

not automatic ← → fully automatic

Decisions Behavior on the **Strong Habits**
Spectrum of Automaticity

On the left-hand side of the spectrum, you have behaviors that are not automatic. They are decisions or deliberate choices. On the right end of the spectrum, you have strong habits—behaviors you do without thinking, like holding a pencil or tying your shoes. The circle in the middle of the spectrum represents a behavior where you deliberate a little bit, so it's not completely automatic. If you do that behavior in the middle of the spectrum and have an emotional reaction to it—a positive feeling as you're doing the behavior or immediately after—then that behavior shifts to the right on the spectrum and becomes more automatic.

Emotions make behavior more automatic

not automatic ← → fully automatic

Decisions Behavior on the **Strong Habits**
Spectrum of Automaticity

Consider this example: using Uber versus getting a taxi. The first time you select Uber, you're probably analyzing the benefits and drawbacks of doing this instead of hailing a taxi. And then you decide. Let's say you choose Uber and have a great experience. They have, after all, made it so *easy,* you almost feel as if you're getting away with something. The first time I used Uber, I was delighted. I pushed a few buttons, and it seemed like a magic carpet had pulled up to whisk me away in luxury. Wow. It exceeded my expectations, that's for sure.

The next time I needed a ride, I barely thought about how I'd get to my destination. I didn't even consider a regular taxi. No decision needed. I just fired up the Uber app and pushed some buttons. Yes, the habit formed that fast: one and done. Most behaviors take more time than this to morph from decision into habit, but I hope you see my point.

The fact that emotions create habits is both good news and bad. Let me start with the dark side.

The overall process of habit formation is exactly the same for "good" habits as it is for those we consider "bad" habits. Your brain doesn't care if society has declared that eating cake at two a.m. is an unhealthy behavior. It still wants the pleasure that comes from eating that cake. There are plenty of behaviors that feel good (hello, video games!) and have slid into habits that we'd rather not have. The point is that your brain's reward system is influenced directly by emotions and less directly by what society labels as "good" and "bad." As humans, we are deeply wired for emotions, which is why most of us are a mixed bag of habits—some we want and plenty we don't.

The good news is that we are not helpless when it comes to our brain chemistry. Using what we know about how the brain functions, we can help our brains help us.

How?

By intentionally creating feelings to wire in the habits that we actually want in our lives. When we hack into the ancient behavioral pathways in our brains, we gain access to the amazing human potential for learning and change. We have an opportunity to use the brain machinery we already have to feel good *and* change behaviors.

You can use many types of self-reinforcement to wire in a habit, but in my research and teaching, I've found that the real winner is creating a feeling of success.

Why Celebration Works Best to Build Habits

Celebration is the best way to create a positive feeling that wires in your new habits. It's free, fast, and available to people of every color, shape, size, income, and personality. In addition, celebration teaches us how to be nice to ourselves—a skill that pays out the biggest dividends of all.

But before you start mixing up the celebration technique with everything you've heard about rewards, let's take a step back.

A word about *rewards*. Okay, maybe a little rant.

Many so-called habit experts have pumped up the idea of motivating a new habit with a reward. They are orbiting the right answer here because, yes, a rewarding stimulus is what activates the reward circuitry, but as with many words that have migrated from academia to pop-science, the meaning of "reward" has gotten muddied to the point of being unhelpful in some cases and downright misleading in others.

Let's say that you have committed to running every day for two weeks, and at the end of those two weeks, you "reward" yourself with a massage. I would say, "Good for you!" because we all could benefit from more massages. But I would also say that your massage wasn't a reward. It was an *incentive*.

The definition of a reward in behavior science is an experience *directly tied* to a behavior that makes that behavior more likely to happen again. The timing of the reward matters. Scientists learned decades ago that rewards need to happen either during the behavior or milliseconds afterward. Dopamine is released and processed by the brain very quickly. That means you've got to cue up those good feelings fast to form a habit.

Incentives like a sales bonus or a monthly massage can motivate you, but they don't rewire your brain. Incentives are way too far in the future to give you that all-important shot of dopamine that encodes the new habit. Doing three squats in the morning and rewarding yourself with a movie that evening won't work. The squats and the good feelings you get from the movie are too far apart for dopamine to build a bridge between the two.

The neurochemical reaction that you are trying to hack is not only time dependent, it's also highly individualized. What causes one person to feel good may not work for everyone. Your boss may love the smell of coffee. When she enters a coffee shop and inhales, she feels good. And her immediate feeling builds her habit of visiting the coffee shop. But your coworker might not like the way coffee smells. His brain won't react in the same way.

A real reward—something that will actually create a habit—is a much narrower target to hit than most people think.

I value precision in my research and teaching. I try to use words with specific and clear meanings. Because "reward" has gotten so muddled in our everyday language, I don't use this word without defining it carefully. It's too ambiguous and ultimately unhelpful.

Regardless of the terminology speed bump I've pointed out, I don't want you to lose the thread: Your brain has a built-in system for encoding new habits, and by celebrating you can hack this system.

When you find a celebration that works for you, and you do it immediately after a new behavior, your brain repatterns to make that behavior more automatic in the future. But once you've created a habit, celebration is now optional. *You don't need to keep celebrating the same habit forever.* That said, some people keep going with the celebration part of their habits because it feels good and has lots of positive side effects.

Another important thing to remember is that celebration is *habit fertilizer.* Each individual celebration strengthens the roots of a specific habit, but the accumulation of celebrations over time is what fertilizes the entire habit garden. By cultivating feelings of success and confidence, we make the soil more inviting and nourishing for all the other habit seeds we want to plant.

Fogg Maxim #2

In chapter 2, I explained Maxim #1: *Help people do what they already want to do.*

I discovered how important this principle was by studying what many successful products and services had in common: They helped people do what they already wanted to do. Without that, the product or service failed.

I took this insight and applied it to how individuals can change their behavior. It mapped perfectly: Success comes from helping ourselves do what we already want to do. When you follow Maxim #1 and match yourself with Golden Behaviors, you don't need to work hard to sustain or manipulate motivation. You are able to say good-bye to the Motivation Monkey and create lasting change.

Now that we are focusing on celebration, the time has come to share Maxim #2. It's every bit as important as the first one.

Fogg Maxim #2: Help people feel successful.

Just four words. But so important.

Note that this maxim doesn't say, "Help people *be* successful." It's about *feeling* successful instead.

Every product or service that is growing and thriving today does this well. They help us feel successful. Look at the products and services you love—from shopping online to the clothing you wear to the apps you use every day for driving, communicating, or playing games. You'll see that you're getting a feeling of success from them.

When Instagram was duking it out with its many competitors back in the day, my former student Mikey and his cofounder won the race because they created the simplest and best way to help people feel successful.

If you try a product and it makes you feel clumsy or stupid or unsuccessful, you will very likely abandon it. But when something makes you feel successful, you want more. You engage. You make it part of your life.

This also applies to how we design for change in our own lives. Helping yourself feel successful is what Tiny Habits is all about.

How to Celebrate the
Tiny Habits Way

Here's how to help a habit root quickly and easily in your brain: (1) Perform the behavior sequence (Anchor —→ Tiny Behavior) that you want to become a habit and (2) celebrate immediately.

So simple! Right?

But celebration is both simple and sophisticated. So, let's talk a little more about the nuances of this technique.

First of all, when I say that you need to celebrate immediately after the behavior, I do mean *immediately*. Immediacy is one piece of what informs the speed of your habit formation.

The other piece is the *intensity* of the emotion you feel when you celebrate. This is a one-two punch: you've got to celebrate right after the behavior (immediacy), and you need your celebration to feel real (intensity).

When I first started doing my after-pee push-ups, I did a double fist pump and said, "Awesome!" For me, that was a good celebration because it created a positive feeling immediately. However, some people may see my celebration as silly or even embarrassing. That's okay. Just make a note that BJ Fogg's celebration is not the right one for you.

A big physical expression of celebration is not necessary. A simple smile or saying a quiet affirmation in your head can work.

Begin your exploration now: Search for celebrations that feel authentic to *you*. If you feel awkward or phony when celebrating, your attempts will backfire. Your brain doesn't want to feel awkward—it wants to feel good. Celebrations are personal. What makes me feel good (and not lame) is probably different than what makes you feel good (and not lame).

The first part of the one-two celebration punch—immediacy—is usually easy for people to get, but finding a celebration that genuinely creates a good feeling is more challenging. The solution may depend on personality type and culture. Some people are naturally more inclined to celebrate their successes. If you are an enthusiastic and optimistic person, you might find celebrations easy to do—even fun. In fact, you may already be celebrating; you just don't have a name for it. However, if you tend toward self-criticism or have a bit of a pessimistic outlook, celebration may not be as natural.

I've also found that certain cultures (hello to all my British and Japanese friends!) are more comfortable being self-deprecating or self-effacing, qualities that don't lend themselves to celebration quite so easily.

Regardless of where you come from or who you are, you *do* have access to a natural celebration that will help you wire in habits quickly. You just have to discover what works for you.

Take my Uncle Brent. He's a former hard-nosed attorney in Utah now in his mid-seventies. He's more comfortable arguing with people and handing out reality checks than celebrating anything. A few years ago, I was teaching Tiny Habits and explaining the concept of celebration to my huge extended family at a reunion. Uncle Brent gruffly interjected that *he* didn't have a celebration, so this didn't apply to *everyone*, thank you very much, BJ.

I asked Uncle Brent what he did when he realized he'd found his winning arguments. With a grin, Uncle Brent jabbed a finger in the air, and said, "Bingo!"

Everyone laughed because it was such an Uncle Brent thing to do, but I said, "There! Saying bingo is your natural celebration."

So, reader, I'm here to say that if my salty dog of an uncle has a celebration so do you. You've just got to find it.

Your celebration does not have to be something you say out loud or even physically express. The only rule is that it has to be something said or done (internally or externally) that makes you feel good and creates a feeling of success.

What might surprise you is this: In English we do not have a perfect word to describe the positive feeling we get from experiencing success. I've read piles of scientific literature on related topics, and I've done my own research in this area, and I am convinced that we are lacking a good word. (The closest label is "authentic pride," but that's not an exact match.) So, with the encouragement of three of the world's experts on human emotion, I decided to create a new word for this feeling of success.

Ready?

I call this feeling Shine.

You know this feeling already: You feel Shine when you ace an exam. You feel Shine when you give a great presentation and people clap at the end. You feel Shine when you smell something delicious that you cooked for the first time.

I believe my celebration technique is a breakthrough in habit formation. I hope you can see why. By skillfully celebrating, you create a feeling of Shine, which in turn causes your brain to encode the new habit.

If I could teach you about Tiny Habits in person, I would start our training by focusing on celebrations. I would help you find celebrations that are natural and effective for you. We would practice them together and it would be a blast. I would train you in celebrations before teaching you about the Fogg Behavior Model, or the power of simplicity, or Anchors, or recipes for Tiny Habits. Celebration would be first—because it's the most important skill for creating habits.

Since I can't come to your home and personally teach you how you celebrate, here are a few exercises to help you find what works for you.

FIND YOUR NATURAL CELEBRATION

A natural and deeply felt celebration will give you superpowers for creating habits.

If you're stumped on what might work for you, put yourself in the following scenarios and watch how you react. This will give you a clue about your natural ways of celebrating. Use that natural reaction to feel Shine and wire in your new habits.

(As you read these scenarios, don't overthink or analyze. Just let yourself react.)

DREAM JOB SCENARIO

You decide to apply for your dream job with a company you love. You make it through the process all the way to the final interview. The hiring manager says, "We'll send an e-mail with our decision." The next morning the manager's e-mail is waiting for you. You open it, and this is the first word you read: "Congratulations!"

What do you do at that moment?

OFFICE SCENARIO

Picture yourself sitting in your office. You have a piece of paper to recycle, and the recycling bin is in the far corner of the room. You decide to wad up the paper and throw it into the bin. You are not sure you'll make it. You aim carefully and toss the paper. Up it goes into an arc. As it comes down, the wad of paper vanishes into the bin. Perfect shot.

What do you do at that moment?

CHAMPIONSHIP SCENARIO

Your favorite sports team is in the championship game. The score is tied and very little time remains. As the time on the clock runs out, your team scores, winning the championship.

What do you do at that moment?

Did you discover a way of celebrating that gave you the feeling of Shine? If not, it's time to try out some other celebrations.

Here are some celebrations that you can try. They include ones you can do in the middle of a crowd or in the privacy of your own home.

- Say, "Yes!" or "Yay!"
- Consider how your new habit helps you achieve your life's purpose
- Smile big
- Imagine your child clapping for you
- Hum an upbeat song you like (maybe the theme from *Rocky*)
- Do a little dance
- Clap your hands
- Nod your head
- Give yourself a thumbs-up
- Imagine the roar of a crowd
- Think to yourself, *Good job*
- Take a deep breath
- Snap your fingers
- Imagine seeing fireworks
- Look up and make a V with your arms
- Smirk and tell yourself, *I got this*

If you want to see a bigger list of celebrations, check out "One Hundred Ways to Celebrate and Feel Shine" at the end of the book.

Celebration in Different Contexts

I encourage you to cultivate a range of celebrations that you can do in public and private. One of my favorite private celebrations came from a Habiteer named Mike. A successful creative director at a marketing firm, Mike was trying to get back in shape and wanted to start with some stretching and short exercises in the morning. In creating his new yoga habit, he focused on a Starter Step. After he put water on for coffee in the morning, he would roll out his yoga mat in the living room. That's all.

Just put out the mat. To lock in this habit, Mike came up with a unique celebration. Pretending the yoga mat was a boxing ring, he'd pace back and forth singing "Eye of the Tiger" with his arms held high like Rocky. When he was singing at the top of his lungs one morning and holding his imaginary boxing gloves aloft, he saw the postman passing by the living room window. He'd seen Mike celebrating the pants off his Starter Step. Mike has a good sense of humor about himself, so he didn't feel too embarrassed, but you can see how *some* celebrations might be done with the curtains drawn.

For habits you do at work, drawing a smiley face after you check your habit off your to-do list might be all you need to feel successful — or think, *Yes, I nailed this!* If you're at the gym and you don't want to make a scene, perhaps you could do a little drumroll on the handlebars of your stationary bike or hum the song "We Are the Champions" in your head.

Sometimes you can even enlist others to help you celebrate. Jill, a Habiteer who wanted to incorporate a daily round of squats into her morning routine, was struggling with celebration. Because her daughter was always trying to imitate her, the little girl would try to do squats right alongside her mom. One day Jill decided to give Emma a high five when they were done. It felt so good that she did it the next day and the next. A celebration was born, one that worked well for that particular habit if little Emma was around.

It doesn't matter whether your celebration is an explosive anthem or a silent focus on your life's purpose. What matters is that your celebration creates the feeling of Shine, the internal feeling of success.

POWER CELEBRATION

When you are creating your range of celebrations, I encourage you to include at least one that is extremely potent — what I call a Power Celebration. You want this option in your back pocket for habits that you need to wire in very quickly.

When I need to feel deep Shine, I think back to Mrs. Bondietti, my fourth-grade teacher in Fresno, California, and I imagine this amazing — and strict — teacher putting her hand on my shoulder and saying to me, "Good job!"

Boom.

This moves me. This makes me feel awesome. This creates a strong feeling of Shine.

I don't overuse this celebration. I save it for when I need to create a habit quickly.

WHAT TO DO WHEN YOU CAN'T *FEEL* IT

The celebration piece of Tiny Habits can sometimes trip people up. They can't get themselves to celebrate or they've tried out a number of celebrations and still feel like a big faker. In these cases, there may be a bigger issue than finding the right celebration. So let's look a little deeper.

Back to Jill.

When Jill took the Tiny Habits course, she struggled with celebration. It wasn't because she didn't have a great way of spotlighting her success. She used to play competitive basketball in high school and would dramatically punch one fist in the air after every basket. (By the way, this celebration likely wired in the habit of shooting baskets accurately.)

The problem was that when she did her tried-and-true celebratory move now it felt silly. "Kind of embarrassing" is how she described it to her Tiny Habits coach. Why? What was the difference between doing her new squat habit and scoring a three-pointer? Jill eventually realized that she didn't think she deserved the celebration. When she'd sunk a sweet shot, she felt like she'd *earned* that celebration. But doing two squats? Come on. Anyone can do that. That doesn't take any skill or effort or talent. It's no big deal, right? It felt silly to Jill to celebrate such a *small* success.

You may be thinking the same thing: *Why should I congratulate myself on two push-ups, or flossing one tooth?*

The answer to this is threefold.

This is how the system of behavior works

Let's say the TV in your living room is old. Sometimes it turns off for no reason. You smack it on the side and it turns back on. This doesn't make sense to you, but it works every time. An engineer could probably tell you why this works, but it doesn't matter because you got what you wanted—to finish watching your show. Behavior is also a system that has invisible components, but we know that dopamine is a key part of making habits stick. That's how your brain works.

Celebration is a skill

Celebration might not feel natural to you, and that's okay, but practicing this skill will help you to get comfortable. When I was learning to play the violin, my teacher showed me the proper way to hold the bow, but I resisted. I wanted to do it my way. She insisted that the only way for me to become proficient was to practice doing it the right way. I didn't listen, and my progress stopped. I learned that she was right.

So tough-love BJ is here to tell you that you can resist learning to celebrate, but be aware that you're choosing not to be as good as you could be at creating habits. For most people, the effort of learning to celebrate is a small price to pay for becoming a Habit Ninja.

You *are* doing something worthy of celebration

This is the most important answer because recognizing that you are doing something worthy of celebration will change so much for you. Your ability to ignore self-criticism and embrace *feeling good about your successes* will ripple out into your life in positive ways that go far beyond the habits you create and celebrate.

As I tell all my students, it is *not* a small accomplishment to perform a new habit exactly as you designed it. I would argue that making a change is a pretty darn big deal no matter how small and incremental. Why *wouldn't* that be something to celebrate?

If celebrating the small stuff is hard for you, the go-big-or-go-home mentality is probably sneaking up on you. Shut it down. It's a trap. Celebrating a win—no matter how tiny—will quickly lead to more wins. Think about all those times you could have changed but didn't, and here you are, two squats in—changing.

It also helps to find the deeper meaning in what you are doing. Tiny Habits can *seem* small on the surface, but if you dig deeper, you'll find the real reason you wanted to do them in the first place, and you'll discover that the value of the actions is definitely worth celebrating. Jill wanted to create a habit of wiping down the counter after breakfast. But she was having a hard time feeling Shine when she celebrated, which made the habit difficult to lock in. So she thought more about what the habit meant in the larger context of her life. Why was she actively trying to cultivate this habit? Why was it important?

Her answer was that it was important to her husband, who was important to her. Colin did the cooking in their house. And when he would get home from work and find a messy countertop, it took the wind out of his sails. This dampened his desire to pull stuff out of the fridge and whip up something delicious for his family—the mess Jill left stopped him short. He'd asked her a number of times to do a better job cleaning up, but she kept forgetting or running out of time. It was one of those small things that people fight about—you know, the things that crop up when tensions and stress are already peaking and result in a blast radius bigger than you ever thought possible. On the days when she did manage to do her habit, Jill discovered that the evenings went noticeably smoother. Colin would get home, cook a nice dinner, and they'd all eat together as a family. It was a little thing, but a big thing at the same time. When Jill framed it as a habit she was doing to create a more harmonious family for little Emma to grow up in and a way to strengthen her relationship with her husband, she saw that wiping those silly counters really *was* something to feel good about doing. And *that* was the key that gave her access to the meaning that was always there—the meaning that fueled her celebration and ultimately helped her to lock in that habit.

A Fast Way to Feel Successful

It's time for someone to say it: You've got to lower your expectations.

When I say this, people sometimes gasp. Or they smirk. Or they think I'm joking.

But I'm serious.

Yes, in our hyperachieving, go-getter world, I'm telling you to lower the bar. Not because I don't want you to achieve great things, but because I know that you need to start small in order to achieve them. But you can't succeed with starting small if you're looking down your nose at it. Why do we clap for a baby when she is taking her first step? Not because she is doing it perfectly, or because she "earned it," or because she did it bigger and better than the baby next door. We clap because we know it is the first small step that she is taking toward a lifetime of walking and running—and *that* is hugely important.

Accepting this, *believing* that it is the way we succeed at change, may be a challenge for some of you out there, and that's okay. Here are some strategies you might try that help people cultivate that feeling of success even when they are having difficulties doing so.

+ Recruit a kid to celebrate with you (they are so good at it!). Jill found that involving her three-year-old in the celebration helped her feel Shine more genuinely.

+ Do a physical movement: smile, raise your fists in victory, or take a Wonder Woman stance (fists on hips, chest out). Sometimes physical movements generate a positive feeling. Tune into the feeling of Shine and see if movement amplifies it.

+ When you're celebrating, imagine that you're celebrating someone you love. What would you say to them? Would you feel genuinely proud of what they're doing? Yes, you would. Use that as a way to access the feeling of Shine.

One Surprising Solution
to Two Habit Problems

Now seems the ideal time to answer two of the most frequently asked questions I get from people doing Tiny Habits: *How can I wire my habit in fast?* and *I keep forgetting to do my habit; how can I help myself remember?*

I'm pretty sure my answer will surprise you, but once you realize that creating a habit is a skill, my answer will make perfect sense.

Ready?

To wire in a habit fast or help yourself remember, you need to rehearse the behavior sequence (the Anchor, then the new habit) and immediately celebrate. Repeat this sequence seven to ten times.

By doing this drill—by rehearsing—you are supercharging the speed of habit formation. I know this sounds crazy today, but I believe this technique will be common practice in the future. When you rehearse your habit, you are training for the very moment you will do the habit in real life, just as you would rehearse for a dance recital or sales pitch. If you didn't rehearse for these things, your dance performance would suffer and your sales pitch might fail. When it comes to peak performance, rehearsal matters.

How many three-point shots has Stephen Curry practiced? More than a million? He's rehearsing so he can shoot from downtown without thinking. He's wired in this habit. *Swoosh!*

When you rehearse in Tiny Habits, you are both training muscle memory and rewiring your brain to remember. And you can drill and wire in a habit quickly if you have an effective celebration.

Let's say your wife is mad at you because you never put the TV remote back on the fireplace mantel where she thinks it belongs. If you goof up on this one more time, it won't be pretty. Time to wire in this habit fast with rehearsal and celebration. The recipe would be something like this: *After I push the off button at night, I will put the remote on the mantel.*

Here's how you rehearse.

Sit in the chair where you watch TV. Pick up the remote. Hit off, then stand up and put the remote on the mantel. Then celebrate big-time, pull out your go-to—the *Rocky* theme song or the Wonder Woman pose or the silent affirmation—and make sure you *feel* Shine. Okay, that's once. Let's repeat it. You sit back down with the remote. You hit the off button, you stand up . . .

You get the idea.

My Recipe — Tiny Habits Method

After I . . .	I will . . .	To wire the habit into my brain, I will immediately:
<u>push the "off" button at night,</u>	<u>put the remote on the mantel.</u>	
Anchor Moment	**T**iny **B**ehavior	**C**elebration
An existing routine in your life that will remind you to do the Tiny Behavior (your new habit).	The new habit you want but you scale it back to be super tiny—and super easy.	Something you do to create a positive feeling inside of yourself (the feeling is called Shine).

This sounds wacky, I know. No one has ever advocated that you rehearse behavior sequences followed by celebrations in order to wire a habit into your brain before. But that's what I'm telling you now.

Trust the process and rehearse this sequence seven to ten times. Make sure your celebration creates the feeling of Shine. Now watch what happens later. I predict that when you hit the off button on the TV the next evening, your brain will likely say, *Hey, don't forget to put the remote on the mantel.* You will remember to do it at the right moment because you've trained for it. *Swoosh!*

Three Times to Celebrate

For the sake of simplicity, I tell people to celebrate immediately *after* they do a behavior they want to become a habit. But the truth is, you can become a Habit Ninja faster and more reliably by celebrating at three different times: the moment you remember to do the habit, when you're doing the habit, and immediately after completing the habit. Each of these celebrations has a different effect.

Suppose you have this as a Tiny Habit Recipe: *After I walk in the door after work, I will hang up my keys.* As you are creating this habit, I encourage you to celebrate the exact moment your brain reminds you to do your new habit. Imagine that you walk in the door after work, and

Three moments for celebration

| The moment you remember to do your new habit | While you are doing your new habit | Immediately after doing your new habit |

as you're putting down your backpack, this idea pops into your head: *Oh, now is when I said I was going to hang my keys up so I can find them tomorrow.* You should celebrate at that moment. By feeling Shine, you are wiring in the habit of *remembering* to hang up your keys, not the habit of hanging up your keys.

When you celebrate remembering to do a Tiny Habit, you wire in that moment of remembering. And that's important. If you don't remember to do a habit, you won't do it.

Another time to celebrate is while you are doing your new habit. Your brain will then associate doing the behavior with the positive feeling of Shine. In Jill's case, she was onboard with the idea that wiping the counter was worth celebrating. The next step was to figure out the best celebration to use to help her lock it in. After some experimentation, she landed on celebrating *while* she was doing it. What most reliably prompted the feeling of Shine for her was picturing the meal that her husband would make that night and imagining him giving her a kiss and saying, "Nice work, babe." For Jill, the celebration was directly connected to the action. Her visualization allowed her to connect her small action with positive feelings of family togetherness. This celebration wired in the remembering and increased her motivation to wipe the counter in the future. Fast-forward to today: Jill wipes the counter without even thinking about it.

Keep the Habit Roots Strong

After a habit becomes automatic, you no longer need to celebrate. But, dear reader, you may need a spritz of celebration here and there to keep your habits well hydrated. There are at least two scenarios where celebration can help keep your habit firmly rooted.

1. You haven't done your habit for a while because you've gone on vacation or changed locations. Or life has simply gotten in the way.

2. You are rocking this habit and increasing its intensity. Perhaps your baseline habit was two push-ups, but one day you decide to go for twenty-five push-ups to see what happens.

The first point is pretty obvious: Use celebration to rewire the habit back into your life.

Point number two is less obvious. When you increase the intensity or duration of a habit, you are exerting yourself more. This is a good time to bring back celebration. Consider my easy habit of two push-ups. That's all I'm required to do. That said, my push-up habit grew naturally over time, and today I typically do eight or ten push-ups at a time. No sweat. However, some days I decide to do a lot more—twenty-five or thirty. When it hurts a bit, when I push into the pain, I bring celebration back. I think about it this way: If I do a habit and it's painful or awkward or unpleasant in any way, then my brain is going to rewire and lead me to avoid the habit. Negative emotions seem to shrivel the roots of automaticity. So I keep my habit healthy and alive by celebrating extra hard to offset the pain of doing thirty push-ups. And that injection of Shine keeps the habit alive.

Celebrating without a Recipe

We have the opportunity to take actions every day that accumulate and drive our self-conception. Am I the type of person who brings a shopping cart back or leaves it in the parking lot? Am I the type of person who leaves a mess on the floor for my partner to pick up? Am I the type of person who shovels the walkway of an elderly neighbor? These are small moments that determine who we really are. Some of the time we'll fail, and maybe we'll be fleetingly disappointed in ourselves. Other times we'll do a good job and momentarily feel good about ourselves. But what if we could easily make it more likely that we'd do the good behaviors again and again? What if we could quietly build on the moments when we're being our best selves until we *are* our best selves? (At least most days.)

I'm going to explain a way to do just that by using celebration without a Tiny Habit Recipe. You do this by celebrating in the course of your everyday life. It's pretty simple. But it requires paying attention to the moments when we do the good stuff and self-reinforcing those good behaviors with celebration.

I'll give you an example.

Sarah, a single mom raising two kids, had already used Tiny Habits to cultivate some habits that helped her work more efficiently and eat more healthy food.

After she put the kids to bed, one of two things usually happened. Either she fell asleep next to them in her work clothes and full makeup, or she made it to her bedroom and collapsed on her own bed—still in her work clothes and full makeup. Sometimes she'd manage to get undressed and throw her clothes on the chair in her bedroom, and sometimes she'd even brush her teeth and change into pajamas. But she almost never washed her face. This nagged at her—everyone knows you're not supposed to go to bed with makeup on. People told her, "It will clog your pores! And give you wrinkles!"

Sarah had heard all that, but she had more pressing concerns, like keeping her kids fed and the lights on. She didn't think too much about it until one night when the kids were with their grandparents and she had a surplus of energy. So she washed her face before bed. It was a little thing, but after she dried her face and looked in the mirror, she smiled. She felt that same sense of Shine that she had felt when she celebrated her other habits, so she invoked a different internal narrative—one that said, *Good for you, Sarah. You washed your freaking face! You're the kind of woman who takes care of herself.* She took a moment to feel good about herself instead of bad.

Sarah didn't design a Tiny Habit Recipe for washing her face, yet her celebration still helped wire in the habit of taking care of herself as a way to wrap up the day. That's great. But Sarah's story continues.

Now that she felt like someone who invests a bit of time for self-care, Sarah did more than wash her face. She started putting her clothes away at night instead of tossing them on the chair. She celebrated this and kept going, letting the effects of feeling good expand to other areas of her life. Notice how Sarah's evening rituals got wired in because she took the opportunity one night to celebrate a behavior she wanted in her life. This simple beginning became a powerful way to change how she felt about herself.

My point is this: You can use celebration at any moment in your life. No need for a plan. No need to write down a Tiny Habit Recipe. Just notice any good behavior you do and self-reinforce by celebrating it. If you can feel Shine, you are on your way to making that good behavior automatic. But more important, you've gained the ability to impact your emotional life for the better by finding opportunities to feel positive emotions instead of focusing on negative ones. Remember that you change best by feeling good, not by feeling bad.

Celebration Is the Bridge from Tiny Habits to Big Changes

Celebration will one day be ranked alongside mindfulness and gratitude as daily practices that contribute most to our overall happiness and well-being. If you learn just one thing from my entire book, I hope it's this: Celebrate your tiny successes. This one small shift in your life can have a massive impact even when you feel there is no way up or out of your situation. Celebration can be your lifeline.

When Linda first started doing Tiny Habits, she wrote off the celebration part of the method. Making things smaller and easier made sense to her pragmatic, analytical brain. But celebrating after every little thing? Not so much. That didn't seem compelling or comfortable to her, so she carried on with the habits she had constructed. She had some successes and some failures, but she wasn't seeing the big changes that others were talking about.

When Linda and I worked together to make Tiny Habits more transformative in her life, I kept seeing that she needed to embrace celebrations in her practice.

Feeling successful isn't just a skill we use to lock in a habit — it's also an antidote to the go-big-or-go-home culture and a new lens through which to see yourself.

To get herself over the celebration hump, Linda tried one of my favorite techniques for feeling positive emotions — the Celebration Blitz. I encourage everyone to do this if you need a score in the win column: Go to the messiest room in your house (or the worst corner of your office), set a timer for three minutes, and tidy up. After every errant paper you throw away, celebrate. After every dishtowel you fold and hang back up, celebrate. After every toy you toss back into its cubbyhole — you get the idea. Say, "Good for me!" and "Wow. That looks better." And do a fist pump. Or whatever works for you. Celebrate each tiny success even if you don't feel immediate impact, because as soon as that timer goes off, I want you to stop and tune into what you are feeling.

I predict that your mood will be lighter and that you will have a noticeable feeling of Shine. You will be more optimistic about your day and your tasks ahead. You may be surprised at how quickly you've shifted your perspective. I guarantee that you will look around and feel a sense of success. You'll see that you made your life better in just three minutes. (That's worth repeating. *You made your life better.*) Not just because the room is tidier, but because you took three minutes to practice the skills of change by exploring the effects of tiny celebrations done quickly.

Linda trusted in the process enough to give it three minutes. And that was all it took. She became a self-proclaimed "celebration convert." After a couple of months, she noticed that she was even celebrating things that *weren't* habits. She'd sail through a green light on a morning when she most needed to, and scream, "Yessss!" in her empty car. As she folded the last bit of laundry, she'd say to herself, "Nice job, Linda!" These moments wouldn't have warranted notice before. What she *used* to notice was all the annoying stuff—the red lights and the cashier who shuts down the lane she'd been waiting in for five minutes. But now the little wins popped out at her. And she started celebrating them. Linda told me that this wasn't even a conscious choice. And that's because her brain had learned that celebrating felt good. She had unwittingly made a *habit* of celebrating.

Remember, our brains *want* to feel good. Celebrating small wins gives them something to repattern our life around. Linda told me that she has "retrained her brain to think positively as opposed to negatively." Which is exactly right. Even in difficult situations, she now looks for small things that she can attach a positive emotion to through celebration. It helps her look for the good and focus on that instead of getting stuck in the negative. Amy did a similar thing in the last chapter when she flipped the script on her husband and used his negativity as a prompt for doing something positive. Because Amy had practiced celebrating so many other habits for all those months, her brain was primed to be on the lookout for the opportunity to feel good—even in unusual circumstances.

Little alarm bells might be going off in your head now. You see the words "positive" and "negative" and are getting a little twitchy. You've heard people say, "Think positively!" or "Find the silver lining!" And you might have rolled your eyes at this because if it were that easy, wouldn't everyone see the glass half full? Yes, they would.

But let's get one thing straight. What Amy did was not magical thinking. What Linda did was *not* a matter of snapping her fingers and putting a positive spin on things. Both of them went through a tried-and-true process, experimented with it, and found evergreen tools to call on when things fell apart. By hacking the reward center of their brains, they shifted their mindsets. It was a thoughtful, deliberate process that blossomed beautifully over time.

But this is by no means the end of Linda's story.

By the fall of 2016, Linda felt herself circling the depression drain once again. Her husband's Alzheimer's had worsened, and he required care that they couldn't easily afford. She felt so overwhelmed that she would put her head down on her desk at work and sob for about fifteen minutes every day. She felt daunted by having to get their finances under control while working and caring for her kids. So she'd allow herself to cry (which, by the way, is a good thing). But eventually she'd say, "Okay, let's get on with it." And she would stand up and do a Celebration Blitz right there in her office. She'd spend three minutes tidying and celebrating—or if she needed a bigger lift, she'd do five minutes. It would blast her out of what she called her "pity party." Having been through enough grief and loss to drown anyone, Linda had learned that you need to let yourself wallow in it sometimes but you can't stay there.

The Celebration Blitz was a lifeline that she threw herself when she needed to drag herself out of the water. Linda did it most every day that fall, and every day she picked her head off her desk and moved forward. She made sure to focus on the fact that she was doing as much as she possibly could for herself, her family, and the people she taught every day as a Tiny Habits trainer. And she celebrated this—a skill she had cultivated and honed. And one that she wishes she had had when she was younger.

Linda's story is harrowing, but the essence of it is very familiar. Teaching Tiny Habits, I have heard many stories where the core message is the same: The feeling of success is a powerful catalyst for change. Your confidence grows when you celebrate not only because you are now a habit-creating machine but also because you are getting better and better at *being nice to yourself.* You start looking for opportunities to celebrate yourself instead of berating yourself. Then, before you know it, something fundamental has changed. You used to believe that you were one type of person. Maybe the type of person who can't stick to an exercise routine, like Mike. Or the type who is prone to leaving things a mess, like Jill. Or the type who can't pick her head up off the desk because it is glued there by her own tears, like Linda. You didn't think that there was much chance that you'd change. But over the course of weeks and months, these tiny, simple habits that you've woven into your life have changed the fabric of your world entirely. You have discovered that you have morphed into a different type of person, the type of person you never thought you'd be. The type of person who gets up before his kids to exercise and scares the postman with his Rocky impersonation. The type of person who brushes off the daily losses and actively celebrates the daily wins. The type of person who knows she can make almost *any kind of change* she wants.

That is the world-changing, life-altering power of celebration. And it very subtly and very effectively alters your life. The type of person you are now can become whatever type of person you *want* to be.

Tiny Exercises to Feel Shine

Earlier in this chapter, there are exercises to help you find your natural celebration. Be sure to do those exercises. It's important.

Below are additional ways to find celebrations that can create authentic feelings of Shine for you.

EXERCISE #1: DIFFERENT MODES OF CELEBRATION

This exercise will help you find new ways to celebrate your tiny successes. Explore these options and see what works for you. If you need more inspiration, check out the appendix at the end of the book: "One Hundred Ways to Celebrate and Feel Shine."

SONGS YOU LOVE

Think of a song that makes you feel happy, successful, and upbeat. Sing (or hum) part of that song as a way to celebrate your tiny successes.

PHYSICAL MOVEMENTS

Explore physical movements that help you feel happy and successful. This could include a fist pump, a short dance, or even an affirming nod of your head. Find a physical movement that helps you feel Shine and practice using that to wire in a new habit.

VERBAL STATEMENTS

Look for phrases you can say that make you feel happy and successful. Some people say, "Woo-hoo!" Other people say, "Awesome!" Explore options and find at least one verbal statement that will make you feel Shine.

SOUND EFFECTS

Find sounds that help you feel a positive emotion—the roar of a crowd, a trumpet fanfare, or the sound of a slot machine jackpot. Pick a sound effect you like and practice using it to wire in your habits.

VISUALIZATIONS

Some people use their imaginations to create a feeling of Shine. This may be harder to do than using the first four options, but it's flexible (you can do it anywhere) and powerful (lots of Shine).

Spend a few minutes listing what you think about that makes you feel happy and successful—the smiling face of your grandchild, snuggling with your dog, the warm sand at your favorite beach. Whatever works for you. Explore your options and find one that seems easy to imagine and is the most powerful in creating Shine. Use this visualization to celebrate your tiny successes.

EXERCISE #2: TRY A CELEBRATION BLITZ

Try this exercise at least once. For extra credit, make it a regular part of your life.

Step 1: Find the spot that is the least tidy in your home or office.

Step 2: Set a timer for three minutes.

Step 3: After you tidy each item, celebrate.

Step 4: Keep tidying and celebrating.

Step 5: When three minutes are up, stop and focus on what you feel. What has changed? What did you learn?

EXERCISE #3: MAKE A REMINDER: YOU CHANGE BEST BY FEELING GOOD

This exercise is a repeat from the introduction. If you didn't do this back then, please do so now. Okay? Thank you.

To help you remember that people change best by feeling good, not by feeling bad, here is a simple task.

Step 1: Write "I change best by feeling good (not by feeling bad)" on a small piece of paper.

Step 2: Put this paper somewhere you can read the phrase often, like taped to your bathroom mirror.

Step 3: Read the phrase often.

Step 4: Notice how this insight works in your life (and for the people around you).

6

GROWING YOUR HABITS FROM TINY TO TRANSFORMATIVE

When Sukumar turned twenty-six, he noticed two things: Everyone around him was getting married and he was growing a paunch. Both came out of nowhere. Only months ago, it had seemed like everyone was single and he was still that skinny guy from Chennai, India. But now

Sukumar's belly spilled over his pants, and after parties, his friends went home with their wives while he went home alone. The same phrase kept echoing in his head: *What girl is going to want to marry me?*

Eventually, Sukumar decided that he needed to do something about his weight. He began watching what he ate more carefully and he tried to exercise more.

Despite Sukumar's attempts at ramping up his diet and fitness regimen, his paunch stubbornly remained. But he kept trying, and the "battle of the paunch" (as he calls it) became less about looks and more about health.

Sukumar had begun to experience back and neck pain so bad that he had trouble sitting at his desk for more than thirty minutes. He was a tech industry innovator, so desk time was unavoidable. He was willing to tolerate the pain, but the long hours he had to put in at work were hard to endure. Worried about his job performance, he finally went to a doctor. His doctor pointed to the extra weight Sukumar was carrying around his midsection. That, he said, was part of the problem.

Sukumar kept trying to be healthy. Exercise more. Eat less.

For years.

Unfortunately, Sukumar was stuck in the all-too-familiar cycle of crash-course diets punctuated by ambitious workouts. He got hungry and sore, but he wasn't seeing results. Sukumar's frustration and physical pain mounted, and he couldn't seem to gain any traction when it came to getting fit. Time and time again, he would quit his ambitious fitness quest and crash back into his easy chair with a bag of chips.

But Sukumar did get married (he found a girl who thought his paunch was cute). When his wife found her own fitness groove, she suggested that he try working with her personal trainer. This plan went great for a few weeks, but Sukumar soon faltered. Work was busier than ever, and taking an hour out of his day was stressful. He told himself, *That's my problem: no time.*

This merry-go-round of fitness attempts and excuses was more than frustrating; it also provoked anxiety. Sukumar was having trouble sleeping and concentrating, yet he felt powerless to do anything about it.

When Sukumar turned forty-three, he realized that he'd been struggling to lose weight for *seventeen years.*

What had started as a small insecurity had grown into a painful cycle that only ended when he discovered Tiny Habits in 2012.

Sukumar started the method the same way many people do—with push-ups. At the outset, he kept things tiny. After he brushed his teeth, he would do two push-ups. He also created a habit of planking for five seconds. And with those tiny first steps, Sukumar was finally on the path to success. As this habit grew and multiplied, he eventually lost twenty pounds, and five inches vanished from his waist. This wasn't yet another flash in the pan for Sukumar because a huge shift in identity made it possible for him to break the old cycle and set the stage for maintaining his weight loss and becoming fitter and stronger over the years.

Now fifty-one, Sukumar regularly does *fifty* push-ups in the morning to kick off his one-hour workout routine that ends with a *five-minute* plank. He still has back pain on occasion, but he manages any flare-ups with strength training and stretches.

When I recently checked with Sukumar about sharing his story, he told me, "BJ, I've transformed myself."

In this book I've shared true stories from people who have gone from *tiny* to *transformative.* In each case, we've looked at one key aspect of their Behavior Design journey—whether it was motivation matching, increasing ability, designing prompts, or embracing celebration. I've walked you through the process of designing new habits, and I've introduced some vital skills that can make you a true Habit Ninja.

But how on earth do you go from doing two push-ups to *fifty* push-ups? How do you win the battle of the paunch for good? How do you run that 10K you've been dreaming of for years? How do you finally save up enough money to cover your bills in case of an emergency? How do you start that business you've been talking about for months? How do you lower your cholesterol levels and keep them there?

I can answer all these questions with good news: When you apply the Tiny Habits method consistently, your habits will *scale naturally*.

This chapter will explain how habits grow and multiply. I will also lay out a framework that will help you to recognize the change skills you already have and how to troubleshoot habits that have gone astray. All of this will help you clearly see your own path from tiny to transformative.

Let's start by revisiting the metaphor I used in chapter 1.

Cultivating habits—good or bad—is a lot like cultivating a garden.

Think of it this way: You could stand on your back porch and wish that your scraggly yard would somehow become beautiful. As the weeks go by, weeds begin to grow. You pull a few out here and there, but this becomes laborious so you stop. But you keep wishing that beautiful things would grow instead.

A much better approach is to *design* the garden (habits) you want. You identify what vegetables and flowers you'd love to have in your garden (motivation), you choose plants you can easily support (ability), and you consider which spot in the yard is best for each plant (finding a place in your routine).

It takes a bit of planning and care in the beginning to get those delicate little sprouts up and out of the ground, but you've made sure the roots are strong by celebrating your tiny successes. Soon it's time to let your rooted habits do their natural thing—grow bigger.

You're still there *doing* things, of course. You are watering and weeding, but you're not engaging in a different process or straining yourself. It's the same with your new habits. It may take some extra experimentation and attention at the beginning, but once you've established new habits in the right way, it doesn't take much beyond doing them consistently for them to flourish.

After you've established your garden, the sunflowers will grow bright and tall, and the strawberries will stretch and spread.

Like plants, each of your habits will scale differently and at its own pace. A push-up habit might grow from two to fifty, but the final size of each habit will vary depending on time and individual human limitations. An eat-an-avocado-every-morning habit may never get any bigger, but this habit might propagate a blueberries-after-dinner habit or a celery-with-lunch habit.

How long does it take for habits to grow to their full expression? There is no universal answer. Any advice you hear about a habit taking twenty-one or sixty days to fully form is not entirely accurate. There is no magic number of days.

Why? Because the formation time of a habit depends on three things:

+ The person doing the habit
+ The habit itself (the action)
+ The context

In fact, it's the *interaction* between these elements that determines how difficult (or easy) it is to form the habit. That's why no one can say for sure that habit X takes Y number of days to become fully realized.

Change is a process, just like growing a flower in the garden or healing a cut on your finger. And like any process, there are things we can do to optimize it—to speed things along and make course corrections along the way. By understanding how our habits grow and what our role is in the growth process, we can reliably design for the change—the transformation—we want in our life.

Let's dig into specifics.

Grow and Multiply

When it comes to the process of scaling habits, there are two general categories: habits that *grow* and habits that *multiply*.

When I use the word "grow" in this context, I mean that the habit gets bigger. You meditate for thirty minutes each day instead of only taking three breaths. You clean the entire kitchen, not just one counter. The essence of these behaviors is the same, but you do more of them. The habits expand.

Like a plant, habits can grow naturally.

As you look at how habits grow, you'll see that each habit will grow only so big. (Same thing with plants.) Sukumar's daily plank habit topped out at five minutes, which is pretty impressive. He either couldn't do it any longer without straining himself or he didn't want to do it anymore —both things that will weaken a habit. Sukumar had found the natural growth boundary of his planking habit.

You might ask: *In the early days, how did Sukumar know when to plank for more than five seconds?*

Good question. We'll dive into that more deeply soon, but for now, the short answer is: *He did more when he wanted to do more.*

The second way that habits scale is through multiplication. This typically happens when the habit you've cultivated is one piece of a larger ecosystem of behaviors. If your overall aspiration is to make each day more productive, you might opt for a classic—the Maui Habit. After you wake up and put your feet on the floor in the morning, you say, "It's going to be a great day." Since this habit is so time specific, it doesn't grow. However, it does multiply, and you can expect ripple effects.

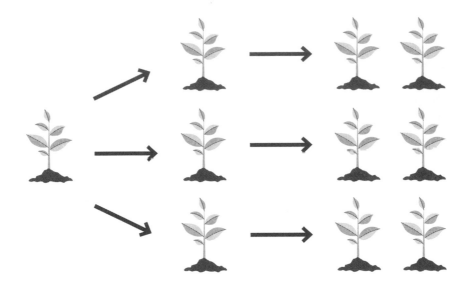

Like a plant, a habit can multiply.

The Maui Habit creates a positive feeling that inspires many people to add other good habits to their morning—like making the bed. As you do the Maui Habit, you can experiment with other habits, like doing the dishes before you leave in the morning or thinking of one thing you're grateful for as you brush your teeth.

I champion the Maui Habit because this simple action helps you to tackle other challenges in the morning. When you succeed with those, you create an upward trajectory for your day that can uplift your attitude and boost your performance at work and beyond.

As people report the positive ripple effects of the Maui Habit, what seems clear is that the Maui Habit doesn't grow so much as it multiplies in the same way a flower's seeds are picked up by the wind and beautiful things get planted in other places. The Maui Habit, and other tiny changes like it, can be easy to create, and they accumulate naturally until your day has transformed (and you don't struggle getting out of bed).

Beginning your habit design process with a clear aspiration will lead you naturally to your own specialized mix of Growth Habits and Multiplication Habits. If one of your big aspirations is to run a marathon, you'll likely design at least one habit that has to do with walking or running—that is a Growth Habit. You'll eventually go farther and faster. At the same time, you will probably create some Multiplication Habits like drinking more water and adding fresh vegetables to your meals. Those habits can multiply naturally and lead to other nutrition-related habits. All of this will move you toward your aspiration of running a marathon.

The Dynamics of Growth

When I first started using the Tiny Habits method, I saw my habits grow and the entire landscape of my life change. But it wasn't until I started to share this with other people in 2011 that I realized the scaling effect of Tiny Habits was universal. As I looked closer, talked to more people, and gathered data, I saw distinct growth patterns arise. You'll see them, too.

You've heard this before, and my research confirms that it's true: Success leads to success. But here's something that may surprise you. The size of the success doesn't seem to matter very much. When you feel successful at something, even if it's tiny, your confidence grows quickly, and your motivation increases to do that habit again and perform related behaviors. I call this success momentum. Surprisingly enough, this gets created by the frequency of your successes, not by the size. So with Tiny Habits you are shooting for a bunch of tiny successes done quickly. Not a big one that takes a long time. The data from my Tiny Habits research show a surprising number of people who tackled big behaviors as a result of succeeding at tiny things. This finding puzzled me at first. But when I asked qualitative questions in later research, I believe I unearthed the dynamic process that creates ripple effects and catalyzes the "big leap" breakthroughs.

We can turn to the Behavior Model to see what's going on here.

We have conflicting motivations for many behaviors in our lives. Part of us wants to do the behavior and part of us doesn't—we want to get up early, but we also want to stay in bed and get more sleep.

To explain this dynamic more vividly, I want to talk about dancing.

Suppose you are at a company holiday party, and a great band is playing music you love. Only a few people are dancing, but part of you wants to dance. A sense of hope motivates you to dance: *I'll have fun and feel good—and maybe be seen as a cool person.* This is the anticipation of good outcomes. However, part of you is fearful. Fear is the anticipation of bad outcomes. You may be thinking, *If I go out and dance, I may look stupid and lose credibility with my colleagues. The boss might see how clumsy I am and think twice about promoting me.*

Hope and fear are vectors that push against each other, and the sum of those two vectors is your overall motivation level.

If you can remove the vector of fear, then hope will predominate, and your overall motivation level will be higher, which may move you above the Action Line—and you do the behavior.

There are a few ways to weaken or remove the demotivator of fear. One common approach to dampen anxiety in social situations is by drinking alcohol. In this case, the normal fear you have will probably be reduced—or removed—and the hope of having fun and looking cool will emerge and put dancing in public above the Action Line.

By the way, this is not a wise approach for a company party.

There are other ways to tackle fear of dancing. You can turn down the lights on the dance floor. You can start a group dance with simple steps that will make everyone look good. You can encourage lots of other people to dance first. At one conference I organized for wellness professionals, I handed out sunglasses to get people dancing. It worked (and it was healthier and more appropriate than alcohol). All of those approaches decrease the fear of dancing in public and allow the overall motivation level to rise.

Another way to get dancing in public above the Action Line is to add motivators. Sometimes this is a good approach, but often you are adding stress and tension to people's lives because the Motivation Vectors are pushing harder against each other.

Suppose no one is dancing, and the big boss, who paid a lot for the live music, gets on the stage and announces that if you don't dance you won't get a year-end bonus. Ugh. So you dance, but it's tense.

Suppose your friends are on the dance floor and you are standing alone by the punch bowl. Suddenly your friends start chanting your name while signaling you to get on the dance floor. You shake your head no. Then everyone in the room chants your name. This would certainly add motivation to do the behavior, but it's not hope that is motivating you, it's social pressure. Despite your significant fear, the Motivation Vector upward is so strong that you are pushed above the Action Line. That means you get on the dance floor and pretend to have fun because social pressure (a powerful motivator) overwhelmed your fear (the demotivator).

This company party shows how conflicting motivators function for a one-time behavior. The same dynamics — vectors pushing against each other — apply to daily habits and long-term change.

One key to designing long-term change is to reduce or remove the demotivators. This allows the natural motivator (often it's hope) to blossom, which in turn can sustain the new behavior over time.

Suppose your boss invites you to lead a daily team meeting each morning. Part of you wants to do it, hoping that this will advance your career, but part of you is fearful of taking this on.

Your boss knows you are a bit reluctant to do this (and he hasn't yet read this book), so he adds an incentive: *If you lead the meeting just once, I'll take everyone to lunch.*

So you lead the meeting.

The first time people do a behavior is a critical moment in terms of habit formation. If you feel like a failure running the meeting, your fear vector will get stronger, moving your overall motivation level down so it's likely that you won't want to lead meetings in the future.

But your story is different. You do an amazing job leading the meeting. You get a lot done, and your colleagues compliment you on your style. This is where the feeling of success plays a powerful role. If you feel successful in running the meeting, the demotivator of fear will get weaker or it might vanish entirely. Your overall motivation level will increase. Now that you are consistently above the Action Line, you say yes to your great new habit of directing more meetings.

But that's not all.

When a demotivator goes away, you open the door to a bigger and harder behavior. The Action Line on my Behavior Model shows that you can do harder behaviors as your motivation levels rise. If you vanquish the fear of running meetings, you are more likely to say yes when your boss invites you to lead company-wide meetings, which is a harder behavior because it takes more time, energy, and thinking—but now your hope surges. As a result, you run big meetings and your career advances.

I now understand why my Tiny Habits data showed so many breakthroughs. When people feel successful, even with small things, their overall level of motivation goes up dramatically, and with higher levels of motivation, people can do harder behaviors.

This is how tiny successes can change the game for you at work, at home, and even inside your own head.

The big takeaway: Start where you *want* to on your path to change. Allow yourself to feel successful. Then trust the process.

But there's more I want to share with you so you become a Habit Ninja—a person who understands *how* to change. I want you to be able to envision any aspiration and achieve it reliably and confidently. Instead of guessing or being distracted by flashy dead-end paths, you will know exactly what to do.

To become a Habit Ninja, you do something familiar: You learn skills.

The Skills of Change

Many people believe that forming good habits and transforming your life is a mysterious or magical process. It's not. As you know by now, there is a system to change. And underlying the system is a set of skills.

I've found that change is a skill like any other skill. This means you won't be perfect at the start, but you will get better with practice. And once you have these skills, you can apply them to all sorts of situations.

When I started mapping out the Skills of Change, I found that they fell into five categories, and I designed the Tiny Habits method to teach skills in each category. As you applied what I shared with you in the previous chapters, you were actually practicing and gaining the Skills of Change. I didn't point that out back then, but now is the time for me to be explicit.

Acquiring the Skills of Change is like mastering any other set of skills. In order to become a top-notch pianist, you need to read musical notation, keep tempo, phrase melodies, memorize music, and expertly finger passages. The more you practice in the right way, the more confident and capable and flexible you become.

You won't become a proficient pianist overnight, just as you won't become a Habit Ninja overnight. But you can get started immediately and watch your skills increase.

Think of any skill you have learned: driving a car, swimming, playing cards, speaking a second language, even walking. You weren't perfect at the beginning—and you didn't expect yourself to be. What was difficult or scary at the start, like merging onto a busy highway, eventually became ordinary and easy. That's how skills work. And that's the right way to think about behavior change.

Learning about the Skills of Change will help you recognize and actively practice them. You don't have to master every single skill to be proficient at changing your life. But the more skills you master, the easier and faster you can turn any aspiration into a reality.

Behavior Crafting is sort of an odd name, but it works. Behavior Crafting skills relate to *selecting and adjusting the habits you want in your life.*

In the previous chapters, you've already been working on Behavior Crafting even though I didn't use that term. You have already learned how to:

- Identify a lot of behavior options (chapter 2)
- Match yourself with behaviors that will lead to your aspiration (chapter 2)
- Make the behavior easier to do (chapter 3)

I hope you can see how far you've already come. Now I want to share a new skill that directly helps you go from tiny to transformative.

Knowing how many new habits to do at once and when to add more

The piano analogy works here as well. To get better on the piano, you need to practice songs. How do you decide which songs to practice and how long to practice them before adding a new tune to your practice routine? You could choose the challenging Fantaisie-Impromptu in C# Minor by Chopin and make sure you can play it perfectly before you focus on a new piece. (This would be a disastrous plan for most people.) Or you could add simple and fun tunes like "Itsy Bitsy Spider" to your repertoire each week. Or you could do something in between. Making this selection effectively is a skill.

A similar selection skill applies to your future habits. Knowing how many new habits to do at once and when to add more is a skill you build largely by diving in, trying stuff, and learning what works for you.

Here are some guidelines for Behavior Crafting.

- *Focus on what interests you.* Some people enjoy cultivating lots of little easy habits. Other people like to tackle habits that are a bit more challenging. What seems most interesting and exciting to you? That's what you should do. If you're feeling lost, here's the default: Start with three super easy habits—that's what most Habiteers begin with—and add three new habits each month.

- *Embrace variety.* The more variety you begin with, the faster you'll learn this and other Skills of Change. Select some new habits that begin as Starter Steps—putting on your walking shoes. Select other habits that are scaled-back versions—flossing just one tooth. It's also good to mix up the general theme—an exercise habit, a food-related habit, a productivity habit. Variety helps you learn more quickly what works best for you.

- *Stay flexible.* If you want to create a list of the habits you want to eventually do, don't get too rigid with your list. Your preferences and needs will change. Today you might put practicing handstands each morning on your list, but in six weeks you might not care about handstands. Be flexible as you progress and leave room for novelty and spontaneity in your life.

Adding Habits Naturally

When Sarika started building habits into her life, she started out with three. She began with turning on the stove burner (Starter Step), sitting on her meditation pillow for three breaths, and drinking a sip of water after she watered her plants. Her larger aspiration was to make her life more predictable so she could better control her medical condition and start incorporating more healthy lifestyle choices. Within a couple of weeks, she went from turning on the stove in the morning to cooking herself a full breakfast every day and eventually cooking *all* her meals —something that before had felt all but impossible. In order to bridge that divide, Sarika had to do a lot more than turn on the stove burner.

So how did she get there? Let's break it down by looking at the "knowing when to add habits" skill we've been talking about.

Once the turn-the-burner-on habit was automatic, Sarika added another habit by putting a pot of water on the burner. This was a natural and easy add-on, and other habits quickly followed—getting rice out of the cupboard, then milk from the fridge, then cinnamon from the cabinet. As Sarika got deeper into the cooking process, she realized that it was hard to cook in a messy kitchen. Last night's takeout boxes and utensils cluttered her countertops—which got in her way when she was trying to make breakfast. This seemed like a natural place for the breakfast habit to multiply.

Sarika felt comfortable and confident enough to branch out. Her next move was to add an evening habit of cleaning off the counter closest to her stove so she'd have space in the morning. That wired in quickly because she felt successful, which made her eager to keep progressing even if that meant adding more steps to the process. Then *that* habit grew, and she started cleaning all the counters the night before. Then she started clearing out the sink and doing all the dishes because waking up to a clean kitchen was so nice. The cascading success of her habits and the natural shape of each behavior inspired Sarika to add more related habits to her initial Tiny Habit recipe.

I walked you through Sarika's process in detail to show you that the skill of knowing when to add more habits isn't a strict formula. It can feel entirely natural. It's not something you need to sweat too much. Start with a variety of habits—I suggest three—and watch what happens.

You know you're doing the right thing if you feel optimistic and see forward movement. Sarika said that the experience was like swimming with the current. After years of waking up to a messy kitchen, skipping breakfast, and starting the day on a disappointing note, she couldn't believe how easy the process was. She said it felt like something was lifting her up and propelling her along, so all she had to do was keep doing what she wanted to do.

SKILL SET #2 — SELF-INSIGHT

Next comes understanding your preferences, strengths, and aspirations. In previous chapters, we've discussed the following skills related to Self-Insight.

+ Clarify your aspirations or desired outcomes

+ Understand what motivates you—i.e., know the difference between what you really want and what you think you should do

Behavior Crafting

Skills of Change

Self-Insight

Here is the next skill that will take you from tiny to transformative.

The skill of knowing which new habits will have meaning to you

Those last two words—"to you"—are important because which habits are significant varies from one person to the next. What you're aiming for is to create new habits that start small in size but are mighty in meaning.

Here are some guidelines to predict if a new habit will be meaningful to you.

+ *The new habit affirms a piece of the identity that you want to cultivate.* If you want to be a person who is loving and appreciative, the habit of saying thank you after your husband makes you dinner is inherently meaningful and will likely propel you toward transformation.

+ *The new habit helps you reach an important aspiration.* If the line from your new habit to your aspiration is clear, your habit will have meaning. A habit of putting on your running shoes may seem small and insignificant, but if your aspiration is to run a 5K, it's decidedly not.

+ *The new habit has a big impact despite being tiny.* Sarika's turning on the stove burner was small, yet it triggered a cascade of changes.

Find the smallest, easiest change you can make that will have the biggest meaning to you.

Here's one from my life: Each morning I fill a water bottle with filtered water and take it with me when I leave the house. This is actually three habits that happen at different times: putting water in the filter, pouring water into a portable bottle, and taking the bottle with me. All these are tiny—and you might find them insignificant—but to me they have important meaning.

Thanks in part to my Stanford students, I became uneasy drinking water from disposable plastic bottles. Being wasteful was not the kind of person I wanted to be. And I didn't want to be the type of person my students saw as uncaring about the earth's future. My identity was at stake.

I explored my options, and these three habits were my solution. Creating these habits was a breeze. And, yes, there are ripple effects, other ecofriendly behaviors I do without thinking, like picking up litter on the beach. (Next habit: carry a small garbage bag in my pocket when I go hiking.)

You can practice this skill by answering one question: *What is the tiniest habit I could create that would have the most meaning?* Write down a few answers even if you don't intend to create any of those habits right now. The more answers you come up with, the more you are practicing this skill.

Getting good at this skill helps you match yourself with habits that you can easily create and maintain. But there's more. As you acquire this skill, you will be more able to identify habits that do not have meaning to you, and you will avoid wasting your time.

If you're having trouble getting a habit to stick, this skill will come to the forefront. Remember when Jill was reflecting on her wiping-the-counter habit? At first it was tough for her to remember—after all, it's a pretty mundane and boring habit on the surface. But when she looked deeper, she realized that this small action had a connection to her larger aspiration—a more harmonious family life and a better relationship with her husband. Once she made that important connection, she was able to generate the meaning necessary to power that habit. She was leveraging the skill of knowing which habits will have meaning to her.

This skill can be vital for habits that are motivationally tricky, the ones that teeter precariously between "I want to do it" and "I should do it." Sometimes you can shift a behavior more firmly to the "want to do" camp by uncovering the meaning. Maybe you think, *I should cultivate a habit of eating vegetables with every meal, but I don't really like them, and I don't know how to cook them so they taste good.* Hello, resistance.

Once you identify a deeply held aspiration connected to eating vegetables, you will be more successful in creating the vegetable habit. There could be lots of hidden meaning for you to find. Maybe you are a grandparent who wants to be fit and healthy enough to see your grandkids grow up. Maybe you want to feel confident in your wardrobe at the annual company conference. Either of those larger aspirations might be enough to help bolster your resolve to eat more vegetables.

On the other hand, maybe you realize that eating vegetables doesn't have any meaning at all. The vegetable-eating habit was all your partner's idea in the first place, and you can't think of why it matters to *you* at all. That's fine. Drop the broccoli habit and focus on what's significant to you.

By practicing Self-Insight, you can figure out if a new habit is worth pursuing. If it is, great — you'll have renewed motivation. If it's not, great — you'll free up space for other habits that matter more to you. Mastering this skill directs your energy toward more important changes.

SKILL SET #3 — PROCESS

As the days go by, your habits change, you change, and the world around you changes. Process Skills are focused on adjusting to the dynamic nature of life in order to strengthen and grow your habits.

Here are the skills you've already learned:

+ How to troubleshoot

+ How to revise your approach if a habit isn't working

+ How to rehearse your habits

This new Process Skill relates directly to growing your habit over time.

The skill of knowing when to push yourself beyond tiny and ramp up the difficulty of the habit

As you do a new habit consistently, you will naturally reach for more. At that point, you can learn to find the edge of your comfort and see how it feels to go just a *little* beyond. Knowing your comfort edge helps you do a bigger version of your habit without feeling pain or frustration, which will weaken the habit.

Let's take a look at Sukumar's push-up habit. How did he know when to grow that habit from two push-ups to three? And how the heck did he get to fifty?

For a habit like this, the comfort edge is fairly easy to find because the signs are physical: burning muscles and labored breathing. In Sukumar's case, he started with two push-ups and focused on his form. After a week of doing two push-ups after brushing his teeth, he recognized that his form was better even on that last push-up. That recognition of progress inspired Sukumar to do more. So he did. And he kept going.

Sukumar grew his push-up habit effectively because he became skilled at finding his comfort edge. As a result, he pushed himself *just enough* to make progress. This process repeated itself over the course of days and weeks. However, if there was a time that Sukumar didn't want to do a lot of push-ups, he didn't force himself. He did two and felt good about keeping the habit alive. Part of this skill is knowing when to back off and do only the baseline.

Steps in Behavior Design

Step 1: Clarify the Aspiration

Step 2: Explore Behavior Options

Step 3: Match with Specific Behaviors

Step 4: Start Tiny

Step 5: Find a Good Prompt

Step 6: Celebrate Successes

Step 7: Troubleshoot, Iterate, & Expand

Now it's time to add this skill to our steps in Behavior Design.

Your comfort edge is not a straight line. It's more like a line on a stock market graph that dips and climbs then dips again. If you keep doing your habit over time, you'll move your comfort edge permanently — but don't think too much about that. Focus on finding your comfort edge in the moment so you can make the most skillful choice.

Here are guidelines for knowing how to adjust the difficulty of your habit.

+ *Don't pressure yourself to do more than the tiniest version of your habit.* If you're sick, tired, or just not in the mood, scale back to tiny. You can always raise the bar when you want to do more, and — surprisingly — you can lower it to tiny when you need to. Flexibility is part of this skill.

+ *Don't restrict yourself from going bigger if you want to do more.* Let your motivation guide you on how much and how hard.

+ *If you do too much, make sure you celebrate extra hard.* Pushing yourself too much to expand a habit can create pain or frustration, which will weaken the habit. If that happens (and it will), you can offset the negative feelings by amping up your celebration.

+ *Use emotional flags to help you find your edge.* Frustration, pain, and especially avoidance are signs that something is going on with your habit—that you've probably increased the difficulty too much, too fast. On the flipside, if you become bored with your habit, you might need to ramp things up.

SKILL SET #4 — CONTEXT

Context pertains to what surrounds us. (I use "context" and "environment" as synonyms.)

None of us lives in a habit vacuum. Our environment, which includes people, influences our habitual behaviors more than we recognize or care to admit. Because our habits are the product of our environment to a large degree, getting good at Context Skills is vital for creating change and making it stick.

We've touched on some of these Context Skills in previous chapters, specifically in relation to tools and resources. In chapter 3, we met Molly, who was trying to eat healthily but struggling to plan ahead so she could make good choices during the week. Molly skillfully recruited her husband as a resource and found a tool to make her habits more likely to succeed. By recognizing the opportunities available to her and implementing these contextual strategies, she was able to succeed more quickly with her eating habits.

I want to go deeper into this Context Skill, which I describe in this way:

The skill of redesigning your environment to make your habits easier to do

This skill is vital to lasting change. When I was working with Weight Watchers, I asked the CEO if he thought sustainable weight loss was possible *without* changing one's environment. His answer? No way. We agreed that if someone loses weight and doesn't change his or her environment along the way, that person will eventually regain the weight. We both knew that context is powerful.

There are two questions that will guide you to change your environment and reduce the friction between the world around you and your good habits. The first is *How can I make this new habit easier to do?*

This is a slight variation on what we discussed in chapter 3—but here I want you to focus on what surrounds your habit instead of scaling back the habit to make it easier.

When I first decided to get serious about flossing, I looked around my bathroom. I usually kept the floss tucked away in a cabinet behind the mirror. I wondered: *How can I make this habit easier?* The answer was pretty clear. I took the floss out of the cabinet and put it next to my toothbrush on the counter. That would be its new home. This one-time action was huge in making flossing a solid habit.

Let's say you're a week into your new habit of eating sliced cucumbers as soon as you get home from work. You used to go straight for the corn chips, so your hope is that eating some sliced cucumber will hold you over until dinnertime. The first couple of days this habit works, but then you start skipping a cucumber here and there, and reaching for the corn chips that live right on the kitchen counter. Okay, time to troubleshoot and ask the next question: *What is making this new habit hard to do?*

You then realize that you skipped one of the days because you couldn't find any cucumbers in the fridge. You fumbled around for fifteen or twenty seconds, cursing under your breath about how no one but you ever cleans out the fridge. The cucumbers are gone—just the excuse you needed to reach for the chips. Another day, you found the cucumbers easily enough, but they weren't ready to eat. You were tired and not in the mood for washing and cutting. So chips again. Now you've got some important clues for a habit redesign.

+ Make a new habit of washing and cutting cucumbers the night before (ongoing habit)

+ Tell everyone to leave your cucumbers alone (one-time action)

+ Make sure the fridge is sufficiently tidy so you can find your cucumbers immediately (once-a-week habit)

By layering your habit with environment redesign, you will reduce friction and set your habit free to go above the Action Line. All hail the mighty prewashed, presliced cucumber.

Some of these environment redesign moves are one and done—telling your family to back off the cucumbers and moving the floss to the counter.

In pursuing one habit, you may be inspired to create other ones that deal with your environment. Remember Sarika? When she noticed that her cluttered counter was getting in the way of her breakfast-making habit, she recognized that design flaw and addressed it with another habit—cleaning the night before.

You'll get better and better at finding ways to redesign your environment to support your good habits. Once you start looking at the world this way, you will see how miniscule obstacles can get in the way of your good habits.

When you consciously and thoughtfully design your environment to accommodate new habits, you make your whole life easier.

Here are some further guidelines for redesigning your environment:

+ When you design new habits, invest time in redesigning your environment so they're easier to do.

+ As you begin doing your new habit, make the environmental adjustments as you go along, redesigning as needed to make your habit easier to do.

+ Question tradition. Who says you have to keep your vitamins in the kitchen or floss in the bathroom? Maybe your vitamins need to be next to your computer. Or maybe flossing works best when you keep floss next to your TV remote. You're a Habit Ninja, not a conformist. Find what works for you.

+ Invest in the gear you need. Suppose you want to bike seven miles to school even when it is raining and cold. Design out these demotivators by buying what you need to make biking in the rain and cold less painful.

So far, I've focused on systems and principles. In this book I'm sharing a process, not prescribing specific habits for specific outcomes. However, I now want to shift gears and share a technique to help you eat healthier food.

Given that I suspect some people reading this book want to lose weight and keep it off—or you have a loved one who does—I want to share my best weight-loss solution from the last ten years.

I call it SuperFridge.

Weight loss happens mostly through changing how we eat. Although exercise is beneficial in many ways, it is not the key to weight loss. Focusing your time and energy on nutrition makes all the difference, but eating better by relying on willpower is a bad approach—we already know why: too many conflicting Motivation Vectors make it nearly impossible to stay the course over time. Unfortunately, the food environment in today's world works against our aspirations to eat better. We have so few good options at work, when we travel, and when we dine out. So many factors work against us. That's just the reality.

Now I'm going to give my opinion: One practical way to change how you eat is by redesigning your food environment, especially your fridge at home.

Denny and I have changed a lot of habits together, but SuperFridge may be our best household shift yet. Thanks in part to our fridge redesign, we have each lost more than 15 percent of our body weight, and we've stayed at our ideal weight for years. And the whole process—even keeping the weight off—has felt easy.

Here's what it's like to live with SuperFridge.

When I open our fridge, I see a bunch of glass containers filled with food ready to eat. The broccoli is in one container already washed and cut up. Same with the cauliflower, celery, peppers, and onions. There's a container with cooked quinoa. I see fresh fruit and boiled eggs ready for a quick snack. We have plain full-fat yogurt, various krauts, and condiments like mustard. You get the idea.

The landscape inside our SuperFridge is beautiful. But that's not the point. We designed it so we can see a bunch of healthy eating options quickly. We can eat as much as we want of anything in the fridge at any time. But we don't put anything in the fridge that conflicts with our eating game plan.

Each week we invest time in shopping and preparing so our SuperFridge can do its job. When we get done refreshing SuperFridge every Sunday, I take a minute to breathe it in because it looks like a page out of *Real Simple* magazine. Beautiful!

The next step may be a bit harder because you don't want to ruin the beauty. But this part is key: During the week, you need to dive in and eat all that wonderful food you've prepared. Don't let anything go to waste. Empty every container if you can.

Although refreshing SuperFridge each week takes time and effort, the investment pays off quickly. If I need a quick lunch, I pull out a few things and I'm done. Dinner prep takes only minutes. When I want a snack at any moment (even in the middle of the night), I open SuperFridge and take anything I want. Still hungry? I go back to SuperFridge and find something else to eat. All good food. No deprivation. And no need to tap willpower.

SuperFridge resulted in weight loss, better sleep, and better energy. We weren't perfect at the start of our SuperFridge quest. Not at all. But we learned how to make the fridge our best friend and ally in our quest for healthy eating.

Redesigning your environment can be fun, and the benefits show up immediately. With time, you will be applying this skill without thinking much about it. Eventually, you'll walk into a hotel room, and if it's not arranged to support your good habits, you will take a few minutes to adjust it—and voilà, it's customized to support better eating, sleeping, grooming, and reaching your aspirations.

SKILL SET #5 — MINDSET

The fifth and final category focuses on what I call Mindset Skills. These are about your approach and attitude to change as well as your perception and interpretation of the world around you.

As it turns out, you've already learned some valuable Mindset Skills.

- Approaching change with an attitude of openness, flexibility, and curiosity

- Being able to lower your expectations

- Feeling good about your successes — no matter how small — by celebrating

- Being patient and trusting the process of change

While celebration is the most important Mindset Skill, this next one ranks right up there with it.

The skill of embracing a new identity

When you can let go of old identities and embrace new ones, you will soar in your ability to go from tiny to transformative.

When people start Tiny Habits, I often hear them say, "I'm set in my ways"; "I'm not the kind of person who changes easily"; or "Nothing ever works for me." But many of those same people changed their tune after as little as five days of the program and told me, "BJ, I can't believe it, but I was wrong. I *am* the kind of person who can change" and "I learned that I'm the kind of person who can follow through."

This phrase — *I'm the kind of person who* — kept coming up, so I decided to bake it into the Tiny Habits evaluation process by asking people at the end of my free five-day program to complete this phrase: "After doing Tiny Habits, I now see myself as the kind of person who..."

Once I began gathering that data, I saw how people's self-concepts shifted as they grew more skilled at creating habits. They started the Tiny Habits program thinking they were one kind of person, and by the end of five days, they were starting to embrace a new identity. Many of these identities focused on having the potential to change, but other identity shifts were linked to the types of habits and changes people were making.

If you ask Sukumar, the push-up king from Chennai, identity was the key part of his puzzle. Before he started, he was thinking, *I'm not an exercise guy. I'm not into eating healthy food. I'm the type of person who has trouble sleeping.* To him, these were immutable personality traits — they were simply *who he was.* But when he dropped down and did his first two push-ups, he took the first step toward hacking the psychology of self.

All humans have a strongly rooted drive to act in a way that is consistent with their identity. When a group faces threats, any group member who is unpredictable creates risk for the group. That person gets shunned. There is a good evolutionary reason for this—when food, shelter, and other resources depend on group unity and collaboration, it is critical to reliably predict what a person is going to do. Your life might depend on it. As social beings, we all act largely in keeping with certain identities even if we don't realize it.

When Sukumar started doing push-ups, he increased his physical strength and mental toughness. This made him feel successful at exercising—he started feeling less like a phony at the gym. Trying out different exercise equipment had felt uncomfortable before, and he was constantly questioning himself. Was he strong enough to use the bench-press machine? Would he be embarrassed if he could do only a couple of repetitions?

After experimenting with planks and push-ups, and seeing results, Sukumar's identity shifted. He now understood how strength building worked and knew he was capable of doing it. He went to the gym more and felt better about it. He even signed up for biweekly sessions with his wife's personal trainer. The group exercise classes were surprisingly fun (he had been way too intimidated to try them before), and he even made some friends in the spin class.

So what happened? Growth, obviously. But driving all this change was his ability to embrace a new identity. He let go of the idea that he was the type of person who was bad at exercise. Thanks to feeling successful with Tiny Habits, he saw himself in a new way.

Identity shifts are change boosters because they help us cultivate constellations of behavior—not just one or two habits here and there. This is important because most aspirations require more than one type of habit change. It's a *set* of new habits that will get you where you want to be—especially in the areas of fitness, sleep, and stress.

The type of person who frequents McDonald's and the type who shops at the farmers' market exhibit different eating behaviors across the board. If you start eating like a person who goes to the farmers' market, your brain begins guiding you in the direction of a coherent identity, and adding pumpkin seeds to your salad doesn't sound like such a crazy thing anymore; it sounds natural. Shifting identity helps you consider other new habits you might not have thought of doing that will move you closer to your aspiration.

Successfully embracing an identity shift in one area often promotes change in other areas. Sukumar's early success with exercise emboldened him to challenge the idea that he wasn't a healthy eater, and he began to design eating habits more in line with the overall healthy person he was becoming. He cut his portion sizes for every meal and made small changes to his diet like switching from white to brown rice. This, too, became an identity that shifted—the healthier he ate, the healthier he wanted to eat. He would have said that he had a sweet tooth before, but months into his Tiny Habits journey, that wasn't true anymore. The amazing part about this is that he didn't tackle sugar directly. Losing his sweet tooth was a ripple effect from other changes he had intentionally made. Sukumar had attacked his sugar monster from behind.

He also used to think that he was a bad dresser, but he later realized that shopping without his paunch became a much more enjoyable and inspiring experience. When he looks in the mirror now, he feels sharp.

Sukumar was questioning his negative notions of self that had once seemed so solid—identities that had caused him pain and frustration. If he could change *those* parts of himself, the ones that had seemed set in stone, he reasoned that he could change anything he wanted. This sense of empowerment and optimism was the real transformation for Sukumar. He became more confident in all parts of his life, and he left the company where he'd been working for nineteen years to start his own business that uses Tiny Habits as a key component for enabling transformation in large organizations.

Okay, let's get down to the nitty-gritty to build those identity-embracing skills that are so important.

+ Finish the sentence "I'm the kind of person who" with the identity —or identities—you'd like to embrace.

+ Go to events that gather people, products, and services related to your emerging identity. When I decided I wanted to get into fermented foods, I went to the local Fermentation Festival. I met enthusiasts who were more experienced than I was. I learned about new products. I attended a workshop where an expert showed us how to make sauerkraut. I bought gear to ferment foods. I came home with a much stronger identity about being the kind of person who eats—and even makes—fermented foods.

+ Learn the lingo. Know who the experts are. Watch movies related to the area of change you're interested in. As I learned to surf, I looked up the lingo that described waves and started using it. I paid attention to big surfing events and watched videos of the most proficient people in the sport. I learned to understand the tide shifts and identify local landmarks that showed whether the tide was high or low. There is a volcanic formation in the ocean off of Maui that locals call the "dragon." You can tell what's going on with the tide by looking at the dragon. If his neck is exposed, it's low tide. If only his head shows, then the tide is high.

- Wearing T-shirts is a common way to declare your identity. Nike sends out T-shirts that say RUNNER. I wear T-shirts that have surfboards or show surf scenes. Because I surf more than one hundred times a year, I don't feel like a poser; wearing that identity feels natural.

- Update your social media page. Put a new profile picture up that conveys your emerging identity. (And see how people respond.) Revise your online bio. Post stuff related to your new identity.

- Teach others or be a role model to galvanize your new identity. A social role is powerful.

Don't Just Read This Book — Practice the Skills of Change

Don't worry, you don't have to learn all of the Skills of Change at once to make major strides. Nor do you have to adopt all of them (though I hope you do). But the more you learn, the more confident, efficient, and flexible you will be in making progress and transforming your life. It's also helpful to know that a coach or teacher can do some of the skills for you. But you need a good one. And eventually you may learn these skills and do them on your own. But for some things, having a good coach makes a

difference because (among other things) it reduces how many skills you have to master at the start.

Reading stories and guidelines about change is a good thing. But don't stop there. You don't learn to dance by reading about it; you don't learn to drive a car by studying a manual. I'm thrilled you are reading my book, but please also apply my insights to your everyday life. You can practice change just like other skills you've learned. You will make mistakes, and that's okay.

I realize that this is a new way of thinking about habits — that behavior change is a skill — but this should give you the confidence that you can change by learning skills in the same way you learned to ride a bike, swim, or use a computer. You might flail around a little at first, but if you keep going, you'll get there.

Some of your tiny changes will grow; others will multiply. Along the way, as you feel successful, your identity will shift. And this is how you will go from tiny to transformative.

My prediction: You will succeed faster than you expect.

Skills of Change

EXERCISE #1: LEARN FROM SKILLS YOU'VE ALREADY MASTERED

In this exercise I want you to connect how you learned other skills to learning the Skills of Change.

Step 1: List at least five skills you've learned—i.e., driving a car, speaking French, or using Photoshop.

Step 2: Jot down what you did in order to learn those skills—i.e., hired a teacher, started with easy things, and practiced every day. (I suggest you spend at least five minutes thinking about this and making notes.)

Step 3: Look over your notes and think about using those same techniques for learning the Skills of Change.

EXERCISE #2: PRACTICE A BEHAVIOR CRAFTING SKILL

One skill in Behavior Crafting is knowing how many habits to do at once. That's what you'll explore in this exercise. You'll try to create six habits at once as a way to discover your capacity for creating multiple habits at a time.

Step 1: Create six recipes for new habits using what you've learned so far in this book. You can also get inspiration from the appendix "Three Hundred Recipes for Tiny Habits."

Step 2: Write each recipe on an index card or use my template found at TinyHabits.com/recipecards.

Skills of Change

- Mindset
- Behavior Crafting
- Context
- Self-Insight
- Process

Step 3: For each recipe, make sure the behavior is tiny. If it's not tiny enough, then scale it back.

Step 4: For each recipe, make sure the Anchor is specific. Bonus: Identify the Trailing Edge of each Anchor.

Step 5: Practice these six new habits for one week, revising and rehearsing as needed. (If you don't like a new habit, discard it and add something else.)

Step 6: After a week, reflect on what you've learned about yourself and the Tiny Habits method. As you move forward, keep the new habits you like most, and let the others fade.

To do well on this exercise, you'll need to redesign your environment and rehearse, which are the focus of the next two exercises.

EXERCISE #3: PRACTICE A CONTEXT SKILL

In this exercise, you will practice the Context Skill of redesigning your environment to support the change you want in your life.

Step 1: Look at each new habit recipe from the Behavior Crafting exercise.

Step 2: For each habit, find ways to redesign your environment so that each one is easier to do.

EXERCISE #4: PRACTICE A PROCESS SKILL

One important Process Skill is rehearsing your new habits and celebrating each time. Here is an exercise for doing that.

Step 1: Look at the six recipes you've created for Tiny Habits.

Step 2: For each one, do the Anchor behavior and the new habit.

Step 3: Celebrate as you do the new habit or immediately afterward.

Step 4: Repeat this behavior sequence seven to ten times.

Step 5: Try not to feel too strange doing the habit rehearsal. Remember how top performances in sports, business presentations, and more comes from practice. And that's how you get top performance in behavior change.

EXERCISE #5: PRACTICE A MINDSET SKILL

One important Mindset Skill is being okay with doing only the tiny behavior. It's okay to floss only one tooth or do only two push-ups. Here's an exercise that will help you get comfortable with this concept.

Step 1: Pick any new habit you are doing regularly. (If you don't have one, then select flossing your teeth.)

Step 2: When you do the new habit next time, do only the tiniest version on purpose. Resist the temptation to do more.

Step 3: Congratulate yourself for deliberately keeping it tiny and feeling okay with that.

Step 4: Repeat this for at least three days in order to develop a mindset that even the tiniest of changes is good. (You want to feel good about underperforming on the size of a habit because that is how you overachieve in doing habits consistently.)

EXERCISE #6: PRACTICE A SELF-INSIGHT SKILL

One important Self-Insight Skill is finding the smallest changes in your life that will have the biggest meaning. I believe this exercise is the toughest one I've suggested, and that's why I saved it for last.

Step 1: List an area of life that really matters to you, such as being a good mom or showing compassion.

Step 2: Spend three minutes thinking about the simplest one-time behaviors you could do that would have significant meaning in that area. Make a list.

Step 3: Repeat step 2, but this time consider the tiniest new habits that would have the most significance to you in that area. Make a list.

Extra credit: Decide what items from steps 2 and 3 you want to put into practice.

7

UNTANGLING BAD HABITS: A SYSTEMATIC SOLUTION

On a work trip to Ghana, Juni (whose sweet tooth was legendary) went looking for a place to buy ice cream at seven a.m. After reminding her that she was in West Africa, her colleagues asked why on earth she wanted ice cream for breakfast.

"Because I'm a grown woman, and I can eat whatever I want," she replied.

When Juni tells that story now, she shakes her head in disbelief. How could it have taken so long to recognize what was really going on? It wasn't just ice cream for breakfast, it was a double caramel macchiato for lunch, an onion-flavored corn snack (Funyuns!) for commercial breaks, and more ice cream for dinner—separate behaviors that were an intricate part of her day that amounted to a big problem for her health and happiness.

Juni's denial about the extent of her sugar habit is surprising to her in retrospect, but at the time, she was focused on other things and was incredibly disciplined in almost every other part of her life. In addition to being a successful radio host, she was an avid runner. In fact, she first signed up for Tiny Habits because her goal was to run the Chicago Marathon. During her initial sessions, Juni created a handful of new habits to help strengthen her core to improve her running times. Those new habits went so well that she started creating other habits related to productivity at work, and she even adopted some healthy eating measures that kept some of her sugar pangs at bay.

But then her mom died in 2015.

A focused, get-'er-done kind of woman like her daughter, Juni's mom died of complications directly related to diabetes. Juni flew to Alabama to help her oldest sister make all the final arrangements. Her six siblings — the youngest was just nineteen — were devastated and leaned heavily on Juni. Despite the stress and her own profound sadness, Juni tried to be strong for them, but that took its toll. So when her husband asked what she needed when she got home, Juni didn't hesitate. "I need bubblegum ice cream from Baskin-Robbins."

Two years later and fifteen pounds heavier, Juni realized her unresolved grief, was surging. After her mother's funeral, Juni jumped right back into her busy life. Two kids, a job, a marriage. The needs of her eleven-year-old autistic son seemed to grow in tandem with her rising stress levels. Looking back on it, Juni realizes that the loss of her mother was always in the background as she charged forward and made it through each day at any cost. Instead of confronting her sadness, Juni fed her grief cookie-dough ice cream and cake, which only made the inevitable sugar crash twice as painful.

Sugar eventually started to impede on her life in ways that even Juni could no longer deny. Carrying the extra weight made running harder, and she felt jittery and foggy at work. As a radio talk show personality, she had to be able to riff on responses to questions and field surprise callers who had something wacky to say. In the midst of a sugar high, she was energized, but she also felt scattered and unable to focus.

Juni joined my Behavior Design Boot Camp hoping for professional insights she could share with her team, but she came away realizing that she could apply all of the techniques to her own well-being. Reinvigorated, Juni covered the walls of her office at home with paper and got out the markers. She identified an aspiration for every area of her life, then did a Swarm of Behaviors, then Focus Mapped the heck out of it all. In the last blank space, Juni wrote STOP EATING SUGAR and circled it. She stepped back and drew in a deep breath.

This was it.

This was the most important transformative behavior she could do. But it was something she would have to design *out* of her life. She got a little tingle on the back of her neck and knew that this was the hardest race she'd ever signed up for.

The only snag in her plan was that the boot camp was mostly about learning to engage customers. It didn't focus on breaking personal habits. But because Juni was nothing if not disciplined, smart, and bold, she figured she could use the Behavior Model to reverse engineer these behaviors out of her life.

So that's what she did.

She put specific sugar-eating habits—"I eat ice cream every night for dinner"—on the Behavior Model and figured out the mechanics of motivation, ability, and prompt that were causing her to surge over the Action Line. She realized that fatigue and grief were prompting her to eat sugar. Juni was also using sugar to help keep herself on her toes. And then she would miss her mom, which always seemed to prompt a binge.

To tackle the sugar monster, Juni tried ridding her house of sugary snacks. She tried ignoring her fatigue or replacing ice cream with pretzels, and she stocked her car with an emergency stash of sugar-free snack bars. When she got sad about her mom, Juni would play Pokémon Go instead of eating.

What ultimately worked for Juni was addressing her grief prompt at its root. She first created a handful of positive habits—journaling and reaching out to friends through social media—which helped her mourn her mother in a way that processed the grief instead of suppressing it. The more she dealt with her grief in a healthy way, the better she felt, and her motivation to do her positive habits became stronger. As Juni started to increase the time between sugary snacks, she saw opportunities for celebrating those small successes. Juni could go one meal without eating sugar at first. Then she could go a couple of hours. This might not seem like much, but Juni knew that she had to lower her expectations. And those moments felt like victories to her.

Knowing the importance of harnessing the feeling of success, Juni celebrated when she went one day without sugar. A huge milestone. Even though she wasn't always perfect, she continued on this path until she completed an entire week without eating any sugary snacks.

Juni knew the importance of being flexible and iterative, and she experimented with dozens of new habits. She was challenged by special occasions where sugar was everywhere, and if she occasionally succumbed to the siren call of cookie-dough ice cream, she wasn't too hard on herself—she looked at it as a challenge to study and hack. She came up with work-arounds for moments of vulnerability, and through trial and error, she discovered what worked and what didn't while she remained compassionate with herself and celebrated her wins.

These wins compounded quickly, and Juni's multipronged approach started to pay off and made her feel as if she could choose to eat sugar or not. Her addiction had held her hostage, and now she knew she could change that. Juni had completed Behavior Design Boot Camp in March. At the end of May, she sent me an e-mail telling me that she had done it.

Juni had beaten sugar.

When Juni told me that she had stopped her sugar habit using the skills learned through Behavior Design and Tiny Habits, I was proud of her, and it inspired me to share my methods on stopping bad habits more widely. I had found success stopping my own bad habits throughout the years, but I had kept my focus on helping people create new positive habits. I was also hesitant to wade into the territory of bad habits too deeply because I am not an addiction specialist, and conversations about bad habits often quickly turn to substance abuse and compulsive behaviors. I didn't want to take on the role of a therapist or a medical doctor. I knew that Tiny Habits is not the answer to serious addictions. But for people with bad habits that are not serious addictions, I have good news: Tiny Habits can be game changing.

A helpful way to think about habits is to put them into three categories. I'm talking about *all* habits here—good and bad. Uphill Habits are those that require ongoing attention to maintain but are easy to stop—getting out of bed when your alarm goes off, going to the gym, or meditating daily.

Downhill Habits are easy to maintain but difficult to stop—hitting snooze, swearing, watching YouTube.

Freefall Habits are those habits like substance abuse that can be extremely difficult to stop unless you have a safety net of professional help.

To help you get rid of your Downhill Habits, I've created a new system called the Behavior Change Masterplan. This system provides a comprehensive approach to follow step by step so you don't need to guess at solutions.

My plan is built—of course—on the Behavior Model.

B=MAP is the foundation for designing new habits *and* saying goodbye to habits that are holding you back. In previous chapters, we focused on how to make things easier. Now we'll talk about how to make them harder (decreasing ability). Instead of building in effective prompts, you'll look for ways to remove them. Instead of trying to ramp up your motivation, you'll consider ways to reduce it for an unwanted habit.

Before we jump into the Behavior Change Masterplan, let's step back and deconstruct how we've been taught to view bad habits. This is a major part of the problem, after all.

Like positive habits, bad habits exist on a continuum of easy to change and hard to change. When you get toward the "hard" end of the spectrum, note the language you hear—*breaking* bad habits and *battling* addiction. It's as if an unwanted behavior is a nefarious villain to be aggressively defeated. But this kind of language (and the approaches it spawns) frames these challenges in a way that isn't helpful or effective. I specifically hope we will stop using this phrase: "break a bad habit." This language misguides people. The word "break" sets the wrong expectation for how you get rid of a bad habit. This word implies that if you input a lot of force in one moment, the habit will be gone. However, that rarely works, because you usually cannot get rid of an unwanted habit by applying force one time.

Instead of "break," I suggest a different word and a different analogy. Picture a tangled rope that's full of knots. That's how you should think about unwanted habits like stressing out, too much screen time, and procrastinating. You cannot untangle those knots all at once. Yanking on the rope will probably make things worse in the long run. You have to untangle the rope step by step instead. And you don't focus on the hardest part first. Why? Because the toughest tangle is deep inside the knot.

You have to approach it systematically and find the easiest knot to untangle.

Juni first listed all the tangles in her sugar-habit knot. Then she addressed the most accessible one—going without dessert after dinner on only one day, then two days. Next, she got rid of her break-room ice cream stash. Eventually, she worked up to removing the ice cream from her home freezer. The process of untangling soon gained momentum. What felt so scary before—dealing with grief without sugar—started to feel less panic inducing. Successfully making it through one evening without dessert showed her something important—that she was stronger than she thought. Just as important, she began to see how all the tangles were connected. And that's when things began to transform rapidly. If she had followed conventional wisdom on breaking bad habits —swapping out a donut for a celery stick—she probably would have given up before long because doing something by willpower alone is hard, and hard is often impossible to sustain. Plus, if you don't want to do a behavior in the first place (if she didn't really want celery), then the good habit won't wire in. And then she would have felt terrible about falling short, and this would have reinforced a cycle of failure.

The inability to stop a bad habit can provoke deep feelings of shame and guilt. Why? In many cultures there is a lot of weight put on personal responsibility—the idea that if you can't do the right thing you must be suffering from some weakness of character. This is reductive and unhelpful in the realm of behavior change, but it's also deeply embedded in our psyches.

The first thing to remember is this: If you've followed some misguided advice on breaking habits and failed, I'm here to say it's not your fault. You have inherited a flawed way of thinking and approaching the problem that has led to a cycle of frustration and dysfunction.

The second thing to remember is that you can design for the change you want in a smarter, better way.

And that's why I'm writing this chapter for you.

It's time to set the record straight and acknowledge that bad habits are not fundamentally different from good habits when it comes to basic components. Behavior is behavior; it's always a result of motivation, ability, and a prompt coming together at the same moment.

The Behavior Change Masterplan

My masterplan has three phases for disrupting unwanted habits.

Behavior Change Masterplan

Phase 1

Focus on **creating** new habits.

Next . . .

Phase 2

Focus on **stopping** the old habit.

Next, if needed . . .

Phase 3

Focus on **swapping** a new habit for the old one.

You create new positive habits first. Then you focus on stopping specific behaviors related to the old habit. If stopping doesn't work, move on to phase three, which is all about swapping in a new habit to replace the old one.

There are more steps within each of these phases, which I've mapped out in flowcharts in the appendixes. (They were too detailed to include here.)

Traditional change methods (the ones that work, anyway) also fit in my overall masterplan. Consider motivational interviewing, a counseling method that helps clients get clear on their motivations. This is one of the few traditional approaches I find worthwhile. People who experience motivational interviewing can better understand their reasons for doing or not doing a behavior.

The use of accountability partners can serve various roles. On the surface, being accountable to someone seems to be all about motivation. Yes, motivation plays a big role, but when done well, the use of accountability partners can also affect your ability. A partner can give you ideas on how to make your unwanted behavior harder to do or even impossible. If you're trying to cut down screen time, an accountability partner might suggest you install a timer that turns off your Wi-Fi at eight p.m. That makes surfing the web late harder to do. (Thank you, accountability partner.)

The masterplan shows where a proven change method might fit in with a more comprehensive system for untangling your unwanted habits, and it specifies the order of things. It's not merely a list of techniques or a set of guidelines; it's something more powerful: an algorithm for creating change in your life by untangling habits that are causing you pain.

Are you ready?

PHASE #1 — FOCUS ON CREATING NEW HABITS

First some good news.

By reading this book and practicing Tiny Habits, you are already on your way to disrupting unwanted habits. Creating new positive habits is phase one of the Behavior Change Masterplan, and by focusing on this first, you learn the Skills of Change and see evidence that you *can* change, and this gives you more power to untangle habits you don't want in your life.

Skills of Change

Remember how many of Juni's new habits focused directly on her sugar addiction?

None of them.

Juni "skilled up" by practicing habits that did not carry emotional baggage. The new habits were safe and nonthreatening. This allowed her to learn the Skills of Change without emotional distraction.

Let's suppose you have struggled with your body weight for years. Maybe you were ridiculed for being overweight. Perhaps even your medical doctor makes you feel awful at each visit. So you might think weight loss should be your number one focus.

I champion a different approach in Phase #1. Don't focus first on weight loss or whatever is causing you pain. Create habits that relate to some other domain instead—tidiness, relationships, creativity, or anything that doesn't relate to your body weight.

It's much better to first build your skills and gain mastery over the change process itself. In Phase #1 you should create habits that build on your strengths. That's how you succeed quickly, and that's how you best learn the Skills of Change—by adding key skills and insights for the road ahead. But there's more.

Identity shift

When you create a host of positive changes, you move closer to the person you want to become. If you feel successful in these changes, you will naturally view yourself differently and begin to embrace a new identity. In the last chapter, we talked about how this leads to more positive habits. But it also has the side effect of crowding out the behaviors you don't want, the ones no longer in line with the identity you are embracing and the person you are becoming. As Sukumar added more and more exercise behaviors, certain bad habits got phased out. He took the stairs instead of the elevator now because he thought of himself as the kind of person who did that. Watching TV in the evenings morphed from a habit to an occasional indulgence because his evenings were spent playing racquetball with a friend or going for a walk with his wife and their dog. Sukumar didn't exactly plan on disrupting these bad habits. But by picking up a bunch of positive habits that helped him embrace a new identity, he changed the landscape of his life so drastically that many bad habits no longer fit.

If adding good habits to your life resolved all your unwanted behaviors, we could stop here. But weeds crop up in even the best-tended garden, so let's continue.

It's helpful to view phase one as a time of preparation. I know the word "preparation" sounds boring and tedious. But this phase can be fun if you pick new habits you enjoy and celebrate your successes. Your new habits, new skills, and new identity will be important as you move to phase two. That's when you stare that tangled knot in the face and design your strategy.

PHASE #2 — DESIGN FOR STOPPING A HABIT

The previous chapters have explained how to design your way *into* a habit, but you can also design your way *out* of a habit, and the Behavior Model will again be your foundation.

You can stop a behavior by altering any of the three components of the Behavior Model. You can decrease motivation or ability, or you can remove the prompt.

Making any one of those changes for the long term will stop the habit. Sound easy?

Well, yes and no.

Most people could easily stop their Uphill Habits of daily exercise or getting out of bed at five a.m. But you're not reading this because you want to stop *those* kinds of habits. You want to stop the Downhill Habits that are making you less healthy and happy.

Get specific to stop a habit

When it comes to stopping a bad habit, a common mistake is trying to motivate yourself toward an abstraction, such as "stop stressing out at work" or "stop eating junk food." Those both sound specific, but they are not. They are abstract labels for a tangle of habits, what I call the General Habit. If you focus only on the General Habit, you probably won't make much progress, just like if you focus on the entire knot at once, you can't untangle it. You need to focus on specific tangles in order to make progress. That means finding specific habits to focus on. And the Swarm of Behaviors model will help you do that.

Write the General Habit that you want to stop in the cloud.

I want to stop . . .

_____
_____

_____
(This is the General Habit)

Then list specific habits that contribute to the general one in the boxes surrounding the cloud. To show you what this looks like, I've filled out the next illustration for the General Habit of eating too much junk food.

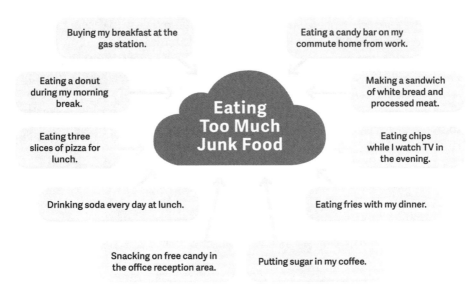

Buying my breakfast at the gas station.

Eating a candy bar on my commute home from work.

Eating a donut during my morning break.

Making a sandwich of white bread and processed meat.

Eating Too Much Junk Food

Eating three slices of pizza for lunch.

Eating chips while I watch TV in the evening.

Drinking soda every day at lunch.

Eating fries with my dinner.

Snacking on free candy in the office reception area.

Putting sugar in my coffee.

Why these steps matter

If you focus only on your General Habit, you will probably feel frustrated or intimidated, and this can cause avoidance: _I don't have time right now_ or _I'll do it later._

However, after you list specific habits that relate to your general habit, untangling this big bad habit will feel more manageable.

When I first used this process to stop an unwanted habit, I was surprised that I could list more than fifteen specific things that contributed to my general habit of leaving things out of place around the house. Let me warn you here: After listing so many specific habits of being untidy at home, I felt kinda bad about myself. I was a bit surprised by the enormity of my clutter habit. Really? Was I that sloppy? Yes, I apparently was.

When you apply this method, I don't want this temporary dark feeling to surprise you. It seems to happen with most people who follow this process because they are facing the reality of their bad habit. However, the dark feeling can soon turn around. As I looked over my specific habits of not being tidy, I found some I could untangle quickly and easily: Yes, I could stop leaving sweaters on the dresser, and I could stop stacking books on the kitchen counter. And that made my dark feeling go away.

With this plan, I felt in control. In fact, I started feeling quite optimistic. And that's what you can expect as well. And with your early successes (no more sweaters on the dresser), you'll be able to tackle some harder tangles.

So I'm saying this: When you see a bunch of specific habits to untangle, don't stop there. And don't get overwhelmed. Keep going. Pick one tangle and design it out of your life. But which specific habits should you tackle first?

The answer is so important, I'll say it three times in different ways: Pick the *easiest* one. Pick the one you are most sure you can do. Pick the one that feels like no big deal.

People are often tempted to pick the hardest, stickiest habit to unwind, but that is a mistake. That's like trying to untangle the tightest snarl deep inside a big knot. Start with the specific habit that will be the easiest for you to stop instead.

And it's fine to pick more than one specific habit to unwind. The choice is yours, but whatever you decide, don't overwhelm yourself. Remember that you are practicing the Skills of Change and learning along the way. Save the tough stuff for when you have more skills and momentum. You'll find that subsequent snarls get easier to untangle as you gain know-how and confidence. And you might not need to address all of your specific habits because some of them will fall away on their own.

The steps here reflect the Behavior Design process I explained earlier in the book. Except now, for stopping a behavior, we are flipping things around. We are reverse engineering the habit. That means we map out what already exists in order to untangle it. In both situations—whether starting or stopping habits—designing for specific behaviors (instead of abstractions) is essential. When you have selected the specific habit you want to stop (the B in B=MAP), move on to the next step. Remember that if you remove motivation, ability, or prompt you can stop the specific habit, and my research shows there is an optimal order in this process. You start with the prompt. And that's our next step in the Behavior Change Masterplan.

Focus on the Prompt to Stop a Habit

Sometimes all you need to do is tackle the prompt and you're done, and there are three ways to do this: remove the prompt, avoid the prompt, or ignore the prompt.

Remove the prompt

Removing the prompt is the simplest option for stopping an unwanted habit. And the best way to remove a prompt is to redesign your environment.

Let's say that you want to stop checking social media while you are at work. You can turn off your phone, put it on airplane mode, or turn off notifications for the social media app. Any of these will remove contextual prompts. And that might resolve the habit right there.

A Tiny Habit Recipe for this would be *After I sit down at work, I will turn off notifications for my social media app.*

My Recipe — Tiny Habits Method

After I...	I will...	To wire the habit into my brain, I will immediately:
sit down at work,	turn off notifications for social media.	☺
Anchor Moment	**Tiny Behavior**	**Celebration**
An existing routine in your life that will remind you to do the Tiny Behavior (your new habit).	The new habit you want but you scale it back to be super tiny—and super easy.	Something you do to create a positive feeling inside of yourself (the feeling is called Shine).

You could also remove the social media app from your phone. This is a one-time behavior, which is usually more effective than a daily action because it's done only once and there's no need to wire in a habit.

When you're designing to undo prompt, you can either use the Tiny Habits method to remove the prompt on a regular basis, or you can do a one-time behavior that removes the prompt forever. When it comes to using social media, the Tiny Habits approach might be better because using social media on your train ride home from work can sometimes be relaxing, so deleting the app entirely might not be the best path.

Avoid the prompt

If you can't remove the prompt for your bad habit, then try avoiding the prompt. If you want to end your habit of grabbing a sugary pastry with your morning coffee, stop going to the coffee shop and make coffee at home, where there's no built-in temptation.

Ways to avoid prompts include:

* Don't go places where you will be prompted

* Don't be with people who will prompt you

* Don't let people put prompts in your surroundings

* Avoid media that prompts you

You'll remember how one of my Tiny Habit Recipes helps me avoid eating too much bread at a restaurant. When the server approaches, I say, "No bread, please." In that way, I take control of my context, and I can avoid the prompt of a bread basket on my table.

However, you might not be able to avoid all situations where you are prompted. What if you *work* at a coffee shop that sells pastries or the person prompting you is your boss and you can't avoid her?

Ignore the prompt

Your final option is ignoring the prompt, but this relies on willpower, which can be problematic because you have to exert extra effort to ignore a prompt for a habit above the Action Line (i.e., when you have sufficient motivation and ability).

But you've done this before. Despite being prompted to indulge, you have resisted and pushed back. But you can say no to the prompt only so many times before your willpower weakens. You can say no to a drink at a party one or two times. But if people constantly offer you a drink (and you want one), you might eventually cave in. This is because with each "ask" that you resist, you're relying on willpower.

This is especially true when you are anxious. You forgot your healthy breakfast at home one morning, and you're not going to make it through your meetings without something to eat so you grab that blueberry muffin at the coffee shop. Or you have a moment of anxiety and your urge to escape on social media soars.

Ignoring a prompt is probably not the best solution in the long term. However, if you find yourself particularly strong-willed and up to the task, make sure you celebrate your achievement when you successfully ignore the prompt and forgo the unwanted habit.

There you have it. You can deal with prompts in three ways: removing them, avoiding them, or ignoring them.

If any one of these works for you, that's great. You've found the simplest solution to redesign a specific habit out of your life.

After you successfully resolve a specific habit, return to your Swarm of Behaviors and select another specific habit to unwind. If you've stopped your habit of buying breakfast at the gas station, you can tackle eating free candy in the office's reception area.

But what if you can't remove, avoid, or ignore the prompt?

Well, that happens.

When you can't design a prompt out of your life, move on to the next component in the Behavior Model.

Redesign Ability in Order to Stop a Habit

The next step in the Behavior Change Masterplan is to focus on making the habit harder to do.

In chapter 3, I explained the five factors in my Ability Chain model: time, money, physical effort, mental effort, and routine. We used this chain to help us make a new habit easier to do, but now we're going to weaken or break the chain to make your habit harder to do. Let's consider each of these five links and how you can redesign them.

High

Make habit harder to do

Motivation

Habit

Action Line

Low

Hard to Do Ability **Easy to Do**

1. INCREASE THE TIME REQUIRED

You can make a habit less likely if you change the environment so the bad habit requires more time. Let's say the general habit you want to stop is eating sugary snacks. You created a Swarm of Behaviors, and you found a specific habit to stop "eating ice cream while watching TV in the evening."

You can't remove the prompt because it's internal. Something inside you was saying, "Hey, ice cream would taste great right now." And you can't ignore that kind of prompt because your sweet tooth always wins out over willpower. So what's next?

Break the Ability Chain

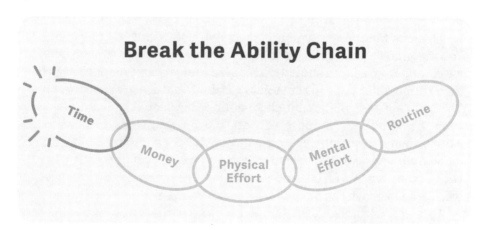

Time Money Physical Effort Mental Effort Routine

One option is to redesign your environment so you don't have any ice cream in your home. About fifteen years ago, Denny and I created a policy of *no ice cream in our freezer—ever.* Perhaps you can make this a policy in your home as well. That means the next time you start binge-watching a new Netflix series and that inner voice pipes up, you can't get out the entire container and grab a spoon. You'd need to put on your shoes, get in the car, drive to the store, find the ice cream, buy it, and come home. All that takes a lot of time. In the ideal scenario, the extra time might be enough to make you say, "Hey, that's too much trouble. I just wanna watch *Modern Family* reruns." This redesign can reduce —or eliminate—your evening habit of eating ice cream.

2. INCREASE THE MONEY REQUIRED

The next factor in the Ability Chain is money, and the question then becomes: How can I make this habit more expensive?

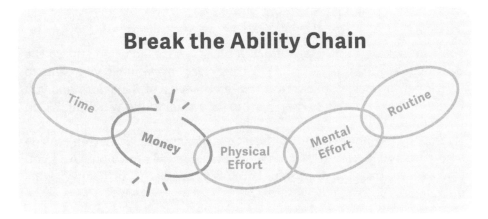

Break the Ability Chain

This is a bit tricky if you are designing habits out of your own life. You are probably not going to charge yourself ten dollars to eat a bowl of ice cream. Even so, you should consider making a habit more costly, then move on to other links in the Ability Chain if this doesn't work.

If you are designing habit change for *other* people, then money may be a viable option. Suppose you don't want your kids to play video games so much, so you charge them five dollars an hour to play. If you don't want your employees to drink so much soda, you raise the price in the vending machines. If you don't want your university staff to drive to work, you increase the price of parking on campus.

This approach should be familiar to you as there are taxes imposed on cigarettes and soda. When the price goes up on these kinds of products, people buy less and overall consumption declines. This works because charging more money decreases some people's ability to do their bad habits.

3. INCREASE THE PHYSICAL EFFORT REQUIRED

To make a habit harder to do, you can change how much physical effort it requires. The ice cream example required more time but also some physical effort. This double whammy is one reason that the "no ice cream in the freezer" policy works so well in our home.

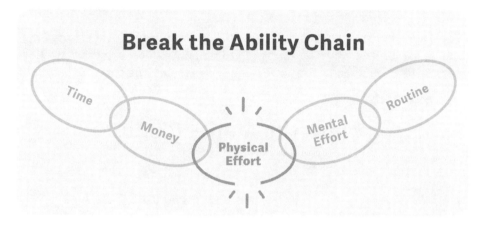

Break the Ability Chain

I don't have a desk chair in my home office in California. I removed it by design in order to make sitting all day harder to do. Yes, I can sit in my office—it's not forbidden. But I'd have to go to another room and drag a chair into my office. Too much work. For the most part, I just keep standing.

In our Maui home, we don't have a TV that's easy to watch. We have one, but it's stored away. And that's by design. In order to watch TV, I have to get it out of storage, physically carry it to a spot in the living room, and plug in the cables. Making this hard to do means that we never turn on the TV randomly. We watch only when we decide it's worth the trouble.

If you want to take this concept to the limit, you could do what I did in my twenties. When I was studying for my master's degree, my younger sister moved in with me. I didn't own a TV, but Kim brought one along. I didn't want either of us to watch lots of TV, and I couldn't imagine trying to study with the TV blaring so I came up with a plan. I bought an old exercise bike and hired an engineering student to rewire the TV so it would turn on only if the bike pedals were moving. After spending sixty-five dollars, we had our solution: the Bike-TV. If we wanted to watch, someone had to get on the bike. If the pedaling stopped, the TV would turn off. This Bike-TV worked much better than I expected. Not only did we watch less TV, we also got in better shape.

Of all the factors in the Ability Chain, physical effort is my favorite one to leverage in stopping a bad habit. You can redesign at a time when your motivation is high and you're not tempted to do the habit. Then, when your mood changes and you want ice cream or TV or wine, you realize that your habit is harder to do and maybe not worth doing at all.

4. INCREASE THE MENTAL EFFORT REQUIRED

For some habits, the best solution is to require more mental effort. This factor exploits our human tendency to be lazy, which is a crass way of saying we've evolved to conserve our energies when we can.

Break the Ability Chain

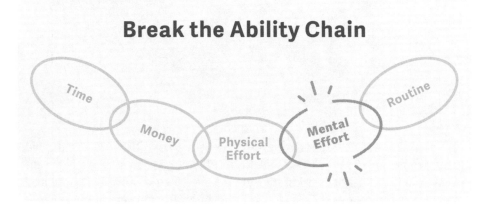

Consider how this might work with social media. If you reset your password to something complicated like 1Lik3be1ng0uT51de (translation: *I like being outside*) and don't allow your system to save it, you'd need to enter this crazy string of characters each time you want to access your feed or post something. Since true habits are behaviors we do without thinking, requiring yourself to concentrate can be a good way to stop a habit or reduce its frequency.

When people count calories or track points, as they do in Weight Watchers, they eat less in part because they have added an extra step that requires thinking.

Does this always work? No. But does logging calories require more mental effort than mindlessly eating? Yes. And that's one reason it can work.

5. MAKE THE HABIT CONFLICT WITH IMPORTANT ROUTINES

The final factor in the Ability Chain is routine. This is the subtlest of the bunch, and it is one of the hardest to apply. But it's worth considering. Look for ways to make your unwanted habit conflict with an important habit, a routine you value more than the habit you want to stop.

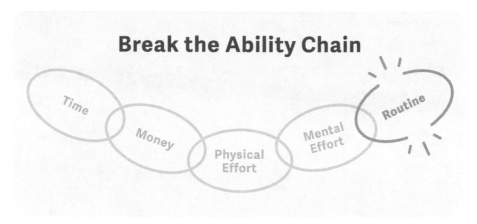

Break the Ability Chain

Surfing at daybreak became an important habit for me, and it's part of my identity now. My new surfing routine made some of my old habits harder to do in the evening because I had to be alert and ready to face the waves early in the morning. I started eating dinner earlier. I avoided blue light from screens, and I went to bed early. These were all good changes that came from creating a morning routine that conflicted with my unhealthy evening habits.

So far, we've focused on changing prompt and ability to disrupt specific unwanted habits. But if you're stuck on a habit where redesigning prompt and ability isn't enough, there's more you can do.

Next up in the masterplan: adjusting motivation.

Adjust Motivation in Order to Stop a Habit

Many people start with trying to influence motivation when they want to stop a habit. In most cases, this is a mistake. Why? Because adjusting motivation levels for Downhill Habits can be difficult (and almost impossible for Freefall Habits).

That's why you don't want to mess around with motivation if you can solve the problem by focusing on prompt or ability. You try to adjust motivation only if these previous steps didn't resolve your bad habit.

Consider this example: If you can reduce your craving to smoke, then you might be able to quit smoking entirely. Let's say you get a nicotine patch, or convince all your friends to quit at the same time, or maybe even find success with hypnosis. Doing these things is worth the old college try and sometimes they work.

OPTION A: REDUCE MOTIVATION TO STOP A HABIT

Another example: Let's say you drink too much in the evening because you are stressed from work. In this case, you might be able to change what happens during the day so you don't have such a strong motivation to drink in the evening. Perhaps you can meditate before leaving work to regain emotional balance. Or perhaps you can listen to calm music on the way home from work to reduce your stress so you aren't motivated to drink all that wine later.

Here are a range of examples that show how a behavior can reduce the motivation for a habit.

+ Going to bed earlier can reduce your motivation to hit the snooze button

- Putting on a nicotine patch can reduce your motivation for smoking

- Eating healthy food before going to a party can reduce your drive to eat bad food at the party

- Getting acupuncture once a week can reduce your motivation to use painkillers

An intriguing example of reducing motivation comes from my former student Tristan Harris, who has urged people to stop using technology mindlessly. One way to do this, he says, is to change our phone screens to show only grayscale. When you don't see vivid colors on your screen, his hypothesis goes, those Internet memes and social media posts become much less exciting and less motivating to your brain.

OPTION B: ADD A DEMOTIVATOR TO STOP A HABIT

The second approach is to add a demotivator, but I do not advocate taking this path. It might work in some cases, but I think that it often does more harm than good.

Here are some examples of behaviors that could decrease your overall level of motivation by adding a demotivator.

- Promise on Facebook that you will never drink again

- Pledge to give $1,000 to a corrupt politician if you ever smoke again

- Visualize how miserable your life would be if you continued playing video games all night

Note how these actions don't address the root cause of your behavior. You are only adding a conflicting motivation that might get you to stop doing your habit.

Motivation versus demotivation is a battle, and this tension creates stress and leads to frequent failures, making you look bad on Facebook, leaving you $1,000 short, or vividly burning into your brain how miserable your future is likely to be.

And demotivators can push us into self-criticism. If you want to cut down on calories, putting a note on your fridge that says, STOP! YOU'RE OVERWEIGHT would certainly be demotivating, but it's also demoralizing. We change best by feeling good, not by feeling bad, so make sure your attempts at demotivating behavior don't morph into guilt trips.

Creating demotivators is easy. That's probably why it's such a popular technique. But if this was a winning plan, then very few people would have bad habits. In most situations, punishing or threatening yourself is a bad way to stop a habit because the shrapnel you'll take is not worth the risk, especially when you have other options. We'll talk more about this in the next chapter when we look at the ethics of helping other people to change.

Scaling Back the Change

If the approaches we've discussed so far don't stop your specific habit, don't give up. You have more options. The next step in the masterplan is to scale back your ambitions, and you can do that in the following ways.

- Set a shorter time period for stopping habit (stop smoking for three days instead of forever)

- Do an unwanted habit for a shorter duration (watch TV for thirty minutes instead of four hours)

- Do fewer instances of the unwanted habit (checking social media once a day rather than ten times)

- Do the unwanted habit with less intensity (pace your drinking rather than downing shots)

Why does this scaling back work?

People are often conflicted about stopping a habit. Part of them wants to stop but another part doesn't. By scaling back, you won't freak out that part of yourself that wants to keep the habit. Let's say you want to quit using Facebook but you're scared of missing out on opportunities to connect with friends. Work with that tension by scaling back.

Tell yourself that you're going to stop using Facebook for only three days. Your specific habit is now a variation: You might find that abstaining for a limited time is easier than trying to stop forever. And with that, you start succeeding and become open to a bigger change. During the three days of not checking Facebook, you might discover that giving it up wasn't as difficult as you'd feared and that this change makes you feel good. Or you discover that stopping Facebook doesn't make much of a difference in your life, so ending this habit is no longer a priority. Either way, you're gaining skills and insight to make other changes easier.

If the above methods aren't working, move to the next phase of the masterplan: swapping a new habit for an old one.

PHASE #3 — DESIGN FOR SWAPPING A BEHAVIOR

Swapping out a bad behavior for a good behavior is a common approach, and many so-called experts will tell you to start here. But it's not entirely true that the only way to stop a habit is to replace it. Many habits can be *stopped* by skillfully using the steps we've just walked through. But there are some habits where swapping may indeed undo whatever Gordian knot you're working on. If you've explored the earlier master-plan phases first and nothing has worked — well, welcome to swapping land. You've arrived here systematically, which means you're focusing on the right thing and that the time and effort you invest is much more likely to pay off.

Get specific to swap a habit

As you did in phase two, you need to get specific about the habit you want to stop and the new habit that will replace it, and it's vital that you choose the new habit wisely. Otherwise, the swap won't work. If you choose something new only because you think it's "good for you," the swap is probably going to fail. If you want to stop your habit of reading political news at work, you *could* try using that time to file paperwork, but that's not likely to work. Why? Because the new habit of filing paperwork is much less motivating than reading the news and it's harder to do physically and mentally. With both motivation and ability lower for the filing habit than the news habit, the replacement habit is doomed from the start. When swapping behaviors, you've got to bring your habit creation skills to bear in order to find a new habit that is easier to do and more motivating than the old one.

In this part of the masterplan, you match yourself with a new habit by using methods from chapter 2: Create a Swarm of Behaviors, then Focus Map the results to find a Golden Behavior.

Let's say I walked through these steps for swapping out my news habit, what might success look like? For me, instead of reading news that raises my blood pressure, I could watch surfing videos. I would be motivated to do this because I love surfing and want to get more skilled. And watching videos is easier than reading. So I've found a new habit that will replace my old one. Success!

Here's a quick reminder from chapter 2 about the three criteria for matching yourself with a Golden Behavior.

+ Impact: the behavior is effective

+ Motivation: you *want* to do the behavior

+ Ability: You *can* do the behavior

Now that you've matched yourself with a Golden Behavior, what's next? Prompts.

Remapping prompts to swap a habit

Remapping the prompt means doing the new habit instead of the old one when you are prompted. Let's say you want to stop snapping at your teenage daughter. That's the old habit. The prompt is your irritation whenever she does something careless. The next time that happens, you replace snapping at her with a new habit of saying something sincerely positive.

The next night, she grabs a yogurt and forgets to shut the refrigerator door. You feel that familiar surge of annoyance, but this is now your prompt for a *new* behavior. Instead of snapping, "Shut the door, for the millionth time!" you might say, "I'm glad you're eating a healthy snack."

As you do this new habit, don't forget to celebrate and feel intense Shine. This is a new habit you're creating, so you've got to wire it in. After you praise her choice of a snack, you've got to *feel* that you just did something good for your daughter. Congratulate yourself for supporting her and being the kind of parent that you want to be. If she looks at you in total shock and smiles, then shuts the fridge door—that's a win, too. (Though maybe that's not the point!)

> **Troubleshooting Guideline: If you forget to do the new habit, then physically or mentally rehearse the swap multiple times and celebrate in order to connect the old prompt to the new habit.**

If you can't remap the old prompt to the new habit, your choice of a new behavior might not have been so "golden" after all. That's okay. You won't always nail it the first time. Maybe you have an unusually steep Downhill Habit that you're trying to replace. Perhaps you can't make the old habit harder to do or you can't make it less motivating. If this is the case, a good next step is to go back and select another new habit to swap in.

If you're still having trouble, then move on to the next step.

Adjusting both ability and motivation to swap a habit

If remapping the prompt doesn't stop your old habit, then you arrive at this step. At this point, you can be pretty sure that your old habit is either more motivating or easier to do than the new habit—or both. Mapping the bad habit and the new habit to the Behavior Model helps you see what's going on. The old habit is farther above the Action Line, which means the old habit is more compelling to you, and so you will keep doing it instead of the new habit.

To change that, you have four options as shown in the next graphic.

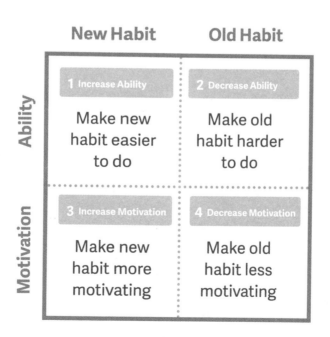

Focusing your energies on any of the boxes will help you make the swap, but if you make all four adjustments, you will be even more successful in swapping your new habit for the old one. The next graphic shows the ideal scenario.

However, not all the adjustments will work. You may not be able to reduce motivation for your old habit. That's okay. As long as you can make the old habit harder to do and the new habit easy to do and motivating, you will probably succeed in making the habit swap.

If Nothing So Far Has Worked ...

Don't despair. You still have options. This process is about finding what works for you. It's like shopping for new shoes. The first pair of shoes you try on looked good on the shelf, but when you put them on your feet, they don't fit right. Don't force the fit, and don't blame yourself or give up. Find another pair of shoes to try on instead.

And here are some other options to try.

+ *Option A:* Find a better new habit to swap in and follow the steps again.

+ *Option B:* Try the swap in a limited way. See how it goes for three days, then decide what to do next.

+ *Option C:* Return to phase one of the masterplan and practice other new habits to build your skills and confidence and shift your identity. Address this persistent bad habit later.

This Process Is a Skill

There is no single technique that works for stopping all habits. But now there is a process, and you can start using my Behavior Design Masterplan immediately. And you will get better with practice. You will become more proficient at pinpointing pivotal issues and resolving problems.

You might have a bad habit of always being late. Or perhaps you have a bad habit of procrastinating. These are special cases because those bad habits are created by behaviors you are *not* doing. When you are dealing with habits of omission or avoidance, you need to get behaviors to happen rather than stopping them. For these types of bad habits, the skilled Habiteer will focus on phase one and loop back to create new habits until the problem is resolved.

This process is a skill. When you find what works for you, future challenges will be easier to tackle. So keep going.

With each successful result, revisit your Swarm of Behaviors diagram to find another specific habit to unwind. This is how you unravel the unwanted general habit in a steady, predictable, and reliable way.

You'll find patterns like I did when I discovered that for me it's often most effective to make the unwanted habit physically hard. And you'll recognize situations that make a bad habit easier to do and you'll learn how to avoid those.

You will also find people in your life who make bad habits easier to do. In some approaches to behavior change, those people are called enablers. They are not to be underestimated! I'll never forget a woman I'll call Martha—someone I met when I was doing Weight Watchers a few years ago (partly because I was training their product team and partly because I wanted to lose some weight). Martha had been doing Weight Watchers for a number of years with varied success. She'd lose a few pounds here, gain a few pounds there, but overall, she couldn't seem to gain any traction. One day in our group meeting, someone brought up the topic of food temptations created by other people. Nearly everyone had a story about birthday cakes in the break room or a coworker who always invited you to eat half of her cookie, and Martha shared a story from her week. During football season, her family gathered every Sunday to watch the games on TV, and her sister-in-law would make cheese dip and her husband would order pizza. This was a big hurdle for Martha.

She explained how she'd eaten a big healthy meal before the game last Sunday so she wouldn't be tempted. She was happily sitting on the couch with her son, cheering on their favorite team. The pizza arrived at halftime, and her husband grabbed a big slice. As he walked by her, he waved it under her nose, and said, "Oh, Martha, doesn't that smell good?" Everyone laughed. Everyone but Martha, that is. She had a good sense of humor about his jokes, but this time she was mad. It wasn't the first time he'd teased her by pressuring her to eat whatever he was having. Sometimes she caved, sometimes she didn't. She thought that the pizza incident felt different because it embarrassed her in front of the rest of the family. She told us that her husband slept on the couch for a few days—but more important, it made her realize that he had been undermining her success with Weight Watchers by enabling her bad habits.

You can't always redesign every single aspect of your world. You can't redesign a movie theater so it doesn't sell soda, and you can't redesign a bar so it doesn't offer cheap drinks during happy hour. And you probably can't redesign your husband or colleagues so they stop offering you sugary snacks. (Wait. Maybe you can. But that's another chapter.) But with the Behavior Design approach, there are multiple ways to loosen every knot. While every bad habit is unique, the approach to untangling them is the same—a concrete set of steps and techniques that are customizable to your specific situation. No guesswork needed—just a little curiosity and plenty of Shine.

The Beauty of Disruption

In the last chapter, we talked about the joy that comes with watching the natural growth and effects of the positive habits you create. I promise that you'll be equally happy when you see the bad habits you've uprooted from your life lying on the compost pile. And while that's a wonderful thing, what's even more awe-inspiring (to me, at least) is what crops up in the new spaces that you've created in your life. When you get rid of unwanted habits, what rises to fill that space could be more time to devote to a passion project, greater productivity at work, the deepening of a relationship, or the expansion of a new identity. Some of what fills that space you will choose, and some of it will come from those around you.

Here's a beautiful example.

A month after Juni untangled her sugar habit, she heard a sound filtering through a window from outside one afternoon. When she went to investigate, she discovered her eleven-year-old son, Elijah, sitting outside in the sun singing a song he had just made up about dolphins. Autistic and quiet, he had never sung before, at least not that she'd heard. When he looked up at her in the doorway, he smiled. As Juni walked over to join him, she had to hold back tears. She realized that had this occurred six months earlier she would have been sleeping on the couch crashed out from a day fueled by sugar. She would have missed hearing her son's beautiful voice.

She could now sit beside him and encourage him to sing more, asking questions and telling him about how she used to sing, too.

When she told her husband how surprised she was at the change in their son, he reminded her that they had all changed in the last few months. It wasn't a coincidence that her son had started singing, or that her husband had given up his lifelong soda habit. They had seen how much she was changing, how happy she was, and were inspired to change with her. Elijah flourished with more structure and attention, and idolized his mom. Juni had gone from celebrating a no-sugar meal to crossing the finish line at her second marathon in Austin, Texas. Everyone in her life, from her colleagues at work to her family and friends, were impacted in ways small and large by the changes she had made.

This was a gift and a side effect of all Juni's hard work—one she had never imagined.

Behavior Design is not a solitary pursuit. Each behavior that we design, each change that we make, is another drop in the pond that ripples out. We shape our families, communities, and societies through our actions. And they shape us. The habits we create and perpetuate *matter*. This book has focused largely on how our behaviors matter to the individual, but that's only part of the story. It's not just about losing ten pounds or putting the phone down during dinner. Behavior Design is about creating change and venturing in the direction of our best selves. Yes, it's for us. But it's also for the people we love and the world we hope to create.

That's why the next chapter may be the most important of all. It's where we learn what it really means to change *together*.

Tiny Exercises to Practice Stopping and Swapping

You can do the exercises below in any order.

EXERCISE #1: PRACTICE CREATING A SWARM OF BEHAVIORS FOR STOPPING A BAD HABIT

Pick a bad habit you don't have. Why? Because the exercise will be less threatening and you'll probably learn more.

Step 1: Pretend you are someone else who has a bad habit.

Step 2: Draw the Swarm of Behaviors graphic or download the template from TinyHabits.com/resources.

Step 3: Write down this person's general bad habit inside the cloud.

Step 4: Write down at least ten specific habits around the cloud. This will require some imagination.

Step 5: Look over your Swarm of Behaviors and pick two or three of the easiest specific habits to resolve.

Note: By creating an imaginary Swarm of Behaviors, you'll build your skills. And when you apply this approach to a real challenge in your life, you will be more confident, less fearful, and more efficient.

EXERCISE #2: PRACTICE REMOVING A PROMPT FOR ONE DAY

Step 1: Pick a social media or sports app you use often.

Step 2: Go into the settings and turn off the notifications for that app.

Step 3: Watch what happens (and doesn't happen) over the course of twenty-four hours.

Note: If you find your life is better without the notifications, leave them off. If it's worse, turn them back on. In any case, you've learned something.

EXERCISE #3: PRACTICE SWAPPING A HABIT AND CELEBRATING TO MAKE IT STICK

Step 1: Find a container that can serve as a temporary trash bin.

Step 2: Set the new bin in your workspace in a different spot from the bin you typically use.

Step 3: Tell yourself to use the new bin instead of the usual bin.

Step 4: When prompted to discard or recycle something, use the new bin, not the old one. In the beginning, you probably won't completely switch to using the new bin. To make the shift happen faster, go to step 5.

Step 5: Rehearse using the new bin seven to ten times and include a celebration each time. Feel Shine.

Step 6: As you go back to work, observe what happens with your new habit. Noticing how your habit shifts—what it feels like to swap a habit—is the point of this exercise.

Note: If you forget to use the new bin, do more rehearsals of the new habit with celebrations. (After a few days of practicing your habit swap, go back to your old habit if you want to.)

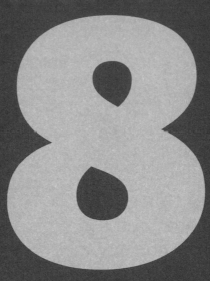

CHAPTER

8

HOW WE
CHANGE
TOGETHER

Mike and Carla felt trapped.

Their son was twenty-one, living at home, and struggling to meet even the smallest demands of adulthood. After Chris bombed out of university at eighteen, they figured he would find a job or get back on track with school. But he didn't. Despite all their financial and emotional support, Chris never seemed to get out of his own way. Though he had a part-time job, his inability to do basic things like pick up after himself, pay his bills, and get along with his younger brother created a tension that was suffocating everyone in the house.

The longer Chris stayed at home, the worse Mike's relationship with him got. Chris was aloof and distant at best, and in the worst of times, he lashed out in anger. Attempting to get Chris to clean up or do his dishes would set off a weeklong cascade of nagging and outbursts as predictable as they were infuriating. Mike would start off with a simple request that Chris tidy his room, which got ignored for days. He'd ask again, a bit more demanding. His son would say something to the effect of *Yeah, yeah, I'll do it.* But he never did.

Unfortunately, Mike's home office was right next to Chris's bedroom so Mike frequently saw the utter chaos in his son's room and thought, *My son doesn't listen to me; he doesn't respect the space he's in or appreciate what I do for him. He doesn't care.* Then Mike would read Chris the riot act and demand that he live by the house rules, find a better job, respect their belongings, and pay his bills on time so they didn't have to float him even bigger loans to pay the late fees. After this, Chris would storm off and ultimately *not* clean his room (or do anything else he was asked). He'd put on his headphones and play video games with people halfway across the world instead.

Mike and Chris wouldn't exchange more than a few words for days, sometimes weeks. An undercurrent of hostility and disappointment swirled around every interaction. And Mike began wishing that he didn't work from home. And when Mike's other son was prompted to clean his room, he would respond, "Why do I have to? Chris doesn't."

That was usually when Mike would put on his running shoes, burst out the front door at a full sprint, and fantasize about never coming back.

When they did manage to get Chris to join the family for dinner, Mike looked at his son across the table and felt a desperate sadness. And no small amount of guilt. Chris had been born when Mike and Carla were in their first year of university. They didn't know what the heck they were doing, and he had basically grown up alongside them. Chris was always a special kid. He understood everything like an adult and joined their conversations. Chris went to classes, dinner parties, and on road trips with Mike and Carla. They felt lucky that he was such a bright little guy. Yet he'd have these angry outbursts that perplexed them even back then, and he'd often act out or be unable to control himself.

Chris did predictably well in school. All he had to do was show up, which ultimately worked against him in other areas. Because what Chris didn't learn was a set of skills as necessary as math and English. Mike had tried to tell Chris that life was about more than grades, that it was about interacting with others, having a work ethic, showing up reliably, and being accountable—all things that Chris struggled with mightily.

Chris's intellectual capacity had always outstripped his emotional capability. It took several years of family therapy for Mike to realize that Chris felt things deeply and didn't have the right tools to deal with that. Even though Mike knew Chris's coldness and distance were defense mechanisms, they still hurt—partly because Mike wanted to be close to his son and partly because Mike felt he had failed as a father to help Chris manage his emotions better.

And now look where they were.

Out of options.

Living at a cool distance in painful tension.

Mike and Carla's marriage was becoming increasingly strained. They had been on the same page at first. They had gone to counseling, tried incentives, and come up with an elaborate plan based on books they had read, but nothing had worked. And now they were at odds about what to do next. Should they kick him out? Carla was wavering, but Mike kept reminding her what had happened in high school when they had backed off—Chris had started working for the mob. Literally. His all-boys private school was populated by an unusually high number of mafioso progeny, so when Chris became a "messenger" for a friend's father, Mike knew exactly what was going on. He and Carla pulled Chris out of that school, but now they were afraid that Chris would fall back on what was easy (and lucrative). That's what made Mike and Carla feel trapped— you can't punish a twenty-one-year-old; you can only kick him out—and if you don't feel as if you can do that, what option is left? How do you get your adult son to help himself? To change? Chris was a good person, funny and insightful, and Mike knew that his son could do something special with his life. He also knew that Chris didn't *want* to be living with his parents. He wanted his own place, his own life — he just didn't know how to get there.

Mike racked his brain, and it made him crazy that he couldn't find a solution. He was a capable guy, after all. No matter how much he might be failing at home, Mike was thriving at work. He was a successful strategist who had helped grow his small nutrition company into an industry leader. He specialized in solving big challenges in innovative ways, and he was always looking to improve, and Mike eventually found his way to my Behavior Design Boot Camp.

Mike was one of those people who "gets it" immediately. He was one of those systems thinkers who are fast at plugging in new knowledge to solve old challenges. I assumed Mike's eagerness to learn the intricacies of Behavior Design was about increasing his professional excellence. But I found out later that the excited energy I'd felt from him was the realization that he could finally help Chris. The Behavior Model made total sense to Mike — many behaviors of Chris's were suddenly explicable, and he saw exactly why his own interventions hadn't been working. Mike realized that he needed to shift his focus from motivation to ability. Motivation, especially in a teenager, is not dependable. He also saw that giving his son a memorable, immediate prompt would be far more effective than the abstract nagging he'd been using.

Excited to try out what he'd learned and mindful of the importance of starting tiny, Mike decided to tackle the coffee maker problem first. This was a seemingly small domestic battle, but one that was a daily source of aggravation. Mike had bought a nice coffee maker for himself. He had done a lot of research and took pride in owning it, so he liked to keep it clean and in good working order — which meant that after each use the fancy filter needed to be rinsed so it wouldn't gum up the works. Chris *never* remembered to do this. Mike laughs about it now, but it was one of those things that drove him nuts. He'd come downstairs to make his second cup and discover that Chris had left his steaming grounds in the machine. After taking care of what his grown-up son wouldn't, Mike would pass Chris's room on the way to his office and make a snappish comment to the effect of *How many times do I have to ask you to clean the filter?* or *If you can't treat my stuff with respect, you can't use it.*

Chris would give him an eye roll or a snarky reply, an interaction that started the day off on the wrong foot and thrust them into a corrosive cycle of frustration and resentment.

But equipped with important Behavior Design tools, Mike broke this problem down. His aspiration was clear — he wanted Chris to respect his stuff. In this case, the specific behavior was taking care of the coffee maker. So Mike asked the Breakthrough Question: *How can I make this easier to do?* When he thought about it, what he wanted Chris to do was a three-step process. Take the coffee filter out, clean it, then put it back. Asking Chris to do all of this at once clearly wasn't working, so Mike decided to make the task easier by breaking it down and asking his son to do only the first specific step.

"Hey, Chris, next time you use the coffee maker, could you take the filter out and put it on the counter?"

Chris gave him a funny look. "Sure."

The next morning Mike came downstairs for his caffeine injection and grinned. The coffee filter was on the counter. Tipped on its side and spilling some grounds, but it was there. Mike felt a surge of pride. As he walked upstairs with his coffee, he remembered my maxim: *Help people feel successful.*

"Hey, Chris, thanks for putting the filter on the counter. That means a lot to me."

Chris flashed him the dad-you-are-so-weird look he'd perfected in eighth grade. "No big deal."

The filter was on the counter again the next day. This blew Mike's mind—he hadn't even reminded Chris to do it. Mike said a quick thank-you to Chris before resuming work. Chris continued to do this small task, and Mike started to believe that his approach was working—that it wasn't a fluke. After a couple of weeks, Mike asked Chris to rinse the filter before putting it on the counter, and Chris agreed to do this because taking the filter out had turned out to be a breeze and it had made his father oddly happy.

A week later there was no filter on the counter, and Mike's heart sank —Chris's not following through was familiar territory. But he reminded himself that his son was still learning this habit, and he resolved not to nag Chris. But when Mike removed the filter, it was clean. Chris had removed it, cleaned it, *and* replaced it without being asked.

Mike let out a quiet *Woo-hoo!*

He felt like he had gotten an unexpected promotion or a great birth-day present, which might seem totally out of proportion to the small task that his grown-up son had completed, but as Mike told me later, it wasn't about the coffee filter—it was about hope. This was the first time in years that Mike felt hopeful about his relationship with Chris. The tenor of their mornings had totally changed. Instead of exchanging harsh words with his son before work, Mike got to feel proud. He got to build his kid up instead of nagging him or fighting. He finally felt like a good dad—someone who could help a person he loves be happier and learn how to live with others in harmony.

What started with a coffee filter soon extended to all sorts of behaviors that were contentious. Mike and Carla saw that Chris's anger and frustration were expressions of his being overwhelmed. When they asked him to do big things like clean his room or pay his bills on time, Chris didn't know where to start, and he was ashamed and resentful, and felt incapable. But when they broke down specific things into tiny behaviors and asked questions such as "Could you put your used towel in the hamper?" or "Could you put your dinner dish in the sink?" Chris got a toehold on the larger task. By feeling successful at those smaller tasks, he gained the confidence to do more. Mike and Carla were with him the whole way, gently celebrating his wins. Not only did this make Chris feel good, it made *them* feel good. No one wants to nag their kids or feel disappointed; we *want* to celebrate them. This is surprisingly easy to achieve when you keep the behavior tiny and set someone up to feel successful.

I recently talked to Mike about his business, but he was more excited to talk about the changes at home. Chris is still living there, but he has two part-time jobs and is saving up for a deposit on an apartment. Their relationship is the best it's been since Chris was little. The tension balloon has popped, and they all feel more connected. Chris shows up at meals, and he laughs more and confides in them. His little brother can no longer use Chris as an excuse not to do his own chores, so the level of nagging overall is diminished. Chris feels better understood, and his parents feel more capable of helping him navigate life. On some days, Mike looks around and can't believe that they've achieved a harmony that had once seemed so far out of reach.

And then there is this: Mike received a birthday gift from Chris for the first time in years (a couple of days late, but who's counting). He unwrapped three vinyl records to add to his soul collection: Stevie Wonder, Ray Charles, and James Brown. Mike gathered his son in a bear hug, thanking him and trying to choke back tears.

Chris smiled. "No big deal, Dad."

Designing for Group Change

We all know that social dynamics are powerful drivers of behavior. The effects are all around us: how we act watching a football game, how we talk about politics, how we treat one another online or in person. Since humans have pretty much always lived in communities, social influences have always been with us. But with social media magnifying and multiplying those influences, our lives have become increasingly connected. That's why it's more important than ever to think deeply about how those social forces are shaping our individual and collective behavior, and ultimately impacting *all* life on planet Earth.

What you've learned in this book gives you the power to defend yourself against undermining influences and design new habits that lead to a more harmonious, healthy, and meaningful life for everyone around you.

You now can figure out what is shaping the habits you don't want, including those created by social pressure. Maybe your family can't eat together without everyone looking at their phones. Maybe your workplace is so competitive that no one takes a vacation day. Maybe your book club is more of a wine club. The habits and norms that exist in any group can feel even more entrenched than individual habits. But it's important to remember that we can *change together*.

Now that you know how behavior works, you can identify what's underpinning those habits you want or don't want. And you have three main approaches when it comes to changing group behavior. You can design a change in your own behavior to distance yourself from a group's negative influences. You can work together with others to design a change in your collective behavior. Or you can design a change for others that will benefit them—just as Mike did with Chris. The last two approaches are what this chapter is about, and we'll talk more about what each means and how we can tweak the process to suit the situation.

By using Tiny Habits and Behavior Design, you can be a force for good in the lives of others. It takes only one skilled and caring individual (you!) to transform a group, but I would suggest that you not start by trying to change your entire country even though with Behavior Design you could transform culture. Build your change skills and begin closer to home instead—a work team or your family. I've long advocated that we view the household—not the individual—as the unit of change. So as behavior designers, we should design products and services to help everyone in a household change together.

Before Mike helped Chris gain traction in his daily habits, he did a good job of changing his own behavior. Mike modified what he asked Chris to do and how he asked him to do it, changing his tone and posture from one of frustration and preordained defeat to one of empowerment and support. The success he found had an outsize effect not only on Chris's behavior but also on his own. We live and work with others, and every change has a general effect on everyone for better or worse. We are always changing together whether we design for it or not.

But I don't think you should leave changes to chance. Design for your future deliberately and efficiently so things change *for the better* in every part of your life.

When you set out to change your family, work team, or community group, you ideally should get total cooperation and support. But that's not likely to happen. When I first started studying changing together as a year-long project in my Stanford research lab, I naively assumed that everyone had a household like mine. Whenever my partner or I wanted to change something, such as how we eat or use technology, we would support each other. When I was a child, my mom dramatically changed our eating habits to help my younger sister with her learning disabilities. We hated giving up Wonder Bread (no fiber) and Tang (full of sugar), but we did it as a family.

As I shared these personal examples with researchers in my Stanford lab, they were quick to come up with their own examples that made the opposite point. I heard about one parent who replied to his son's desire to meditate with "You're going through another phase. Let me know when this one is over." I heard from another lab member that her spouse had told her, "Hey, honey. Can we hold off on your little plan until after the kids are back in school?" From these stories, I saw that members of households can undermine you as well as support your aspirations.

If you are having trouble effecting change in your household, the principles of Behavior Design can help. One way to break through is to apply my Maxim #1: *Help people do what they already want to do.* What does your spouse already want to achieve? What aspirations does your work team have right now? (If you don't know, ask them!) Then help them achieve those aspirations.

Maybe your spouse doesn't want to eat healthier food right now, but he wants a tidier house. Start there. Remember this truth: *Change leads to change.* You start people on the path to change from the place they want to begin. As they build confidence and skills, they will open up to other types of changes, I promise. Don't give up on changing how your family eats, but maybe your starting point isn't what you'd thought. Perhaps you start by leading change for a tidier home, or any aspiration that you and your spouse share. Chances are your spouse will be energized by the positive changes and start coming up with habits of his or her own that are more aligned with what you wanted. *Hey, I was thinking that maybe we should stop drinking so much soda.*

If you can't be the leader of change, don't give up. Behavior Design and Tiny Habits are methods for changing together in any situation for any group. They offer a workable framework even if you're not given the authority or support you need. After all, every group situation is unique—and group change, like individual change, is most successfully approached with a process, not a prescription.

The Ethics of Changing Others

A quick word on "changing others"—a concept that can make people feel a little nervous. First of all, we have to understand that we are influencing the behavior of others all the time, often without realizing it—that's the nature of living in communities—and no one frets too much about that.

People often try to help a family member with a new eating program or a coworker with productivity issues. But if you challenge people to do something very difficult, they will probably fail, and this failure makes change harder in the future. My view is that the most ethical approach is to be mindful of our influence on others while using the best possible methods to help them.

When you use Behavior Design and Tiny Habits, you can be confident you're setting people up to succeed.

When supporting other people in the change process, let my two maxims be your guide.

#1 Help people do what they already want to do.
#2 Help people feel successful.

If you are helping a spouse, a work colleague, your boss, your customers, or your kids do what they aspire to do, you're likely on solid ethical ground. And it's almost never a bad thing to help someone feel successful. Once you feel good about the change you want to help others implement, you're ready to jump in.

How to Change Together

Earlier I specified two ways to change together that I'll discuss in this chapter. I want to make these clear and memorable by giving them fun names. You could approach a group change either as the Ringleader or the Ninja.

THE RINGLEADER

As the Ringleader, you take the lead in helping your group change by sharing what you have learned about Tiny Habits and Behavior Design and acting together. This happens a lot in families or informally at work. You're in the break room, talking about how to solve some intractable problem, and it hits you—*we need to do a Swarm of Behaviors and a Focus Map!* You explain the methods to colleagues, and the next day you all come to the table with the problem mapped out and ideas about creating change. Another way to be the Ringleader is to help others learn Tiny Habits and Behavior Design. Sharing this book is a simple and effective way to do that.

Or you could take a stealthier approach.

THE NINJA

As the Ninja, you sneak Behavior Design in subtly. Others in your family or group don't even have to know you're doing it. This was Mike's approach with his son and the coffee maker. He didn't *tell* Chris he was breaking down the steps and making them easier to do or that he was intentionally celebrating his wins—but it worked nonetheless. Using Behavior Design techniques like the Swarm of Behaviors or making a behavior easier can be used ad hoc to help others change—no need to make an announcement.

Whether you're the Ringleader or the Ninja, you flow through the same steps outlined in this chart.

Design Process for Group Change

While the methods you use to create change in a group are essentially the same as those for an individual, how you put those methods into practice can differ.

1. CLARIFY YOUR ASPIRATION TOGETHER

Behavior Design always begins with getting clear on your aspiration. This is your first step if you are designing a product, designing habits for yourself, or helping a group change together.

The Ringleader

If you're helping your family change how they eat, you can propose an aspiration and see if people buy in by asking, "As a family we want to eat more fresh fruits and vegetables. Is that a good description of what we hope to achieve?"

On a business project, you might be given an outcome to achieve —increase sales by 20 percent next year—or you might be given a less specific aspiration—reduce employee stress. And there you have your starting point. As the Ringleader, get your team clear on what you all hope to achieve and make sure everyone understands it in the same way.

The Ninja

You don't need to say you're using Behavior Design to get the clarity you need. You can start right off with the objective.

"Just to clarify, we're designing for X, right?"

"Yes, that's correct," someone replies.

"Okay, great! Just wanted to be on the same page. Thanks!"

This Ninja move may seem like a no-brainer, but you will be doing everyone a favor by making the objective clear.

2. EXPLORE BEHAVIOR OPTIONS TOGETHER

Once the aspiration is clear, then you explore behavior options.

The Ringleader

When leading a group in Behavior Design, you can either run a session of Magic Wanding, which I explained in chapter 2, or you can use the Swarm of Behaviors worksheet and ask people to fill in the boxes with different behaviors that will lead to the aspiration.

I find that Magic Wanding produces a broader range of behaviors in a carefully guided small group. But if you have more than twenty people, the moderating gets unwieldy. For large groups, hand out the worksheet for the Swarm of Behaviors. With minimal instructions, your family, your work group, or your entire company—I've done this with more than a thousand people at the same time—can succeed in finding behaviors to fill in the swarm. Your choice of method depends on your group and your leadership style.

The Ninja

You can Magic Wand on the sly by asking questions like these at the right moments.

+ What do you want to happen? If we had magical powers, who would do what?

+ Imagine we could get anyone to do anything. What's the ideal action we would get them to take?

Consider this scenario of Ninja Behavior Design: You are in a meeting about your local parks. You're a volunteer. The director wants more people to use the parks. You recognize this as her aspiration.

To help the meeting succeed, you affirm her aspiration then use the Magic Wand questions outlined earlier.

When you invite your team to think in this way, the meeting will get more interesting for everyone because you've done two things. You've helped everyone go beyond the abstract by focusing the meeting on a specific objective. And you've helped everyone see many potential solutions. As a result, the group won't settle on the first idea.

Thanks to your Ninja use of Magic Wanding, what felt like an intractable problem five minutes ago now feels solvable.

3. MATCH YOUR GROUP WITH GOLDEN BEHAVIORS

Once you have a big set of potential behaviors, you are ready to figure out which ones you will turn into realities. As I explained in chapter 2, you want to match people with behaviors that will have an impact, are easy to do, and are motivating. Ideally, the behaviors you select will have all three characteristics. These are your Golden Behaviors.

The best way to match your team with Golden Behaviors is with the Focus Mapping method. You can do this as a group. Collaborating as a family or a work team will give you the benefit of many brains. And when you reach consensus during the Focus Mapping process, your group will be primed to support one another as you turn the Golden Behaviors into realities. Of all the methods in Behavior Design, Focus Mapping as a group is my favorite.

The Ringleader

I've taught hundreds of teams how to use the Focus Mapping method to pinpoint the Golden Behaviors for their projects or their own self-improvement.

Focus Mapping as a group uses the same overall framework that I described in chapter 2, but there are some important additions.

As with individual Focus Maps, you begin with a set of behaviors written on cards. The behaviors written on these cards come from Magic Wanding or the Swarm of Behaviors worksheet.

As the Ringleader, explain that there are various rounds in the Focus Map and that in round one they will be placing each card along a vertical axis, putting behaviors with a high impact toward the top of the spectrum and behaviors that won't have impact toward the bottom.

Have your team members take turns putting a card onto the Focus Map until all the cards are placed. Then have people take turns re-sorting the cards up or down without having them explain why they moved a card. On each turn someone can move one card. They just read the card and move it. Sometimes a card will get moved multiple times when people disagree on where it should be placed. That's normal. (Don't worry. Just keep the process moving.)

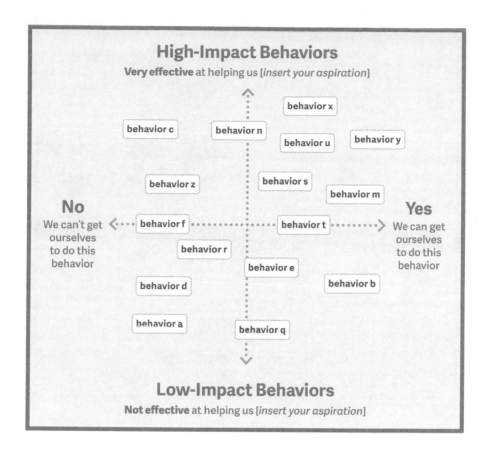

High-Impact Behaviors

Very effective at helping us [*insert your aspiration*]

behavior x

behavior c   behavior n   behavior y

behavior u

behavior z   behavior s

behavior m

No
We can't get
ourselves
to do this
behavior   behavior f   behavior t   **Yes**
We can get
ourselves
to do this
behavior

behavior r

behavior e

behavior d   behavior b

behavior a

behavior q

Low-Impact Behaviors

Not effective at helping us [*insert your aspiration*]

Keep going until everyone is happy with the arrangement of the cards. When you have consensus, you're done with round one.

In round two, your team will take turns sliding cards side to side along the feasibility dimension. Explain that they should put behaviors that they think they could get themselves to do toward the right and behaviors that they don't think they can get themselves to do toward the left.

Have your group take turns, and one by one people can move the cards side to side until everyone is happy with the arrangement.

At this point, after some brief comments and adjustment of the behavior items, you will find your Golden Behaviors in the upper right-hand corner of the landscape. Lead your team in a discussion of how many Golden Behaviors you want to make into a reality. You might pick only one or two. (Picking more than five is rather ambitious.)

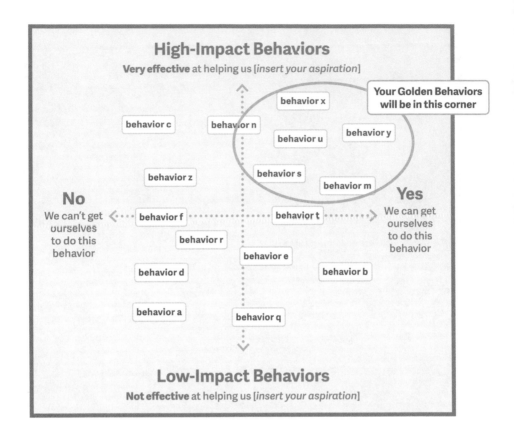

The surprise for most teams is how quickly and easily they reach a consensus about which behaviors to focus on and which to forget about for now. What might have been a long and tense process gets streamlined into a session the Ringleader can run in about thirty minutes. And everyone walks away happy about the result in most cases. (To get more guidance on running a group Focus Mapping session, see my instructions at FocusMap.info.)

Note: If the Golden Behavior your group comes up with is a habit, then go into Tiny Habits mode in the next steps. But not every Golden Behavior will be a habit. Some will be one-time behaviors.

The Ninja

Let's say you're in the middle of a family discussion or a company meeting and you need to get your team focused and aligned, but you can't lead an official Focus Mapping session.

In that case, I have a Ninja solution for you. After your group suggests different ideas, perhaps prompted by your Ninja Magic Wanding, then you can ask, *Which option can we realistically get ourselves to do?*

This question combines the motivation and ability components of my Behavior Model, and it's the fastest way to find behaviors that may well be Golden.

4. START TINY BY MAKING THE GOLDEN BEHAVIOR EASY TO DO

If the Golden Behavior for the group is intended to be an ongoing habit, go into Tiny Habits mode and make the behavior as simple to do as possible. But don't forget that one-time behaviors like everyone attending a training seminar should also be made as easy as possible.

The Ringleader

Ask your group what is making the desired behavior (or habit) hard to do and how they can make this behavior (or habit) easy to do. Let's suppose that two weeks ago you started a new effort with your project team. As the manager, you want each person to e-mail you once a day and share the biggest project roadblock they are facing at that moment. It could be that the legal department hasn't reviewed the new agreement, or there's not enough in the budget to do quality user research, or the Internet keeps going down. Whatever. As a manager, you want to know the roadblocks so you can resolve them and help each person move forward efficiently. This sounded like a great plan, and your team seemed enthusiastic, but the results were not good over the last two weeks. Time to ask the Discovery Question.

At the next project meeting, you ask your team about the roadblock e-mail: What is making this daily routine hard to do?

You can get even more specific, asking about each link in the Ability Chain: Do you have enough time? Money? Mental capacity? Physical capacity? Does this conflict with our existing routines? By working together this way, your group can help you—and each other—see the weak links. As it turns out, it's not actually a time issue. Instead, most people on the team don't know how to think about roadblocks. And with that insight, you realize it's a mental capacity issue (but you don't say that out loud!). You have options: You can make this daily routine easier by skilling your team up in identifying roadblocks. Or perhaps you give them a checklist that walks them through various options: *project clarity, legal issues, budget constraints, collaboration issues, technology problems.* Once addressed, this weak link in the Ability Chain can become a strong link, helping everyone succeed more often with the daily roadblock e-mails.

Side note: When writing this book, I wanted to share a lot more about how to use Behavior Design for business success, but that would make my book too long. Even so, I want to offer you my special chapter on Tiny Habits for Business Success, which you can get for free by going to TinyHabits.com/business.

The Ninja

Suppose you want to get your spouse to exercise with you every day, and he's not quite on board. Ask him a version of the Discovery Question: *What do you think makes it hard to exercise every day?*

If your spouse is like most people, he will say, "I don't have the time." As a skilled Ninja, you realize that time may or may not be the real issue. But assume it is, and ask: *If you could find a way to exercise with me just ten minutes each day, do you think you could do it?* If he says yes, find that ten-minute exercise. However, he might come up with another issue: *I am just too tired to work out.*

And there you have it: The problem isn't time; it's physical effort. Then suggest exercises that require less exertion, like dancing to a disco song each morning or doing a simple yoga move. And don't forget to redesign the environment so exercising is easier for him — set out the yoga mat before you go to bed. Don't worry too much about the health benefits of just one sun salutation because getting someone started on a healthy habit — no matter how tiny — is a big deal. If your spouse feels successful doing one sun salutation, he will naturally expand his exercise habit.

In Ninja mode, you informally yet systematically figure out what makes a behavior hard for someone to do, then you take steps to strengthen those weak links.

Good job, Ninja.

5. FIND A WAY TO PROMPT THE GOLDEN BEHAVIOR

You've read chapter 4, so you know there are three types of prompts: Person Prompts, Context Prompts, and Action Prompts. In this step, you need to figure out which will reliably work for your group.

The Ringleader

If you're helping your group create a habit, use the Tiny Habits approach first and ask your group: *Where might this habit fit naturally in your daily routine?* If you're helping your team e-mail you each day with their number one roadblock, then ask them: *What existing routine can remind you to do this new habit?*

The group can explore options together, but each person can pick their own Anchor. The recipe for some may end up looking like this: *After I return from my lunch break, I will get out my checklist on road-blocks and write a quick e-mail.*

My Recipe — Tiny Habits Method

After I . . .	I will . . .	To wire the habit into my brain, I will immediately:
return from my	_get out my checklist_	
lunch break,	_on roadblocks and_	☺
	write a quick e-mail.	
Anchor Moment	**Tiny B**ehavior	**C**elebration
An existing routine in your life that will remind you to do the Tiny Behavior (your new habit).	The new habit you want but you scale it back to be super tiny—and super easy.	Something you do to create a positive feeling inside of yourself (the feeling is called Shine).

As you know, there are other ways to prompt a behavior. You could have the new intern walk around and remind people to send you the e-mail. But that's not a great solution for the long term. Maybe you send a daily e-mail reminder? Yes, that could work, but it's not as elegant as using an existing routine as a prompt.

The Ninja

The Ninja's approach to this step is the same as the Ringleader's. If that doesn't work, you could get less elegant, and ask, "What do you think would be a good reminder for this?"

I'm a fan of finding what works and then scaling that approach. Let's go back to the roadblock e-mail habit. After the task has been made easy to do, see what happens. After you discover who is succeeding on this task, ask them what prompts them to do the behavior. They *will* have a prompt (even if they don't recognize it). When you find a successful pattern, suggest that everyone use the same prompt.

Let's suppose that you walk around and talk with ten of your teammates who are trying to send you the roadblock e-mail. Five are succeeding. You learn that four of the five are setting the checklist card on their keyboards before they leave for lunch. The checklist then reminds them to write the e-mail when they return from lunch. So the recipe then becomes something like this: *After I pick up my wallet to go to lunch, I will put my roadblock checklist on my keyboard.* You share this technique with everyone. You've found what works and scaled it to the rest of your team.

6. CELEBRATE SUCCESS
TO WIRE IN THE HABIT

This step applies only if you want to create a habit in your group. If your solution is a one-time behavior or decision, you can skip this step.

The Ringleader

One of my hopes for this book is to change how leaders interact with their teams, how parents interact with their children, and how doctors interact with their patients. When you understand one of my key points —that people change best by feeling good, not by feeling bad—you can put that into practice in your own life, but you can also use this to help people around you change whether they are employees, kids, spouses, or patients.

Feedback from authority figures is powerful, and approval from authority figures can open the door to transformation. If you can give feedback at the right moment to help people feel successful, you can create a habit of the good behavior. But that's not all. As I shared in chapter 5, the effects of feeling successful ripple out. There is no more powerful praise than what comes from someone we admire and trust. And for some people, that person is you.

I see three approaches to using the power of Shine to create group habits and ultimately change culture when you are the Ringleader.

First, teach your group how emotions create habits. Explain that you've found a new way to wire in a habit by firing off positive emotions on demand by celebrating and feeling Shine. Use one of the exercises at the end of chapter 5 to help your group members find their own authentic celebrations and encourage them to develop and apply this skill.

Second, *you* can be the source of Shine for your group. This happens naturally for parents helping babies walk, and it's natural for good teachers. You'll also find examples of this in everyday life even when you don't expect it. At a spot on Maui where people learn to surf, the spectators (mostly friends and parents) will cheer for the newbies when they catch their first waves.

Most of us can up our game in this area. We can be more prolific and immediate with positive feedback. If we wait until someone reaches a big milestone, we have missed many opportunities to help people feel Shine.

The third approach is one I've seen emerge naturally in families who have learned the Tiny Habits method: An individual's good habits are celebrated by others in the group. Young kids pick up on this quickly. As mom does two push-ups against the kitchen counter, her daughter claps, and says, "Good job, Mommy!"

The Ninja

As a Ninja, you can be the instigator of Shine in other people much like the Ringleader. However, you go about things in stealthier ways. When someone does a good behavior, you can help wire in the habit by saying, "Wow. That's great. How did tidying up your desk make you feel?" With this question, you help your colleague access Shine more readily the next time they tidy their desk. You can also redefine the meaning of success by helping people recognize that they are succeeding with the process even if the outcome hasn't been reached. Every time someone selects water instead of soda, that's a success even if they don't see the bathroom scale change. When someone practices meditation, they don't need to calm their mind to be successful. Simply sitting quietly is a success, and they can feel good about that.

In my research, I've mapped out thirty-two different types of messages that affirm success. (It's a grid framework with four rows and eight columns.) For example, recognizing that someone has reached a personal best is one of the thirty-two ways to affirm success. *You've done your best job ever!* Another way is to help people see that they did something better than anyone else.

Some people will feel more Shine from the first approach; other people will feel more Shine from being better than others.

If you know what message type creates the most Shine for each member of your group, you can use this power to help them wire in habits and perform better and better.

Here are a few more elements from my framework written as though I'm giving feedback to a student.

+ You have shown remarkable *consistency* in your homework

+ You got a *perfect* score on the exam

+ Despite the terrible score on your first exam, you really *came back strong* this time

+ You are learning this material *faster than anyone else* in class

+ You improved your score *more than anyone else* in the class

Check out all of my thirty-two messages that affirm success in the back of the book. But also pay attention to everyday life to learn more. When you give positive feedback, what has the biggest impact? Try different approaches and see what happens.

People react differently to how messages are framed, but I've learned that there is one approach that applies to everyone.

What I'm sharing next can be used in powerful ways, both good and bad. This is the first time I'm sharing it in written form. Please use what's next only for the most noble of purposes.

The feedback that has the most emotional power has two characteristics: It relates to a domain you care about, and it's in an area where you feel uncertain. I created a graphic to show this overlapping space that I call the Power Zone.

Feedback Power Zone

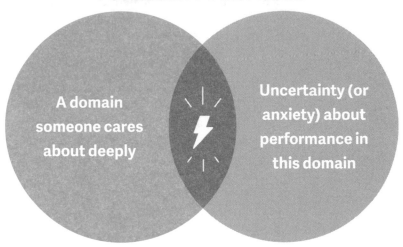

Any feedback you give someone in the Power Zone will be amplified because they care about the subject *and* are uncertain. That means you can inspire huge Shine or cast serious shade. Suppose you see a new mom trying to calm her baby. She wants to be a "good" mom, and because she is new to this, she is uncertain. If you say, *That's a good technique! That's what my sister used to do with her babies and she's the best mom I know,* she will beam with Shine.

On the other hand, think of the impact of saying, *Do you want me to try? It looks like your baby is pretty upset.* Oops. To a new mom, the implication underlying this interaction is crystal clear—*you're doing it wrong.* This statement is in the Power Zone, but it's negative and will probably be extra hurtful. And this mom would never forget you—for all the wrong reasons.

One of my personal themes for the last year has been to "strengthen others in all my interactions." And I even have a beautiful painting in my home office with these words on it (thanks, Stephanie). I apply my research insights in pursuing this aspiration, and I try to strengthen others by giving well-timed feedback to people around me: when one of my students gives her first presentation in class, when my partner cooks a new dish, and when someone phones me with a question about my work. In all these situations, I have a huge opportunity to strengthen these people—they care about a topic, and they are uncertain. All I have to say is something positive that is sincere. Too often people give negative feedback in vulnerable situations. *The start of your presentation was too slow. This fish is a little dry; how long did you cook it? I can tell from your question that you really haven't read my work.*

Yikes. Don't do that.

Be a good Ninja.

7. TROUBLESHOOT AND ITERATE TOGETHER

Now we arrive at the last step in Behavior Design. Always embrace iteration, whether designing for a one-time behavior or a habit. If something doesn't work as well as you'd like, take specific steps to troubleshoot.

The Ringleader

When you lead your group in a change process, tell people well in advance that the first attempts to create habits may not work out. Explain that creating lasting change is like buying shoes. The first pair you try on might not be an ideal fit. This analogy sets the proper expectations, and you won't lose credibility if your first designs as Ringleader don't pan out. Expect to correct your course along the way.

Explain the troubleshooting order based on the Behavior Model. *If our attempts to create this habit don't work, we will troubleshoot, starting with the prompt. And we won't blame ourselves for lack of motivation or willpower. What we are doing is all about design—and redesign. If we need to tap into willpower, we are doing it wrong.*

If we revise the prompt and make the behavior as simple as possible, and we still don't succeed, we'll back up and pick a different behavior— one that we actually want to do.

The Ninja

If you're troubleshooting a group behavior Ninja-style, you can bring in the Behavior Model in a new way. As usual, start with the prompt. Then look at ability. And then—as a last resort—fuss with motivation. In the best scenario, you skip motivation and rematch the group with a new behavior that they are already motivated to do.

The graphic version of the Behavior Model can clarify what steps a Ninja should take or avoid. Let's imagine you're in charge of getting people signed up for the company walking program. You invite people to join a thirty-day challenge, and the response is terrible. Fewer than 2 percent join.

Your first step in troubleshooting is to examine the prompt. Are people getting your e-mail with the invitation? Maybe it's going to their spam folders. Perhaps inboxes are jammed. Find another way to prompt the enrollment behavior—personal invitations via phone or hand-written notes.

If you're sure your group is getting prompted (you personally delivered those handwritten notes) and if your results are still miserable, move on to the next step in troubleshooting. In cases like this, I like to map out the situation using discrete segments on the Behavior Model.

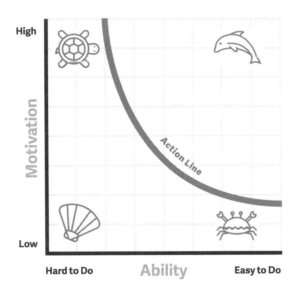

In the upper right-hand corner, envision all the people who have responded to your prompt and joined the walking challenge. I call that segment the Dolphins. They are both motivated and have the ability. They did the behavior—signing up for the challenge when prompted. In the upper left-hand corner are the people who did not sign up when prompted. They're motivated, but for some reason, the walking challenge seems too hard to do. I call this segment the Turtles.

In the lower left- and right-hand corners are the people who are not motivated to join the walking challenge: the Crabs and the Clams. The Crabs have the ability, but they don't want to do it. The Clams have neither the ability nor motivation. As you strive to get more people involved besides the Dolphins, focus first on the Turtles and use the Ability Chain to figure out how to make the behavior easier for them to do. Forget about the Crabs and the Clams for now. They are unlikely to join, and you shouldn't waste time on them.

When I teach this segmentation at my boot camp, I find that this is one of the most enlightening and disruptive insights for people learning

Behavior Design. Innovators often try to solve for all four segments at the same time. Or they figure that they should focus on the toughest segment—the Clams. Both approaches are a mistake. In Behavior Design, you help people do what they already want to do. The Crabs and the Clams don't want to join a walking challenge. The Dolphins and the Turtles do. So you help the Dolphins and the Turtles first.

When you've done that, find a different activity for the Crabs and Clams that they would enjoy—playing table tennis, joining a cooking club, or riding their bikes. Or set them aside and have a blast walking with the Dolphins and the Turtles.

That said, there is one situation when you can try to reach the Crabs (and maybe the Clams). This exception is when there is a behavior someone *must* do, something really important like getting a flu shot. In those cases (and only then) you can shift gears and also appeal to the Crabs.

If for some reason you *must* get the Crabs to join the walking challenge, find an aspiration that would align with their joining. If your initial campaign framed the challenge as having fun while getting healthy, and that is not resonating with the Crabs, find something that *is* meaningful. This may take some research, and not all Crabs will resonate with the same aspiration. But imagine these potential changes to your campaign.

+ Join the walking challenge and *get free passes to the Friday concert series*

+ Join the walking challenge and *talk face-to-face with top management*

+ Join the walking challenge and *get free walking shoes*

In these examples, you are not revisiting the Swarm of Bs and matching people with another behavior. You are doing what I call the Queen B Solution. You keep the behavior (because you have to) and frame it with other aspirations. (You'll see a true example of this in the next story.)

This use of my Behavior Model for segmenting can give you and your team surprising clarity. As you share this way of thinking with teammates, you start raising your colleagues to Ninja status. And they can then apply their energies in areas where they will get results and not waste time pursuing the Crabs and Clams.

Sometimes the process of changing together unfolds in a straightforward way, with you and your crew hitting all the steps I've laid out. But the beauty of Behavior Design and the methods from Tiny Habits is that they are flexible. Now that you've seen the broad strokes of the change-together process, let's see what they look like in real life. Let's call these two true stories "Tales of Two Transformations." The first story brings back a Behavior Change All-Star who has been with us before. The second story is about using the Tiny Habits method to increase resilience in a workplace that is rife with unavoidable stress—a hospital.

Family Change: Succeeding with a Learning Disability

CLARIFY ASPIRATIONS AND OUTCOMES

Amy's daughter was diagnosed with ADHD in kindergarten. A neuropsychologist said that Rachel was the smartest but most scattered kid he'd ever seen. Amy knew her daughter was a deep thinker, but it was as if the ramifications of every little action slowed Rachel down to a snail's pace. She had trouble following directions because she was often lost in thought. Decisions were painful to arrive at. But almost all of Rachel's teachers agreed that she could be successful if she found a way to harness all those thoughts and process them more quickly without losing sight of the need to finish a worksheet or answer a direct question. By fourth grade, Rachel was in Special Education, and Amy was struggling to help her finish her homework every day, and all Rachel wanted to do was play video games or play outside.

Having used Tiny Habits and Behavior Design to grow her business and navigate a difficult relationship with her ex-husband, Amy didn't see any reason why she couldn't use what she'd learned to help Rachel. The first thing she did was figure out Rachel's larger aspirations, which took some time and creative questions on Amy's part. It turned out that getting good grades, earning the teacher's approval, and learning her multiplication tables were not as important to Rachel as doing what she wanted to in the moment. Amy kept pushing to find Rachel's own unique *why* behind the behaviors she wanted to do and those she was avoiding (doing her homework). Knowing that finding the right aspiration was the key, Amy used the Queen B method: She set out to align the homework tasks (a requirement) with an aspiration Rachel already had.

Amy told me that her real aha moment was when she asked Rachel, "I know doing homework is a struggle, but what do you think will happen if you don't learn to tackle it?"

"Well, I guess I'll have more free time," Rachel said.

"True. But how would you feel if it was time to finish fourth grade, and everybody else went to fifth grade and you didn't?"

Rachel's eyes widened. "What?"

"And what if you're still in fourth grade, and they've gone to sixth?"

The wheels turned in her daughter's mind—this was a new concept. "I wouldn't like that."

"Okay, so it sounds like what you want is to finish fourth grade and keep pace with your classmates. That's good—now we know what you want and where you want to go, so we can find good ways to make it happen."

It turned out that this conversation was just as important for Amy as it was for her daughter. What she figured out was that Rachel wasn't actually interested in mastering her homework. *That* was all Amy. What Rachel did care about was keeping up with her friends in school. So Amy put that aspiration in a new Swarm of Behaviors cloud, and from there, she could talk with Rachel about specific behaviors that could help her reach that outcome.

MATCH WITH A SPECIFIC BEHAVIOR

Since doing homework after school was the specific behavior in the swarm that kicked off their change-together journey, Amy and Rachel started with that.

TOGETHER FIND WAYS TO START TINY

The next step was to make it easier for Rachel to do. The biggest stumbling block was attention span. Rachel's learning challenges meant that staying focused was a constant struggle—especially after a day of school. So Amy experimented with breaking up the homework into smaller tasks. They would do things in ten-minute increments—organizing school supplies on the glass table where she did her homework or making a list of worksheets she needed to complete. They tried taking five-minute breaks to jump on the trampoline between work sessions. They tried using flashcards and videos; they tried doing homework on the computer and on paper. Along the way, they strengthened any chink they found in the Ability Chain.

In all of this, Amy made her thought process clear to her daughter and asked for Rachel's input. If Rachel pushed back on something, she'd make a deal with her—they'd try it Rachel's way for five days and Amy's way for five days and take notes on which worked better. Amy understood that she was not only helping Rachel get her homework done but was also teaching her how to experiment and manage her own behavior. She was teaching Rachel the Skills of Change.

FIND YOUR PROMPT

Finding a place in Rachel's after-school routine for homework was critical. When they waited to do homework until after dinner, they were doomed. No matter what "make it easy" techniques they tried, Rachel was too tapped out to focus successfully. So they figured out that homework needed to be done soon after school. With that as a place to start, they got increasingly granular. Amy used the Tiny Habits Recipe format *After _____, I will do _____* for each homework behavior they tackled. They tried moving homework after a few different distractions, and iterated until they found recipes that worked: *After we bounce on the trampoline for five minutes, I will take the worksheets out of my backpack.* Exploring together, they learned it was important to break homework into smaller habits like organizing her school supplies, making to-do lists, and interspersing those tasks with fun bursts of activity.

CELEBRATE WINS TOGETHER

Amy also made sure to incorporate heavy doses of celebration into their Homework Habit Recipes. They played around with high fives, silly dances, and sticker charts to find the celebrations that worked best for each win. A naturally goofy, sweet kid, Rachel was all in on the celebrating. Amy also made sure to connect it very clearly to the behavior her daughter had just completed, giving her a strong sense of Shine and wiring in the new habit more efficiently.

TROUBLESHOOT, ITERATE, AND EXPAND

Rachel and Amy kept going back to the Swarm of Behaviors and incorporating new habits that helped her with homework and led to more and more success in the classroom. Some of these habits ended up embedded in her academic life. One habit that they created in fourth grade helped Rachel manage time and get things done. The recipe was *After I get home from school* (trailing edge: taking off my backpack), *I will check my homework list and write down a guess of how long it will take me.* Her celebration was built in—once Rachel had guessed how much time her homework would take, she could get excited about all the things she could do with the rest of her time that evening. This was only a number written on the top of a list, but it helped her learn time management. Rachel got better at understanding how long certain academic tasks took and prioritizing her to-dos accordingly. At first, Amy would help her review her estimates every few days and talk through what she guessed wrong, why it was wrong, and how she could course-correct.

By helping Rachel take ownership of this habit, Amy was soon able to back off. This took some pressure off their relationship because the more skilled Rachel got at understanding her capacity and motivation, the less Amy had to get involved. Amy also saw how this improved her daughter's overall ability to manage time, whether it was getting ready for school or cleaning her room. The habits she had cultivated in the academic arena spilled over into other parts of her life.

By the time she reached sixth grade, Rachel was no longer in Special Ed classes. Not only did she integrate well into mainstream classes, she went on to take advanced placement courses, and she graduated with honors.

When she had started using Tiny Habits to help Rachel, Amy did not expect or even dream about that kind of transformation. She just wanted her daughter to find a way to use the gifts that she was born with. While it wouldn't have been a crisis if Rachel had gotten held back in the fourth grade, it would have been an abiding source of pain for Amy if she hadn't helped her daughter reach her full potential. And Amy had been careful about how she did that. If she had gotten heavy-handed with Rachel, the effort would have been a constant source of anxiety and tension, and it might have ultimately failed.

Amy found so much joy in the process of changing together and Rachel found so much success that Amy wishes she had known about Tiny Habits earlier so her older two children would have had the same benefits.

Workplace Challenge: Reducing Stress in the Hospital

I was hired a few years ago by a major research hospital to tackle the problem of nurse burnout. I invited Linda, who had become a Tiny Habits coach and trainer, to help me. The project brief from hospital leaders said that the aspiration was to "help nurses form new habits that make them more resilient." "Resilience" was the positive frame for this effort, but everyone understood this was really about employee burnout, a large and growing problem among nurses, doctors, and other medical staff.

I understood that working in a hospital was stressful. Nurses care for people who are ill. Despite excellent care, some patients die, and doctors, patients, and family members can make unreasonable demands. However, as I learned more about the nurses and the reality of their jobs,

I was floored to see how deeply stressful each shift could be and what effect this stress had on every nurse and how it continued to affect their time away from work.

As Linda and I taught the courses via live video conferencing, I was able to see each nurse on my screen. Some were in their pajamas at home, bleary-eyed and flopped on the couch eating takeout. They didn't look like nurses ready for a new patient. They looked like superheroes after a dramatic rescue: totally depleted. At home or at work, the nurses stared into their computer cameras with faces full of fatigue.

Linda and I deeply wanted to help them, and Linda was an ideal coteacher because she was an expert in using Tiny Habits to reduce stress. The nurses fully understood that by taking care of themselves (and one another) they could better care for their patients, but they didn't know how to put that aspiration into practice.

We trained them in the Tiny Habits method an hour a week over the course of a month, and during the week, they practiced making behaviors tiny, creating recipes, rehearsing the Anchor-habit sequence, celebrations, and troubleshooting.

We got to know the nurses as people. We learned about some of their existing habits at work. They almost never took breaks. They used computer software that was old and aggravating. And most surprising to me, they typically wouldn't drink any water during a twelve-hour shift. The nurses knew this wasn't a healthy behavior, but something in the culture of the hospital pushed them to their very limit. If they didn't drink water, they wouldn't need a restroom break. And in that way, they thought they could help more patients and also believed their colleagues would admire their devotion.

But this devotion had a high price. Many would return home after a long shift unable to engage with their spouses and kids. They had headaches, and some had trouble sleeping.

To make the Tiny Habits training easier for them, I created the Recipe Maker tool. Linda and I had the nurses write a list of Anchors (routines they did every day at work) on the left side of a worksheet.

+ After I park my car ...

+ After I log on to the computer ...

+ After I meet each patient ...

+ After I do an EKG ...

+ After I answer the call light ...

+ After I wash my hands ...

Then Linda and I worked with the nurses to discover what tiny behaviors they could do to reduce stress. We came up with a long list, and we put some of the items into the recipe format on the right side of the worksheet.

* I will take a deep breath.

* I will smile at the closest person.

* I will take a sip of water.

* I will ask for help.

* I will say, "Thank you."

With those two parts, the nurses could mix and match. By pairing an Anchor on the left with a Tiny Behavior on the right, the nurses quickly created recipes that they could try out during their shifts. Helping each other, the nurses then shared what recipes were working.

Here are some recipes they created.

* After I park at work, I will close my eyes and take three relaxing breaths.

* After I clock in, I will think, *Today I'm helping people who really need me.*

* After I meet each patient, I will make eye contact and give them a smile.

My Recipe — Tiny Habits Method

After I...	I will...	To wire the habit into my brain, I will immediately:
park at work,	close my eyes and take three relaxing breaths.	☺
Anchor Moment	**Tiny B**ehavior	**C**elebration
An existing routine in your life that will remind you to do the Tiny Behavior (your new habit).	The new habit you want but you scale it back to be super tiny—and super easy.	Something you do to create a positive feeling inside of yourself (the feeling is called Shine).

- After I dock my computer, I will take a sip of water.
- After our team huddle, I will thank the first night-shift person I speak to.

As we taught the nurses to implement the Tiny Habits method in their busy, stressful jobs, we could see that the nurses were changing together despite being so tired and pressed for time.

But that's not all. The nurses embraced celebration. We took one full class to help them understand how to celebrate their tiny successes and why they should do it. This paid off in a surprising way. The nurses started celebrating their own successes, as we'd hoped. But they also started *celebrating one another*—a quick clap for a fellow nurse who took a drink of water, a high five after a colleague sat down in the break room, a "Good for you!" after someone took a deep relaxing breath.

We went on to train different groups of people at the hospital. This included emergency room staff and hospital administrators. And we ran a formal research study to measure the effects that Tiny Habits had on the nurses.

Before the nurses started our training, they had completed an anonymous questionnaire about stress and resilience. Three months after our training ended, the nurses answered the same questions again, and the data showed statistically significant improvements in these areas.

- "I practice stress-reducing habits daily."
- "I am managing my stress well at work."
- "I practice building resilience techniques throughout my day."
- "I practice healthy habits daily at work."
- "I recognize when something goes well at work."
- "I am able to design positive habits at home."

Linda and I were pleased that the Tiny Habits method could help tackle such a challenging problem in the workplace. But we were even happier that our efforts helped these healers be less stressed, healthier, and better able to serve those in need.

And I had a big surprise that didn't come from the research data but from an overall impression: If someone is stressed out, if they are pressed for time, if they feel overwhelmed, *they cannot make big changes.* And they aren't likely to even try. I saw that Tiny Habits was the only realistic path that would work for people in that situation. And it may be the only realistic option for you and the people around you.

The Bigger Picture

When you see the world through Behavior Design glasses—viewing behavior as a puzzle to be solved—the realm of the possible opens up well beyond your home or office. We live in a world with no lack of problems big and small. I believe that with the principles of Behavior Design, the methods of Tiny Habits, and the Skills of Change practiced and ready to use, you have everything you need to start solving whatever challenge you face. I've seen my students and the professionals I've trained use Behavior Design to address problems that seemed intractable. Whether changing together means deepening your relationships, helping your child reach her fullest potential, or improving working conditions for people in high-stress jobs, I hope you see that with the right approach almost *any* change is possible.

Behavior Design is not a solitary pursuit. With each habit we design, each tiny success we celebrate, and each change we make, we reach beyond our personal lives. We shape our families, communities, and societies through our actions. And they shape us. The behaviors we perpetuate matter. Behavior Design is not just about losing ten pounds or putting the phone down during dinner. It's about becoming the person you want to be—and creating the kind of family, team, community, and *world* we want to live in.

Tiny Exercises to Enhance a Group's Skills of Change

EXERCISE #1: SHARE THE BASICS OF BEHAVIOR DESIGN

Step 1: Ask your work team or family to join you for thirty minutes to learn something new that some Stanford scientist invented.

Step 2: Hand out the Swarm of Behaviors worksheet or have them draw one.

Step 3: Ask people to write an aspiration inside the cloud.

Step 4: Ask them to come up with at least ten behaviors that would lead them to their aspiration. (Give people about five minutes—but you might need to help them.)

Step 5: Ask people to put a star by the five behaviors that would be the most effective in helping them reach their aspiration.

Step 6: Ask people to circle any behavior they could get themselves to do. The behaviors with both stars and circles are their Golden Behaviors. Explain what that means.

Step 7: Have the group share their Golden Behaviors and discuss how they could turn them into reality. If you continue on to designing for new habits, help your team use the Tiny Habits method.

EXERCISE #2: SOLVE A PROBLEM TOGETHER USING BEHAVIOR DESIGN

Step 1: Ask your work team or family to join you for thirty minutes to learn something new that some Stanford scientist invented.

Step 2: Have them come up with an aspiration that the whole group shares. Your work team might want better quality meetings. Your family might want more quality time together in the evenings.

Step 3: Pick one of the aspirations from Step 2 and make sure everyone is clear about what it means.

Step 4: Have everyone follow the process for finding Golden Behaviors for the group's aspiration. (See Steps 2 through 6 in the previous exercise.)

Step 5: Ask people to share one or two Golden Behaviors with the group. (Write those down for everyone to see.)

Step 6: Go through the list you've written. Ask your team or family how the group can make each Golden Behavior a reality. Discuss and make a plan.

EXERCISE #3: CREATE TEAM ALIGNMENT ON WHAT BEHAVIOR TO CHANGE

Step 1: Decide what your team's aspiration is before they gather. For a work team, the aspiration might be more positive communication or making progress on projects that really matter.

Step 2: Magic Wand a set of behaviors on your own (or get someone to help you come up with ideas).

Step 3: Double-check that these behaviors are specific, then write each one on a 4 x 6 index card or a half-sheet of paper.

Step 4: Gather your team and explain the aspiration to the group.

Step 5: Hand out the cards so each person has about the same number.

Step 6: Lead the group in a Focus Mapping session as described in this chapter. For more details on moderating a group Focus Map, go to FocusMap.info.

Step 7: Once your team has identified a small set of behaviors in the upper right-hand corner (the Golden Behaviors), ask how the group can make each behavior a reality.

Step 8: Discuss and make a plan.

CONCLUSION
The Small Changes
That Change Everything

I was in Amsterdam speaking at a conference in 2008. I'd given the opening keynote in the morning, then enjoyed the rest of the day at the event. Denny and I had just walked into our hotel room after the evening reception when my phone dinged. It was a text message from my brother. *Garrett died of an overdose.* I blinked and read it again. The text was so short, so painfully to the point, that I knew it had to be real. But my first reaction was to say *no*. I said *no* over and over again, louder and louder. My throat felt like it was closing up, but I managed to croak out the words of the text to Denny. To this day, it is difficult for me to say those words out loud.

Garrett was my sister Linda's son. At twenty, Garrett still called me Uncle Beej and gave me a big bear hug whenever I saw him. He was the sweetest kid in the family, and everyone knew this. His own siblings called him the Golden Child both in jest and in all seriousness. He loved sunflowers, and he could beat most anyone in an eating contest, especially if it was chocolate chip cookies.

A hundred images of him flooded my mind followed by what felt like a million questions.

An overdose? He had completed rehab and had been sober for months. I thought he was free and clear. What happened? Denny and I sat silently on the edge of the bed. Stunned. Several awful minutes passed. I knew my sister was in the worst pain of her life, but I was halfway across the world. I pushed the shock and questions aside, and said: "Let's pack and fly home. Right now."

Denny got up and set out our suitcases. I called the front desk to see how fast we could get to Schiphol Airport. It was just after midnight. We threw everything into our bags, and a few minutes later, we took a taxi to the airport and caught the next plane to Las Vegas.

Linda is my older sister, and one of my earliest memories is of her standing in front of a tiny blackboard in our living room when I was maybe three. I was sitting in a little chair, and she was teaching me a very important lesson: When tape is wet, it doesn't stick. She stuck a piece of dry tape on the blackboard, then she dipped another piece in water and tried to stick it on the blackboard. When it slipped down the board, Linda said, "See, BJ!"

My sister and I have always had a special relationship—maybe because she's the oldest or because our personalities are in sync. We both love to learn and teach, and we always find a way to make our work about helping people. As you probably gleaned from the stories I've already told, Linda is a caretaker at heart—she's a mother of eight, and she's also someone who has suffered more tragedy than anyone I know.

When Denny and I arrived in Las Vegas after hearing the news about Garrett, we went directly to Linda's home. We were there while my sister and her family were enduring unimaginable loss. I gave the eulogy and was a pallbearer.

After the funeral, close friends and extended family gathered at Linda's home, bringing chicken casseroles and expressing their deepest condolences. At one point I saw Linda leave the kitchen and head toward the side porch. After a minute or so, I followed her. When I stepped outside, it was starting to get dark. I saw my big sister sitting on the stone patio. She was leaning against the wall in a fetal position with her arms wrapped around her legs. Her hand was over her face, and she was sobbing and shaking. I slumped down next to her and put my arm around her shoulder. I didn't know what to say, so the two of us sat there alone.

She told me later that she needed to get away from the people, the funeral, and the horrible absence she felt. But when she got to the porch, she realized that there was no getting away from this. And that's when she broke down.

Linda had not only taken care of me when I was a little kid but also when I had turned the corner into adulthood. I came out of the closet when I was a grad student in the early nineties, and my sister was one of the first people I had told. She had handled it more lovingly and gracefully than I could have imagined. We were raised in a conservative Mormon family, so this was no small feat of human compassion. I revealed something that, for a devout woman, was emotionally complicated to say the least. But for Linda, I was her little brother, and she was there to take care of me. So I knew it was my turn that day on her side porch. Before I sat down to comfort her, I thought to myself, *Whatever it takes, I'm going to help her.*

On its face, this was a pure and deep desire—to help someone you love when they are in pain. But it was a galvanizing moment for me that would influence the ultimate direction of my professional work and life. Linda's, too, as it turns out.

After Garrett's death, the waves kept pounding on Linda's shores. The years that followed her loss were filled with struggles: her husband's diagnosis of Alzheimer's and his rapid decline, the loss of the family business, and bankruptcy. Along the way, I tried to be there for Linda in whatever way I could be, but at one point, she found herself at a crossroads. She had worked her butt off to get her master's degree and was doing steady consulting work all over the country, helping parents navigate the new terrain of social media. But after a few years of barely making ends meet and feeling burned out from being on the road and away from her kids, Linda wanted a new direction. Just as important, I knew she needed income to support her family.

At that point, I'd been coaching people individually in Tiny Habits —thousands of people each year. I didn't make any money from my coaching, but it was fun to do and I learned so much about human behavior from this daily hands-on experience.

Interacting with hundreds of people each day took time, my scarcest resource. Even when I was on vacation or traveling to give a talk, I still took time to coach people from all over the world. I loved that my Habiteers were finding success with my method. They told friends about Tiny Habits, who then told their friends. And it just kept going.

While I felt great each day as I helped people, I started worrying about how all this was taking time away from my "real" work—the academic kind. But I couldn't turn away the hundreds of people who signed up for my free program every week.

And then Linda needed help.

She was perfect for Tiny Habits. She already knew a ton about Behavior Design (she was helping me run workshops at Stanford), she was a very good teacher, and she was committed to working in health and wellness. I knew that training coaches in the Tiny Habits method was a great match for Linda's skills and her passions. And I hoped that it could be a source of income for her. At the same time, I wanted to create a skilled group of professionals to help coach all those people who were joining my free five-day program. Would this be a good way to help Linda and also reduce the daily burden on me?

It was, but what I didn't realize then was that it would become so much more. You've read about Linda's amazing successes with Tiny Habits in this book, but working side by side with her to coach others in the Tiny Habits method, I was able to witness her life transform step by step. It was an amazing thing to watch. I saw her master the Skills of Change, I saw the confidence that this mastery gave her, and I saw how all of it radically changed her mindset. Over the course of about six months, I saw her help others change their lives all the while drastically changing her own. She was progressing and thriving, and most important, she had regained hope.

What I knew from coaching people in Tiny Habits was that it makes you happy. It's very simple. You're helping people change their lives, and you see the positive impact of that every day. That feels good—it gives you Shine.

Linda is an inspiring, incandescent example of what I've shared with you in this book—you change best by feeling good. She is living proof of a life transformed.

I had a dream in 2016 that I was on an airplane that was going down.

Was everything in the cabin shaking? Was the person next to me clutching my arm? Were people screaming? Probably. But what I remember is this: I knew that I was going to die. But strangely enough, I wasn't gripped by fear or panic. And sad to say, I wasn't treated to a highlights reel of my life's greatest hits. Instead, I was filled with deep regret. The many insights given me would be lost. With my painful death coming at any second, I thought only of how I had failed in my duty to explain the truth about behavior change. I had failed to help millions of people be healthier and happier.

When I woke up and realized it was a dream, I thought, *Wow. That's strange. I was certain that I would die in a plane crash, and that was my reaction?*

I got the message: I needed to share my insights broadly—and soon. I needed a way to bring all this to the world.

I had been meaning to write a book for years, but other projects consumed all my time, it seemed.

I was running the Behavior Design Lab at Stanford, teaching new courses every year, training industry innovators, and working on a half-dozen other projects at any one time.

That dream was my wake-up call. Up until that point, only a small portion of my work had made it out into the world. And what was out there wasn't as accessible as I wanted it to be. My work in Behavior Design was hard to find online. I was teaching and applying my work every day, but it was limited to my Stanford courses and people who could attend my industry boot camps. Everyone else could get a glimpse only when I gave a keynote or I tweeted. Even worse, I stashed file boxes and notebooks full of my frameworks, flowcharts, and innovations related to human behavior change in the closet in my home office — info *no one* had access to.

It caused me pain when people would e-mail me or call me for help. They would have worthy projects, and they'd ask: "How can I learn more about your work?" I'd lamely reply: "Read my Twitter posts carefully and search for some of my videos online." Ultimately, I didn't have an answer. And I felt pretty bad about that. At the time, there wasn't anything I could offer that brought together the models and methods of Behavior Design. Something that the student in Peru could use to design a better recycling service. Something that would help the county health worker design an effective immunization program. Something families could use to make their lives better. Something like a book.

My airplane dream helped me realize that in the same way Tiny Habits had helped my sister it could help *everyone's* sister, brother, mother, father, son, and daughter. I knew these insights could help anyone feeling defeated by what life throws at them. Anyone mired in shame and self-criticism. Anyone who sees the person they want to be and the life they want to live but doesn't know how to get there. Anyone who doubts that meaningful change is possible in the first place.

If I had given up Tiny Habits all those years ago, and if I hadn't been resolved to help my sister, I might have missed out on a huge realization: My work at Stanford and with industry leaders is important, but that's not what's going to change the world.

You are.

I don't mean that in a kumbaya, hand-holding kind of way. I mean that in a straight-up, these-are-the-facts-Jack kind of way.

By now you know the habits you create using the Tiny Habits method are far from tiny — they are mighty.

Habits may be the smallest units of transformation, but they're also the most fundamental. They are the first concentric circles of change that will spiral out. Think about it. One person starts one habit that builds to two habits that builds to three habits that changes an identity that inspires a loved one who influences their peer group and changes their mindset, which spreads like wildfire and disrupts a culture of helplessness, empowering everyone and slowly changing the world. By starting small with yourself and your family, you initiate a natural process that can create a tidal wave of change.

When I'm really dreaming big (and that's quite often), I think about how Behavior Design can play a role in creating the large-scale changes the world needs by reversing the spiral of failure that is so pervasive today. What if accurate models of behavior and effective methods for change were common knowledge and common practice? The potential for change would be enormous. Young kids could learn about Shine and apply it throughout their lives. Healthcare workers all over the world could learn to help patients succeed with healthy habits and use those same concepts to help themselves manage stress more effectively. Monday-morning meetings at companies could be more productive by framing each business challenge in terms of behavior change. Innovators could use Behavior Design to create products that help people transform into their best selves. Policy makers and civil servants could more easily translate abstract problems into specific behaviors—then empower their communities to create and implement the solutions.

This vision of the future may be a few years away, but the good news is that we can start cultivating a culture of change right now. One of the fastest ways to set off this chain reaction is for you to introduce people to the Behavior Design ways of thinking and doing. This is something you can do tonight at dinner—talk to your friends and family about what you've learned in this book. A shared understanding of change is the foundation for collective transformation. When you frame a problem from an accurate common perspective, you can more quickly and successfully solve it. And Behavior Design excels here. When a work team learns my models, they gain a shared way of thinking about behavior and talking about change. When they learn these methods, they learn a shared way of designing for change on a concrete, practical level. Just as important, it makes them more efficient, more impactful, and it reduces conflict, which keeps them from wasting valuable time. With your help, everyone in your circle can reap the benefits of a shared perspective on how human behavior works and the ways you can design for change.

Here's how you can help create a culture of change right now.

BY SHARING

+ *Engage in conversations about change with the people around you.* Share the most salient insights of the book—my maxims, for instance.

+ Help people do what they already want to do.

+ Help people feel successful.

To make it more personal, you can adapt the two maxims this way.

+ Help *yourself* do what you already want to do.

+ Help *yourself* feel successful.

+ *Share what you've found most helpful about this book.* Maybe you use the garden analogy about how habits work: that our collection of habits is an ever-shifting landscape we can nurture by design or ignore at our peril. And that we start a habit by planting a tiny seed in a good spot, then keep nurturing it. As the gardeners of our habits, we won't be perfect. There will be trial and error—and that's okay. Or perhaps you share the analogy of untangling bad habits like a big knot. This simple image sets the right expectations of how to get rid of a habit, and it also is powerful for helping people let go of shame and self-criticism. These ideas are easy to share, and they open people up to thinking about change and habits in a new, accurate, and helpful way.

BY DOING

+ *Teach and guide others in Shine.* Explain that there's a new word for a powerful emotion. Describe what Shine feels like and what it does (wires in new habits). You can also explain how to celebrate. And you can actively celebrate others when they do something good. You can create Shine at any moment and even (especially!) for *tiny* successes. Your daughter picks up one toy (out of dozens) and puts it away—clap for her or give her a hug.

+ *Share this book or its exercises.* Go online and get my templates for the Swarm of Behaviors and use it with friends and family. You'll find the tiny exercises in this book are effective learning tools at work, church, or school.

+ *Create a family tradition of positive change.* Start now no matter how challenging it seems. By sharing the Tiny Habits method and the concept of Shine, you can begin today to support one another in change. As you learn and practice change skills together, you will create a lasting legacy of empowerment.

In 2007 I taught what is probably my most famous class—dubbed the "Facebook Class" by the *New York Times*. Facebook had just launched its app-hosting platform, and I ran a new course at Stanford to better understand how everyday people using social networks can influence others. Using an early version of my principles and processes, students created apps and set them free in the real world (of social media). They were more successful than I could have imagined. Within six months, the students, without spending any money, had engaged more than twenty-four million people. I saw the awesome potential of Behavior Design to change the world and the awesome responsibility that comes with it.

In this book I've shared some important insights about how to think about and design for behavior change. The way I look at it, it's like many breakthrough discoveries—when you uncover a universal principle, it has the potential to be used for good or evil. You can use the principles of basic chemistry to create fertilizer and life-saving medicines or you can use those same principles to make chemical weapons.

After we wrapped up the Facebook class, I immediately focused on how we could use technology-mediated social influence for perhaps the most ambitious, pie-in-the-sky good of all—world peace. Within three months, I created a new Stanford course called Peace Technology and invited students to join me. This effort expanded after the class ended, and it continues today in research labs and centers around the world under the title of Peace Innovation, with headquarters now based in The Hague.

On a smaller level but with the same lofty ideals, my focus outside of Stanford has been teaching innovators how to create products that improve wellness, financial security, and sustainable practices. The focus on doing good is a natural one for me. I grew up in a religious tradition that made this clear: *Where much is given, much is expected.* I've always believed that.

I recognize that I've been fortunate in my work. Over the years, people have opened doors for me, challenged me, and inspired me. As a result, I could focus my research, my innovation efforts, and my life on discovering and articulating the models and methods you have learned here, including the Tiny Habits method. I feel I've been given an answer to a puzzle piece by piece. And when it snapped together, I recognized something brand-new but yet so familiar.

Then I had the airplane dream, and I realized that I had failed to share much of my work. And I was deeply troubled by that fact. I believe that it's not ethical to have the potential to do good and not use it for the benefit of humanity. It would be like finding a cure for cancer and keeping it to yourself.

But I am thankful and thrilled that this book is now a reality and in your hands. (And I'm certainly glad that I'm sleeping better.) If I had that airplane dream today, I would not feel regret. And I can't wait to see how you'll use these models and methods to make your life happier, help those around you, and make the world a better place.

I believe this book gives you everything you need to meet whatever challenges come your way and realize whatever dreams you've not yet been able to achieve. You now have a system for change, which means you don't have to guess. You can design for whatever aspiration or outcome you want.

But that's not all. You can now filter out all that noise and confusion about habits and human behavior. Because you know how behavior works, you know what to pay attention to and embrace, and what to ignore and discard. If an e-mail from a friend comes through about a new exercise or diet program, a quick scan will tell you all you need to know. Will it help you do what you already want to do? Will it help you feel successful? The answers to those questions are freeing because if the change program doesn't satisfy these two requirements, it's not worth your time.

The quality of our life on planet Earth depends on the choices we make every day—choices about how we spend our time, how we live our lives, and most important, how we treat ourselves and others. I'm sad to see how people seem more bitter, divided, and overwhelmed than ever these days. We are, as a global community, increasingly disconnected from ourselves and other people. The first step toward fixing what ails us is to embrace feeling better.

Habits are a means to this end.

They teach us the Skills of Change, and they propel us toward our dreams, and they add more Shine to the world. By embracing feelings of success and adding more goodness to your day-to-day life, you are making the world brighter not only for yourself but also for others. You are vanquishing shame and guilt, and you are freeing yourself and others who have endured a lifetime of self–trash talk.

The most profound transformations you've read about in this book are not about discrete habits being formed; they are about essential shifts in experience. From suffering to less suffering. From fear to hope. From being overwhelmed to feeling empowered. These shifts were made because Amy, Juni, Linda, Sarika, Sukumar, Katie, Mike, and others decided to embrace feeling good and use it as a lever for greater change. In doing so, they overcame devastating circumstances, cyclical dysfunction, and years of self-criticism. They regained control of their lives and discovered what we all are capable of making—the small changes that change *everything*.

I've created additional materials for you in the appendix. If you want more tools and resources—such as case studies, worksheets, and teaching outlines—you'll find them at TinyHabits.com/resources.

ACKNOWLEDGMENTS

This book became a reality mostly because shortly after my airplane dream Doug Abrams tracked me down, persuaded me to meet for lunch at Stanford, and inspired me to share my work in book form (finally). Giving me invaluable guidance through the writing and publishing process, Doug was more than a world-class literary agent. He became a true friend and an ongoing inspiration. Thank you, Doug, so very much.

Doug introduced me to Lauren Hamlin, who became my closest collaborator in transforming my research insights and hands-on experience into polished prose on the page. She brought her East Coast toughness to my West Coast optimism, and together we created this thing—a book —that exceeded my expectations. Working with Lauren was a delight. During our time together, I know she made personal sacrifices to get these ideas into your hands, and—I hope—into your hearts and minds. Lauren, the words "thank you" are simply not adequate to express how much I appreciate what you've done for me.

My sincere thanks to Lara Love for helping me make the commitment to this book and for providing guidance at critical moments. I also very much appreciate the careful work of Katherine Vaz, who scrutinized every word, every idea, and every transition in this book. I admire your charm when you needed to give me bad news, and your dedication to helping me communicate each idea better.

I will be forever grateful to the entire publishing team at Houghton Mifflin Harcourt, especially Bruce Nichols. Thank you for your confidence in my work and your passion to bring my insights about human behavior to a wide audience. Working with you and your team has been fun and uplifting.

I'd also like to thank all the editors and publishers who are bringing the book to a global market: Joel Rickett at Ebury for his editorial insights; Caspian Dennis, Sandy Violette, and the team at Abner Stein; Camilla Ferrier, Jemma McDonagh, and the team at the Marsh Agency.

Long before I dove into creating this book, people helped me move my work forward. I give thanks to my long-time collaborator and friend, Tanna Drapkin. As we worked together at Stanford and elsewhere for many years, Tanna has provided strengths in areas where I was weak and energy when I was tapped out. No one has supported my work longer or more thoroughly than Tanna.

Others at Stanford University stepped up over the years to champion my research, teaching, and innovation. Many people inspired me and opened opportunities along the way, including Byron Reeves, Terry Winograd, Roy Pea, Keith Devlin, Martha Russell, Phil Zimbardo, and the late Cliff Nass. I'm also grateful to others at Stanford who helped me in ways they may not even realize, including Jennifer Aaker, John Perry, Tom Robinson, Bill Verplank, Tina Seelig, and David Kelley.

When I first shared Tiny Habits with the world in 2011 by posting a simple invitation on social media, I had no idea this would become a huge part of my professional and personal life. I am grateful to early supporters and champions of the Tiny Habits method, notably Liz Guthridge and Linda Fogg-Phillips. There are more people—thousands, in fact—who joined my program and gave feedback and insight. People all over the world have contributed to what you find in this book.

A special thanks to people who shared their stories with me during the writing process. Some of those stories are in this book, and some are not. In either case, your experiences and insights made this book better—and fun to write. My gratitude goes out to Mike Coulter, Emily E., Mallory Erickson, Juni Felix, Linda Fogg-Phillips, TJ Jones, David Kirchhoff, Shirisha N., Margarita Quihuis, Sukumar Rajagopal, and Amy Vest. In addition, I thank others who shared real-life stories and examples with me, including TJ Agulto, Kevin Ascher, Ginger Collins, Roller Derby Renee Schieferstein, Joe Dimilia, Mark Garibaldi, Jonny Goldstein, Kate Hand, Brittany Herlean, Manjula Higginbotham, Maya Hope, Roger Hurni, Judhajit "JD" De, Brendan Kane, Erin Kelly, Ellen Khalifa, Glen Lubbert, Kevin McAlear, Jasmine Morales, Gemma Moroney, Barry O'Reilly, Steve Peterschmidt, Mary Piontkowski, Shirley Rivera, Ramit Sethi, Wingee Sin, Michael Stawicki, Khadija Tahera, Renee Townley, Michael Walter, and Bert Whitaker.

I want to express my deep gratitude to my colleague Stephanie Weldy, who assisted me on most every emergency and every nonemergency in the writing process. She cleared the path for me almost on a daily basis. She oversaw the interviews—real people, true stories—and she helped shape the texture and tone of this book.

The experts I've trained in the Tiny Habits method have moved this book forward in ways that are too numerous to list. If you're a Certified Coach in Tiny Habits, I thank you for investing time in my methods and for your efforts in making this book better for everyone. I'm sure I'll miss naming some of the most influential coaches (sorry), but here are a few who really stepped up (and who come to mind as I write this): Amy Vest, Juni Felix, Linda Fogg-Phillips, Edith Asibey, Joshua Bornstein, Kristiana Burke, Mike Coulter, Judhajit "JD" De, Charlie Garland, Jonny Goldstein, Kate Hand, Katherine Hickman, Manjula Higginbotham, Joshua Hollingsworth, Jason Koprowski, Shelley Lloyd-Hankinson, Martin Mark, Ruby Menon, Shirley Rivera, Christine Silvestri, Dave Spencer, Deb Teplow, Erwin Valencia, Stephanie Weldy, Michelle Winders, and Misako Yok.

I want to give a special note of thanks to the experts in human emotions who inspired and guided a vital part of this book: James Gross, Lisa Barrett Feldman, Aaron Weidman, and Michele Tugade. Thank you for taking time from your busy lives to help me.

On the broader research side of things—making sure I had my facts straight—I have many people to thank, including Elena Márquez Segura, Brad Wright, and David Sobel. (In addition, David also suggested the name Motivation Wave many years ago at one of my boot camps.)

Before arriving at Stanford, I was fortunate to learn from teachers and mentors who shaped my thinking and challenged me to master valuable skills. These people opened the early doors to what you find in this book: Donna McLelland, Clayne Robison, Kristine Hansen, Don Norton, Bill Eggington, Chauncey Riddle, and John Sterling Harris.

I also want to thank a wide range of people who have supported me from both near and far. These people include David Ngo, Derek Baird, Michael Fishman, Ramit Sethi, Rory Sutherland, Jim Kwik, Joe Polish, Tim Ferriss, David Kirchhoff, Amir dan Ruben, Mark Bertolini, Partha Nandi, Vic Strecher, Kyra Bobinet, Jeffrey Bland, Mark Thompson, Rajiv Kumar, Sohail Agha, Ted Eytan, Tom Blue, Benjamin Hardy, Julien Guimont, Jason Hreha, Hiten Shah, Dean Eckles, Margarita Quihuis, Maneesh Sethi, Tony Stubblebine, Vishen Lakhiani, Barry O'Reilly, Andrew Zimmermann, and Esther Wojcicki.

I want to thank friends in Maui who kept me grounded, active, and optimistic throughout the writing process. (I lived in Maui when writing most of this book. And, yes, that was wonderful.) My thanks go out to Dorothy, Jenn, Mitch, Bob, and Wanda and other friends for checking in and cheering me on. I also want to thank the surfers and SUPers in the Kihei Cove lineup—the regulars in the "dawn patrol": Tommy, Glenn, Brandice, Dana, Jeff, Rosie, Mitch, John, and the rest of you. When I surfed with you each morning, I didn't talk much about this book, but your aloha and encouragement energized my mornings so I could work hard the rest of the day. To you, I say mahalo.

I want to give special thanks to my sister Linda, whose generosity in sharing her experiences and heartaches in the service of getting the word out is nothing short of staggering. I am in awe of my big sister once again. A similarly heartfelt thank-you to my parents, Gary and Cheryl Fogg. They have been encouraging me to write this book for ten years. Even at the earliest stages of the Behavior Model and Tiny Habits, they gave helpful feedback and guidance. As you can imagine, when it comes to my life and impact in the world, my family has always been my biggest champions.

And finally, a huge hug to my life partner, Dennis Bills, who has endured my obsession with human behavior every step of the way for more than twenty years. Aside from keeping me nourished and happy, he has lovingly submitted to countless personal experiments and more chatter than is humane about Tiny Habits, Behavior Design, the Behavior Model ... you get the picture. His unwavering support gave me superpowers to research, learn, apply, and teach what I've learned to thousands of people—and with you, the reader of this book.

APPENDIXES

I've included these appendixes to help you better understand and apply my work.

For additional references and resources related to this book, go to TinyHabits.com/resources.
Enjoy!

Behavior Design: Models, Methods, and Maxims

This graphic gives you a visual overview of some models, methods, and maxims of Behavior Design. I created it to help you see the bigger picture better. If you want to use this graphic (or a newer version) in your work projects or your teaching, please go to BehaviorDesign.info to find out how to do that.

Behavior Design

Models
How to think clearly about behavior

Fogg Behavior Model

B = MAP

Motivation–PAC Person

Motivation Wave

Motivation Vectors

Ability—PAC Person

Ability Chain

Prompts—PAC Person

Other Models in Behavior Design

Swarm of Behaviors

Spectrum of Automaticity

The Skills of Change

The Behavior Change Masterplan

Power Zone Model

Methods
How to design for behavior

Tiny Habits (Methods specific to Tiny Habits)

Starter Step

Scale Back

Anchoring (Existing Routine → New Habit)

Recipe Format: After I_____, I will _____

Recipe Maker Tool

Pearl Habits

Rehearsal: Anchor → Habit → Celebration

Celebrating to feel Shine

Other Methods (Also used with Tiny Habits)

Troubleshooting a behavior: P→A→M

Swarm of Behaviors Worksheet

Magic Wanding

Focus Mapping (Behavior Matching)

Discovery & Breakthrough Questions

Design Flow: Easier to do

Maxims
#1: Help people do what they already want to do.
#2: Help people feel successful.

Fogg Behavior Model

If you want to use this graphic or a version of it, please go to BehaviorModel.org to request permission. You will also find other versions of this graphic at the Behavior Model website.

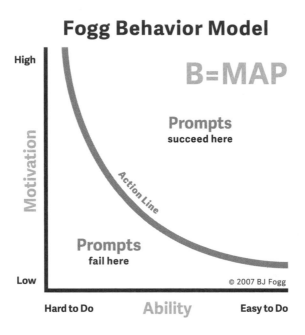

Teaching the Fogg Behavior Model
THE TWO-MINUTE SCRIPT

Step 1: Introduction
Let me explain how behavior works by teaching you the Fogg Behavior Model. This will take about two minutes.

Behavior happens when three things come together at the same moment: Motivation, Ability, and a Prompt.

Step 2: Drawing the graphic
You can visualize this model in two dimensions. Along this vertical axis is the level of Motivation for a behavior, and it can range anywhere from high to low.

Along the horizontal axis is the Ability to do a behavior. It's also a continuum. On the right is high ability, and I'll label that side as "easy to do." On the left side of this axis are behaviors that are "hard to do."

Step 3: An example
Suppose you want someone to donate to the Red Cross. If they have high motivation, and if it's easy for that person to do, they will be here in the upper-right corner of the model. When a person here gets prompted to donate, they will do the donation behavior.

In contrast, if someone has low motivation to donate to the Red Cross, and if it's hard for them to do, they will be here in the lower-left corner. When that person is prompted, they will not do the behavior.

Step 4: The Action Line
There's a relationship between motivation and ability. This curved line, called the Action Line, shows that relationship. If someone is anywhere above the Action Line when prompted, they will do the behavior. In this case, they will donate to the Red Cross. However, if they are below the Action Line when prompted, they won't do the behavior.

If someone is below the Action Line, we need to get them above it for the Prompt to instigate the behavior. Either we need an increase in motivation, or the behavior needs to be easier to do, or both.

Step 5: A brief summary
This model applies to all types of human behavior. In summary, when Motivation, Ability, and a Prompt come together at the same moment, that's when a behavior will occur. If any of the three elements is missing, the behavior won't happen.

The Anatomy of Tiny Habits

The Anatomy of Tiny Habits®

1. ANCHOR MOMENT
An existing routine (like brushing your teeth) or an event that happens (like a phone ringing). **The Anchor Moment reminds you to do the new Tiny Behavior.**

2. NEW TINY BEHAVIOR
A simple version of the new habit you want, such as flossing one tooth or doing two push-ups. **You do the Tiny Behavior immediately after the Anchor Moment.**

3. INSTANT CELEBRATION
Something you do to create positive emotions, such as saying, "I did a good job!" **You celebrate immediately after doing the new Tiny Behavior.**

Anchor

Behavior

Celebration

My Recipes — Tiny Habits Method

You can write your habit recipes on index cards using the Tiny Habits format.

Writing these down and putting your collection of habits in a recipe box will help you review and revise your habits as needed.

To print the graphic below, download the template I've created for you at TinyHabits.com/recipecards.

My Recipe — Tiny Habits® Method

Please revise your recipe as needed. Revision is an important part of Tiny Habits.

After I . . .

I will . . .

To wire the habit into my brain, I will immediately do this:

Anchor Moment

An existing routine in your life that will remind you to do the Tiny Behavior (your new habit).

Tiny Behavior

The new habit you want but you scale it back to be super tiny—and super easy.

Celebration

Something you do to create a positive feeling inside of yourself (the feeling is called Shine).

Make a Behavior Easier to Do

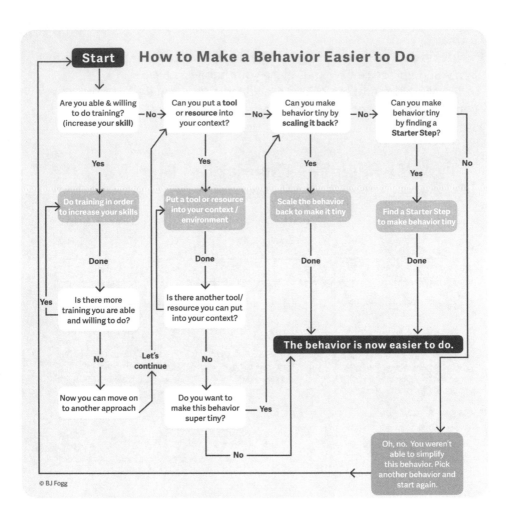

Start · How to Make a Behavior Easier to Do

Are you able & willing to do training? (increase your **skill**) —No→ Can you put a **tool** or **resource** into your context? —No→ Can you make behavior tiny by **scaling it back**? —No→ Can you make behavior tiny by finding a **Starter Step**?

Yes · Yes · Yes · Yes · No

Do training in order to increase your skills · Put a tool or resource into your context / environment · Scale the behavior back to make it tiny · Find a Starter Step to make behavior tiny

Done · Done · Done · Done

Is there more training you are able and willing to do? · Is there another tool/resource you can put into your context?

Yes

No · Let's continue · No

Now you can move on to another approach · Do you want to make this behavior super tiny? — Yes

No

The behavior is now easier to do.

Oh, no. You weren't able to simplify this behavior. Pick another behavior and start again.

© BJ Fogg

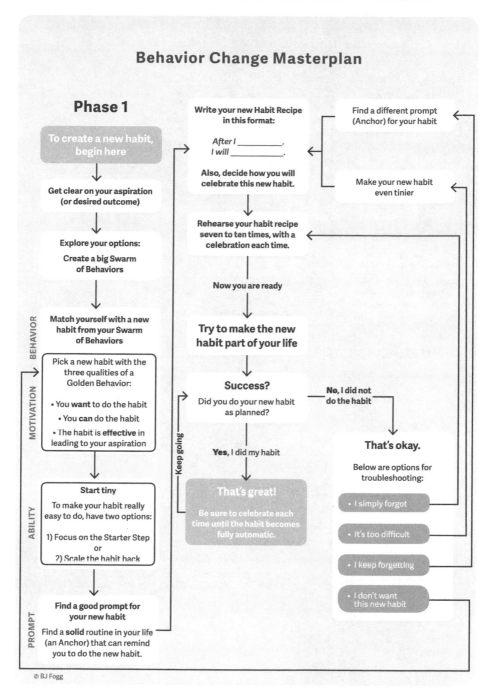

Behavior Change Masterplan

Phase 1

To create a new habit, begin here

↓

Get clear on your aspiration (or desired outcome)

↓

Explore your options:

Create a big Swarm of Behaviors

↓

BEHAVIOR

Match yourself with a new habit from your Swarm of Behaviors

↓

MOTIVATION

Pick a new habit with the three qualities of a Golden Behavior:

• You **want** to do the habit
• You **can** do the habit
• The habit is **effective** in leading to your aspiration

↓

ABILITY

Start tiny

To make your habit really easy to do, have two options:

1) Focus on the Starter Step
or
2) Scale the habit back

↓

PROMPT

Find a good prompt for your new habit

Find a **solid** routine in your life (an Anchor) that can remind you to do the new habit.

Write your new Habit Recipe in this format:

After I _____.
I will _____.

Also, decide how you will celebrate this new habit.

↓

Rehearse your habit recipe seven to ten times, with a celebration each time.

↓

Now you are ready

↓

Try to make the new habit part of your life

↓

Success?
Did you do your new habit as planned?

No, I did not do the habit →

Yes, I did my habit

↓

That's great!

Be sure to celebrate each time until the habit becomes fully automatic.

— Keep going →

Find a different prompt (Anchor) for your habit ←

Make your new habit even tinier ←

That's okay.

Below are options for troubleshooting:

• I simply forgot
• It's too difficult
• I keep forgetting
• I don't want this new habit

© BJ Fogg

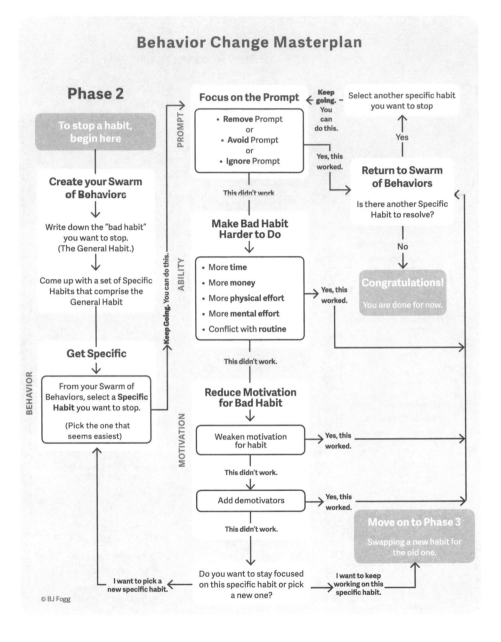

Behavior Change Masterplan

Phase 2

To stop a habit, begin here

BEHAVIOR

Create your Swarm of Behaviors

Write down the "bad habit" you want to stop. (The General Habit.)

Come up with a set of Specific Habits that comprise the General Habit

Get Specific

From your Swarm of Behaviors, select a **Specific Habit** you want to stop.

(Pick the one that seems easiest)

Keep Going. You can do this.

PROMPT

Focus on the Prompt

- **Remove** Prompt
  or
- **Avoid** Prompt
  or
- **Ignore** Prompt

This didn't work.

Keep going. - You can do this.

Yes, this worked.

Select another specific habit you want to stop

Yes

Return to Swarm of Behaviors

Is there another Specific Habit to resolve?

No

Congratulations!
You are done for now.

ABILITY

Make Bad Habit Harder to Do

- More **time**
- More **money**
- More **physical effort**
- More **mental effort**
- Conflict with **routine**

Yes, this worked.

This didn't work.

MOTIVATION

Reduce Motivation for Bad Habit

Weaken motivation for habit

Yes, this worked.

This didn't work.

Add demotivators

Yes, this worked.

This didn't work.

Do you want to stay focused on this specific habit or pick a new one?

I want to pick a new specific habit.

I want to keep working on this specific habit.

Move on to Phase 3
Swapping a new habit for the old one.

© BJ Fogg

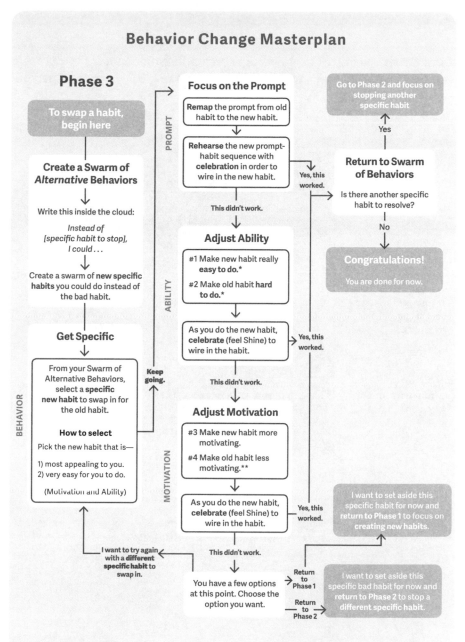

Behavior Change Masterplan

Phase 3

To swap a habit, begin here

PROMPT

Focus on the Prompt

Remap the prompt from old habit to the new habit.

Rehearse the new prompt-habit sequence with **celebration** in order to wire in the new habit.

Yes, this worked.

This didn't work.

Go to Phase 2 and focus on stopping another specific habit

Yes

Return to Swarm of Behaviors

Is there another specific habit to resolve?

No

Congratulations!

You are done for now.

Create a Swarm of *Alternative* Behaviors

Write this inside the cloud:

Instead of [specific habit to stop], I could...

Create a swarm of **new specific habits** you could do instead of the bad habit.

ABILITY

Adjust Ability

#1 Make new habit really **easy to do.***

#2 Make old habit **hard to do.***

As you do the new habit, **celebrate** (feel Shine) to wire in the habit.

Yes, this worked.

This didn't work.

Get Specific

Keep going.

From your Swarm of Alternative Behaviors, select a **specific new habit** to swap in for the old habit.

How to select

Pick the new habit that is—

1) most appealing to you.
2) very easy for you to do.

(Motivation and Ability)

BEHAVIOR

MOTIVATION

Adjust Motivation

#3 Make new habit more motivating.

#4 Make old habit less motivating.**

As you do the new habit, **celebrate** (feel Shine) to wire in the habit.

Yes, this worked.

This didn't work.

I want to try again with a **different specific habit** to swap in.

You have a few options at this point. Choose the option you want.

Return to Phase 1

Return to Phase 2

I want to set aside this specific habit for now and **return to Phase 1** to focus on creating new habits.

I want to set aside this specific bad habit for now and **return to Phase 2** to stop a different specific habit.

* To adjust ability, consider these factors: time, money, physical effort, mental effort, and routine.

** You can reduce motivation by weakening whatever is motivating the old habit, adding demotivators, or both.

© BJ Fogg

Thirty-Two Ways to Give Positive Feedback

Because the feeling of success helps create lasting change, I've mapped out thirty-two different ways to give positive feedback so that a person will feel successful.

	A. One time	B. Best ever	C. Compared to last time
1. Your excellent performance	You succeeded in selling a lot of widgets.	You sold more widgets this week than ever before—a personal best.	You sold 20 percent more widgets this week than last week.
2. Your performance compared to others	You sold more widgets today than your colleagues.	You sold more widgets than anyone, ever—a new record.	Over the last month, you improved your sales more than anyone else.
3. Your performance when collaborating	Because of you, your sales team had a great result.	You were a key player in helping your team set a new company record.	You helped your sales team beat last month's performance.
4. Good news despite poor performance	Even though you didn't sell any widgets, you did a great job finding prospects.	Although you didn't sell any widgets, you found more new prospects than ever before.	Even though you didn't sell any widgets, you found more prospects this month than last month.

Not all thirty-two types are equally impactful for everyone. My research suggests that some people like feedback about their own performance. Others respond more strongly to a favorable comparison with their peers. And others (though only a few) prefer to hear good news despite a poor performance.

Here is my framework with examples relating to sales performance.

D. Milestone reached	E. Trending in the right direction	F. Consistent effort	G. It could have been worse	H. Despite the challenge you faced
You sold your entire set of widgets and reached a key milestone.	During the last quarter, you have sold more and more widgets each week.	You have consistently done the necessary work to sell widgets.	At least you sold enough widgets to cover your expenses.	Despite having a new sales territory, you performed well.
You are the only one to reach the million-dollar sales level.	You are improving your sales results faster than anyone else.	You consistently work harder than your peers.	Everyone else selling this new widget gave up early, but you persisted.	Despite not having support from HQ last week, you still outsold all your colleagues.
With your help, your sales team reached the million-dollar level.	You are helping your team get increasingly more efficient at closing sales.	Your consistent efforts helped everyone on your team succeed.	Your team didn't close any deals this week, but with your help everyone learned a lot.	Despite having a smaller team, you helped your team be successful.
Even though you didn't sell any widgets, you have now reached the one-year milestone with our company.	Even though you didn't sell any widgets, your ability to find prospects continues to increase over time.	Even though you didn't sell any widgets, you worked hard and followed procedures faithfully.	Even though you didn't sell any widgets, you came back strong after your terrible flu.	Although you didn't sell any widgets, you didn't let this fact set you back.

One Hundred Ways to Celebrate and Feel Shine

There are many ways to celebrate in order to feel shine and wire a new habit into your brain.

Below are some celebrations suggested by expert coaches I've trained in Tiny Habits. As you read through this list, you'll probably see many celebrations that won't work for you. Some may seem downright crazy. That's okay. You don't need one hundred celebrations. You only need one. If you find more than one, that's even better.

You can use this list to consider your options and find the right celebrations for you.

1. Say, "Yes!" while you do a fist pump
2. Drum a happy beat on a wall or desk
3. Imagine your mom giving you a big hug
4. Do a subtle head nod
5. Pretend you just nailed a half-court shot
6. Visualize fireworks going off for you
7. Smile big
8. Do a double thumbs-up
9. Draw a happy face and feel it
10. Hum a few seconds of a peppy song
11. Think of your favorite teacher saying, "You did a great job!"
12. Raise your arms and say, "Victory!"
13. Think of your best friend being happy for you
14. Briefly massage your own shoulders or neck
15. Think, *Yes, I am succeeding with change*
16. Imagine opening a beautiful thank-you gift
17. Say, "That's what I'm talking about!"
18. Do the floss dance
19. Throw imaginary confetti
20. Say, "I nailed it!"
21. Clench your fists and say, "Yes!"
22. Smile at yourself in the mirror
23. Pump your fists and say, "Awesome!"
24. Hear a roaring crowd
25. Say, "Way to go!"
26. Put your palms together in gratitude
27. Say, "Got this one," and snap your fingers

28. Put your hands on your hips and puff out your chest
29. Say this to yourself: "Yes, I'm good at creating habits"
30. Strut around the room in a proud and playful way
31. Say or think, "Good job!"
32. Tap your fist on your heart three times
33. Imagine a teacher handing you a trophy
34. Think of your child smiling at you
35. Do alternating fist pumps
36. Do a celebration dance
37. Think, *Yes, I got this!*
38. Imagine the taste of chocolate
39. Look at something that is bright yellow
40. Rub your hands together in glee
41. Imagine your father saying, "Wow. That was excellent!"
42. Fist-bump yourself and explode both fists
43. Give yourself a high five
44. Hear trumpets in your head
45. Say, "It's a good thing" in your best Martha Stewart voice
46. Snap your fingers
47. Imagine getting the news that you got a new job
48. Say, "You got this!"
49. Lift your chin and smile toward the horizon
50. Imagine an audience applauding
51. Say, "Nice!" and nod your head
52. Pause, breathe deeply, and appreciate your success
53. Raise your hands and say, "Yay! Yay! Yay!"
54. Do repeated thumbs-ups
55. Say, "I love it!"
56. Sing, "Celebrate good times, come on!"
57. Give yourself a compliment: "I'm so good at . . ."
58. Whistle a happy song
59. Breathe out and say, "Yes!"
60. Brush your shoulders off with pride
61. Clap for yourself briefly
62. Imagine getting a big hug from someone you love
63. Say, "Yesssss!"
64. Think, *Nicely done!*
65. Strike a power pose
66. Imagine your own facial expression when greeting a loved one
67. Jump up and down with your hands in the air
68. Pose like a muscleman
69. Inhale and think of energy entering you

70. Do "spirit fingers" for a few seconds
71. Say, "Touchdown!" and raise your arms like a referee
72. Smell some flowers (which you keep nearby, of course)
73. Imagine being on your favorite beach
74. Bow gracefully
75. Give a high five to your child
76. Imagine the sound of a slot machine jackpot
77. Look in a mirror and say, "I'm so proud of you!"
78. Pound your chest
79. Chant this while getting your groove on: "S-U-C-C-E-S-S! That's the way I spell success!"
80. Sing, "Hey now, you're a rock star."
81. Think about the good feeling you get when you are with your dog
82. Pose like Usain Bolt does after he wins a sprint
83. Give a high five to yourself
84. Imagine a smiling feeling inside
85. Do the *Kung Fu Kids* pose
86. Smile big and say, "Woot! Woot!"
87. Give yourself a pat on the back
88. Snap your fingers multiple times
89. Stretch your arms wide and imagine yourself embracing change
90. Whisper, "Thank you, Lord."
91. Blow kisses like a movie star
92. Do a quick dance spin
93. Say, "Right on!"
94. Imagine you have a dog's tail and wag it with joy
95. Flash a peace sign and say (or think), "Victory!"
96. Do a fist bump and bow
97. High-five your reflection in the bathroom mirror
98. Imagine a sparkling aura around you
99. Laugh out loud
100. Channel Fred Flintstone and say, "Yabba dabba doo!"

Three Hundred Recipes for Tiny Habits — Fifteen Life Situations and Challenges

You can see more recipes at TinyHabits.com/recipes

TINY HABITS FOR WORKING PARENTS

1. After I hear my alarm, I will turn it off immediately (no snooze).
2. After I put my feet on the floor in the morning, I will say, "It's going to be a great day!"
3. After I walk into the kitchen, I will drink a big glass of water.
4. After I start the coffee maker, I will get out the lunch boxes.
5. After I get the eggs cooking, I will set out my vitamins.
6. After I turn on the shower, I will do three squats (and maybe more).
7. After I make my bed, I will put clothes into the washer and set a timer.
8. After my children leave for school, I will get out my to-do list for work.
9. After I buckle my seat belt, I will press play on my audiobook.
10. After I pull into the parking lot at work, I will park in the farthest parking space.
11. After I sit down at my desk, I will put my phone on airplane mode.
12. After I sort through my spam folder, I will walk around and quickly greet my teammates.
13. After I get back to my desk after my morning meeting, I will list my top priority for the day.
14. After I eat lunch, I will walk around the building at least once.
15. After I put my computer to sleep at the end of the day, I will tidy my work desk quickly.
16. After I drive out of the parking lot at work, I will turn toward the gym.
17. After I walk in the door after work, I will give my children a hug.
18. After I start the dishwasher, I will tidy up at least one thing on the counter.
19. After I say good night to my children, I will think of one person I love whom I might call.
20. After I get in bed, I will open the scriptures and read at least one verse.

TINY HABITS FOR BETTER SLEEP

1. After I hear my alarm in the morning, I will get up without hitting snooze.
2. After I put on my shoes in the morning, I will go outside to soak in the natural light.
3. After I finish eating lunch, I will get outside into the natural light of the sun.
4. After I decide to take a nap, I will set an alarm so I don't sleep for more than thirty minutes.
5. After I see it's past three p.m., I will drink water instead of coffee.
6. After I arrive home from work, I will charge my phone in the kitchen, not in the bedroom.
7. After I put dinner in the oven, I will take a magnesium supplement.
8. After I turn on the dishwasher in the evening, I will dim the lights around the house.
9. After I turn on the first light in the evening, I will put on glasses that block blue light.
10. After I turn on the TV at night, I will take a melatonin supplement.
11. After I finish watching *Jeopardy!* on TV, I will start my bedtime ritual.
12. After I see it's past eight p.m., I will stop using electronics and staring at screens.
13. After I lock the doors at night, I will turn down the thermostat to seventy degrees.
14. After I floss my teeth at night, I will turn on my white-noise machine.
15. After I turn on my white-noise machine, I will close my curtains so the room is entirely dark.
16. After I close the curtains, I will spray a little lavender scent in my bedroom.
17. After I get into bed and I'm not sleepy, I will open a relaxing book to read in a dimly lit room.
18. After I want to get up in the middle of the night, I will lie back down for about fifteen seconds.
19. After I keep looking at my clock at night, I will turn the clock around so I can't see it.
20. After I start to worry about a problem at night, I will say, "That can wait until tomorrow."

TINY HABITS FOR ACTIVE OLDER ADULTS

1. After I make a cup of tea, I will get out my medications.
2. After I get the morning paper, I will take three deep breaths.
3. After I finish the paper, I will turn on a favorite album and dance a bit.
4. After I sit down for breakfast, I will take one medication.
5. After I clean my breakfast dish, I will put on my walking shoes.
6. After I set out on my walk, I will call a sibling.
7. After I get on the walking path, I will turn on my camera and shoot a single photo.
8. After I get back to my street, I will check the mailbox.
9. After I open the garden gate, I will pause and say, "Every day is a gift."
10. After I put on my garden gloves, I will pull three weeds.
11. After I see a beautiful blooming plant, I will clip a few blooms to put in a vase.
12. After I take off my walking shoes, I will fill my water glass.
13. After I sit down on the couch, I will launch my photography app.
14. After I open a photograph to edit, I will make one adjustment.
15. After I turn on the shower, I will think one positive thought about my body.
16. After I turn off the water, I will grab hold of the safety bar to exit the shower.
17. After I hang up my towel, I will apply my skin cream to a patch of dry skin.
18. After I put on my undergarments, I will do a stretch and touch my toes.
19. After my friend arrives at my house, I will pay him a genuine compliment.
20. After we turn on the dance music, I will whisper, "Dance like no one's watching."

TINY HABITS FOR CAREGIVERS

1. After I get up to check on Mom at night, I will whisper a word of support to her even though she can't hear me.
2. After my alarm goes off, I will put my feet on the floor and say, "It's going to be a great day—somehow."
3. After I feed the dog, I will read at least one verse from the New Testament.
4. After I bring morning tea to Mom, I will ask her to tell me one of her favorite things.
5. After I see my partner has made me breakfast, I will give him a big hug before sitting down and eating.
6. After I see my husband drive away to work, I will sit down and take three deep breaths.
7. After I see Mom's appointments for the day, I will remind her so they're not a surprise.
8. After I bring in the sponge-bath supplies, I will hold Mom's hand and smile before starting.
9. After I e-mail the doctor a question, I will make a note of what I asked in my care journal.
10. After I help Mom do her physical therapy, I will compliment her on one thing she did well.
11. After I give Mom a medication, I will note it in my care journal.
12. After I see Mom has fallen asleep for a morning nap, I will open a great book and try to get lost in it.
13. After I start to change a bandage, I will talk about something fun we did as a family in the past.
14. After I log on to Facebook, I will post one challenge I'm facing as a caregiver.
15. After I hear my mom criticize my care or cooking, I will say exactly this: "Mom, you are entitled to your opinion," and nothing more.
16. After I have a good cry, I will wash my face, look in the mirror, and say, "You can do this."
17. After I get frustrated with the healthcare system, I will think of one friend I can call for a listening ear.
18. After my neighbor comes over to give me a break, I will hug her and say how soon I will return.
19. After my kids ask, "How is Grandma?" I will share one true thing about her situation.
20. After I get Mom in bed for the night, I will tidy one item in the kitchen or den—and call it good enough.

TINY HABITS FOR NEW MANAGERS

1. After I sit down for breakfast, I will open my calendar app and review the day's agenda.
2. After I get dressed for work, I will read a positive affirmation.
3. After I walk into the office, I will smile and greet each person I see.
4. After I close my office door for a one-on-one meeting, I will ask a specific question about how my colleague is doing.
5. After I notice a colleague getting frustrated, I will point out a strength of theirs.
6. After I wrap up a one-on-one meeting, I will highlight one positive contribution from my colleague.
7. After I learn about a new project from my manager, I will create a new channel in Slack for it.
8. After I launch the weekly staff meeting, I will ask a fun check-in question and hear a brief response from each team member. (E.g., What's the last city you traveled to? What's your favorite condiment? What's one album on repeat in your household?)
9. After I notice a meeting topic getting stuck in abstractions, I will say, "Just to clarify, we're designing for X, right?"
10. After we go through all the agenda items, I will ask if my colleagues have any additional items for discussion.
11. After our meeting adjourns, I will ask my team members to e-mail the group with their action items.
12. After I close my lunch box, I will put on my walking shoes.
13. After I enter the office after lunch, I will walk up to someone on my team and ask, "How can I support you today?"
14. After I head out for a meeting, I will offer a positive comment to the front-desk associate.
15. After an employee comes to me with a problem, I will say, "What do you think is the best way forward?"
16. After I complete the hiring paperwork for new employees, I will add their birthday to my calendar.
17. After I receive a complimentary written remark, I will move the e-mail or document into my Performance Review folder.
18. After I turn off my computer for the day, I will file one set of papers on my desk.
19. After I pack up my work bag, I will lock my filing cabinet drawers.
20. After I close my office door, I will think about one accomplishment I achieved that day as I walk to the train.

TINY HABITS FOR SUCCESS IN COLLEGE

1. After I hear my alarm, I will put one foot on the floor and try to wake up.
2. After I get in the shower, I will say, "It's going to be a great day."
3. After I start the coffee maker, I will tidy up one thing in our apartment.
4. After I put my books in my backpack, I will add a healthy snack from the fridge.
5. After I get to my bike, I will put on my helmet (even if it messes up my hair).
6. After I walk into the library, I will sit at a table in the far corner away from other people.
7. After I get out my homework assignment, I will put my phone on airplane mode.
8. After I leave morning class on Monday, Wednesday, and Friday, I will phone my mom or grandma.
9. After I sit down for lunch, I will launch LinkedIn to read nursing news and get better connected.
10. After I wrap up a study group, I will thank my teammates sincerely.
11. After I sit down for class with my laptop, I will turn off Wi-Fi.
12. After I walk into the campus bookstore, I will turn away from the candy corner (too much temptation!).
13. After I gear up for the climbing wall, I will cross myself and give thanks for challenges in my life.
14. After I pick up my plate in the dining hall, I will fill most of it with veggies and protein.
15. After I put my dinner tray on the conveyor belt, I will go to the quiet lounge and open Ramit's new book about personal finance.
16. After a friend asks if I want to go out clubbing, I will smile, and say, "Thank you, but not tonight."
17. After any professor sends me an e-mail, I will respond immediately even if it's just this: "Got it. Thank you."
18. After I get a good grade on a paper or exam, I will send a photo of my result to my mom and grandma.
19. After I arrive home from church on Sunday, I will sit down and explore one summer internship in STEM.
20. After I feel discouraged (for any reason), I will reread my personal statement of purpose.

TINY HABITS FOR PARENTS WHO WORK FROM HOME

1. After my feet touch the floor in the morning, I will say, "It's going to be an awesome day."
2. After I walk into the kitchen, I will drink fresh lemon juice with water.
3. After I pour my first cup of coffee, I will put on my running shoes.
4. After I finish drying off from my shower, I will apply at least a little bit of lotion.
5. After I see my kids sit down to breakfast, I will ask them, "What good thing do you want to happen today?"
6. After I notice my wife cleaning up the kitchen, I will give her a hug and a thank-you.
7. After I take my vitamins, I will feed the dog.
8. After my partner and kids leave for the day, I will sit down and meditate for at least three breaths.
9. After I wake up my computer, I will review my team updates on Notion.
10. After I see a teammate has completed a project, I will send a quick note or emoji.
11. After I select my top priority for the day, I will start my Pomodoro timer.
12. After my phone rings, I will answer it and walk around outside while I talk.
13. After I hang up the phone, I will do a quick set of push-ups or squats.
14. After I clean up lunch, I will walk around the block (and maybe call my parents).
15. After I wrap up our team meeting, I will send out a reminder of to-dos for each person.
16. After my kids arrive home, I will ask them to share one surprise from their day.
17. After I see the sun go down, I will put on my glasses that block blue light.
18. After I see the first TV commercial in the evening, I will get out my foam roller.
19. After we turn off the TV, I will unplug it until the next evening.
20. After I turn on the shower, I will think of one thing that went well that day.

TINY HABITS FOR REDUCING STRESS

1. After I wake up in the morning, I will open a window and take a few deep breaths.
2. After I turn on the shower, I will say a quiet prayer of gratitude.
3. After I pour my coffee or tea, I will sit down on my meditation pillow.
4. After I get the kids on the school bus, I will express a thought of gratitude to a neighbor.
5. After I sit down with my coffee, I will open my journal.
6. After I start my exercise, I will say, "Peace is every step" (Thich Nhat Hanh).
7. After I realize I have X amount of time before I need to leave, I will set a timer on my phone.
8. After I finish my lunch at work, I will walk outside.
9. After I arrive at my appointment, I will put my phone away and be with my own uplifting thoughts.
10. After I pack my work bag, I will tidy my workspace for five minutes.
11. After I sit down on the train, I will launch my meditation app.
12. After I receive an e-mail from the PTA asking for help, I will reply, "Sorry I can't help this time around, but please ask me again in the future."
13. After I get upset with a family member, I will take a walk to the mailbox alone.
14. After I take the dog on a walk, I will identify a bird or plant that I see.
15. After I clean up from dinner, I will make an herbal tea.
16. After I put my kids to bed, I will light a candle and turn off the overhead lights.
17. After I run my bath, I will put in a few drops of essential oils.
18. After I get my pajamas on, I will set out one item for work the next day.
19. After I get in bed, I will close my eyes and chant, "Om."
20. After my head hits the pillow, I will think about one thing I'm grateful for from the day.

TINY HABITS FOR WORK TEAMS

1. After we arrive at work, we will park in the farthest spot.
2. After we turn on our computers, we will check our voice mail.
3. After we draft an e-mail with sensitive information, we will double-check that it's being sent to only necessary recipients.
4. After we submit the quarterly update, we will high-five a contributing team member (virtually or in person).
5. After we hear negative feedback from a customer, we will say this exact script: "Thank you for the valuable feedback. I will share that with my team."
6. After we receive positive feedback from a customer, we will print the e-mail and pin it to the kudos board in the break room.
7. After we schedule a team meeting, we will send out an e-mail asking for agenda items.
8. After we return to our desks from using the toilet, we will clear one item from our desks.
9. After we arrive at a meeting, we will put our phones on do not disturb mode.
10. After we adjourn a meeting, we will push in the chairs in the conference room.
11. After we clean the whiteboard, we will check the table for trash or loose papers.
12. After an employee brings up a problem, we will say, "What do you think is the best way forward?"
13. After a meeting is about to end, we will ask, "What's one surprise from today's meeting?" and hear each team member's reply.
14. After we take the last item of an office supply, we will e-mail the administration lead with details about the item in need.
15. After we select the date for the monthly staff potluck, we will send out the who's-bringing-what sign-up sheet.
16. After we finish eating in the break room, we will wipe down one countertop.
17. After we onboard a new hire, we will walk them around the office and make brief one-on-one introductions.
18. After we close our computers down, we will file one stack of papers.
19. After we shut down our computers, we will lock our filing cabinets.
20. After we close the office for the day, we will make sure the lights, fans, and heaters are all powered down.

TINY HABITS FOR BEING MORE PRODUCTIVE

1. After I open my calendar for the day, I will get out one file related to the day's agenda.
2. After I sit down at my desk, I will put my phone on do not disturb mode.
3. After I close my office door, I will organize one item that's lying around.
4. After I finish reading e-mail, I will close the e-mail browser tab.
5. After I launch a new Word doc, I will hide all other programs running on my computer.
6. After I find myself mindlessly browsing social media, I will log out.
7. After I sit down at a meeting, I will write the title, the date, and the attendees at the top of my notes.
8. After I notice a call going on for longer than expected, I'll say this script: "It's been great to talk, but I need to wrap up. What haven't we covered yet that's important?"
9. After I read an important e-mail, I will file it in a folder for the designated project.
10. After I read an e-mail I can't deal with immediately, I will mark it as unread.
11. After I read an e-mail that's time sensitive, I will reply with this script: "Got it. I will review in detail and get back in touch soon."
12. After I shut down my computer, I will ready one file for the next day's agenda.
13. After I pack my work bag, I will review my whiteboard and calendar.
14. After I leave the office, I will think about one success from the day.
15. After I walk in the door at home, I will hang my keys on the hook.
16. After I walk into the kitchen, I will plug my phone into the charger.
17. After I change out of my work clothes, I will hang or organize one item I was wearing.
18. After I review a bill, I will add it to the to-pay envelope.
19. After I get out my stack of bills, I will get out the basket with my checkbook, pen, envelopes, and stamps.
20. After I start the shower at night, I will think, *Why am I so incredibly productive?*

TINY HABITS FOR BRAIN HEALTH

1. After I put my feet on the floor in the morning, I will say a brief prayer.
2. After I turn on the shower, I will do a full body stretch.
3. After I press the brew button on my coffee maker, I will do one table tennis rally with myself.
4. After I finish my morning coffee, I will put out my yoga mat.
5. After I open the newspaper, I will do one item on the crossword puzzle.
6. After I make my breakfast plate, I will add a few slices of avocado.
7. After I sit down on the bus or train, I will look at one Hawaiian language flash card.
8. After I leave my house for a walk, I will press play on my podcast player.
9. After I finish listening to a podcast episode, I will think of one takeaway that I got from it.
10. After I notice negative thoughts popping up, I will ask myself if they are true.
11. After I open my calendar to plan for the week, I will choose a recipe with curry to cook.
12. After I make a grocery list, I will add one new fruit or veggie.
13. After I enter the grocery store, I will walk to the produce aisle first.
14. After I prepare my afternoon snack, I will make a cup of green tea.
15. After I get back home after errands, I will open the Duolingo app.
16. After I feel hungry in the afternoon, I will eat a handful of blueberries.
17. After I turn on the oven, I will play a classical music album.
18. After I take my evening vitamins, I will strum my ukulele.
19. After I sit down on the couch after dinner, I will open my gratitude notebook.
20. After I set my alarm at night, I will read one verse of Scripture.

TINY HABITS FOR STRENGTHENING CLOSE RELATIONSHIPS

1. After I make the bed, I will give my spouse a hug.
2. After I finish flossing, I will write a little love note on the mirror in dry-erase marker.
3. After I take a coffee break midday, I will text my spouse a message of appreciation.
4. After I listen to a great podcast, I will send the link to the episode to my best friend.
5. After I see a neighbor, I will wave and ask them, "What's new and what's good?"
6. After I sit down to coffee with a friend, I will ask her a specific question about her life.
7. After I see the card aisle at the grocery store, I will select one "thinking of you" card to send to someone I love.
8. After I see online that a close friend has a birthday, I will send that person a quick audio text with a happy message.
9. After I balance the monthly budget spreadsheet, I will compliment my partner on one specific aspect of how they contributed to our success.
10. After I arrive home from work or errands, I will hug my spouse and kids.
11. After I hear my partner complain about an ache or pain, I will offer to rub their back for a moment.
12. After I hear about my spouse's stressful day, I'll say this: "I'm here for you."
13. After I thank God for the dinner we are about to eat, I will express gratitude for my spouse and family in my prayer.
14. After I leave church, I will call my parents on the ride home.
15. After I make a special trip to see family, I will share a few photos in an e-mail note to say a quick thanks.
16. After I leave an event with a close friend, I will send them a quick text of thanks.
17. After I make a homemade baked good, I will take a portion of it to a neighbor or friend.
18. After a gift arrives from my kids, I will send a quick text saying, "Got X. Wow, so thoughtful. Thank you!"
19. After I plan a day trip for my partner and myself, I will ask my partner if there's anything special he or she would like to see or do.
20. After I pack for a weekend away, I will pack a special surprise for the people I'm visiting.

TINY HABITS FOR STAYING FOCUSED

1. After I walk in the door at work, I will switch my phone to airplane mode and store it in my backpack.
2. After I set my backpack down at work, I will pick an important task that I want to do immediately.
3. After I pick my important task, I will clear my desk of all distractions.
4. After I clear my desk, I will set a timer for forty-five minutes.
5. After I set my timer, I will put on my headphones to signal to others that I shouldn't be disturbed.
6. After I put on my headphones, I will close all the unnecessary windows on my computer.
7. After my timer goes off, I will list what my next task should be and take a break.
8. After I sit outside during break, I will meditate for three breaths or longer.
9. After I come back into the office, I will pour some fresh coffee.
10. After I check for urgent messages, I will turn on the e-mail autoreply that says I'm away from e-mail.
11. After I decide to go to lunch, I will write down the next step on my project (what to do immediately after I return).
12. After I sit down for lunch in the cafeteria, I will check for any urgent personal messages.
13. After I put away my lunch utensils, I will walk around outside and recharge.
14. After I check for urgent e-mails after lunch, I will turn on the e-mail autoreply that says I'm away from e-mail.
15. After I pick the next project to do, I will quickly list the steps in the project.
16. After someone asks me to run an errand with them, I will say, "I can't right now. Sorry."
17. After I finish my afternoon snack, I will set a timer for a ten-minute nap.
18. After I go into our project room, I will close the door and put up the DO NOT DISTURB sign.
19. After the project meeting begins, I will start taking notes (so I stay tuned in).
20. After I walk out the door to go home, I will say, "Why am I so good at staying focused?"

TINY HABITS FOR STOPPING HABITS

1. After I shave, I will put bitter nail polish on one nail.
2. After I put my belongings in the car, I will put my phone in the trunk.
3. After I get ready for bed, I will plug my phone in a different room to charge overnight in order to stop scrolling Facebook in bed.
4. After I put my computer to sleep at night, I will sweep the papers off my desk into a box in order to stop adding to the clutter.
5. After I leave the house for work, I will drive a route to work that avoids fast food restaurants.
6. After I finish dinner, I will immediately brush my teeth in order to stop my snacking in the evening.
7. After I start cooking dinner, I will pour myself a nonalcoholic beverage.
8. After I get a snack, I will close and store the snack container.
9. After I finish a glass of wine, I will put dish soap in the glass.
10. After I arrive at the party, I will leave my cigarettes in the car.
11. After I arrive at my desk, I will put my phone on airplane mode.
12. After I sit down in the car, I will turn my phone on do not disturb mode.
13. After I finish dinner, I will brush table crumbs on my dinner plate to avoid eating seconds.
14. After I finish my entrée, I will pour pepper over the remaining fries.
15. After I arrive at a party, I will tell the host, "I'm not drinking tonight."
16. After I get up from a slot machine, I will give my friend what money remains and say, "Don't let me gamble again, okay?"
17. After I arrive at a restaurant, I will turn off my phone completely.
18. After I sit down at a restaurant, I will say, "No bread or chips, please."
19. After I pee, I will put the toilet seat down.
20. After I turn off the TV in the evening, I will turn off my Wi-Fi router.

TINY HABITS FOR BUSINESS TRAVEL

1. After I print my boarding pass at home, I will update audiobooks and movies on my iPad.
2. After I pack my suitcase, I will list what I need to do in the morning before leaving home.
3. After I go through security, I will buy a Cobb salad to take with me on the flight.
4. After I get to my departure gate, I will stretch my legs and shoulders.
5. After I sit down in my seat, I will put on headphones and turn on a TED talk.
6. After the attendant offers me an unhealthy snack, I will say, "No, thank you."
7. After I touch down at my destination, I will text my wife with an emoji that I've landed.
8. After I walk into my hotel room, I will unpack my business materials and most of my clothes.
9. After I see the snack bar in my hotel room, I will hide it in the closet or a drawer.
10. After I unpack in my hotel room, I will find the fitness facility so I know where it is.
11. After I hang up the DO NOT DISTURB sign, I will turn on the white-noise app on my phone.
12. After I get into bed, I will call my wife.
13. After my alarm goes off in the morning, I will get up and open the curtains.
14. After I floss, I will smile at myself, and say, "It's going to be a great day."
15. After I sit down with coffee, I will take out my notes to prep for my meeting.
16. After I hear people's names in the meeting, I will write them down and use them.
17. After I get through security on the way home, I'll go to a shop to find a small gift for my kids.
18. After I sit down at the departure gate, I will text my wife about the flight status.
19. After I sit down on the plane headed home, I will make a list of people to thank from my business trip.
20. After I walk in the door at home, I will unzip my suitcase immediately to make it easy to unpack.

Maxims in Behavior Design

It took me more than ten years to figure out the most important principles when designing for behavior change. I eventually found my answers, and I call them my maxims. The evidence is clear: If you don't do these two things, your product or service will not engage people over time.

These two maxims also apply to how we design change in our own lives. As I explain in this book, we all need to do two things: (1) *Help ourselves do what we already want to do*, and (2) *Help ourselves feel successful.*

If you want more tools and resources — such as case studies, worksheets, and teaching outlines — you'll find them at TinyHabits.com/resources.

Fogg Maxim #1

Help people do what they already want to do.

Fogg Maxim #2

Help people feel successful.

ABOUT THE AUTHOR

BJ Fogg, PhD, founded the Behavior Design Lab at Stanford University. In addition to his research, Fogg teaches industry innovators how human behavior really works. He created the Tiny Habits Academy to help people around the world. He lives in Northern California and Maui.

For more about the author, see bjfogg.com/about.